The Making of a Terrorist

The Making of a Terrorist

On Classic German Rogues

✦

Jeffrey Champlin

Preface by Avital Ronell

NORTHWESTERN UNIVERSITY PRESS
EVANSTON, ILLINOIS

Northwestern University Press
www.nupress.northwestern.edu

Printed in the United States of America

ISBN 978-0-8101-3438-6

The Library of Congress has cataloged the original, hardcover edition as follows:

Champlin, Jeffrey, author.
The making of a terrorist : on classic German rogues / Jeffrey Champlin.
pages cm
Includes bibliographical references and index.
ISBN 978-0-8101-3010-4 (cloth : alk. paper) — ISBN 978-0-8101-6794-0 (ebook)
1. Goethe, Johann Wolfgang von, 1749–1832. Götz von Berlichingen. 2. Schiller, Friedrich, 1759–1805. Räuber. 3. Kleist, Heinrich von, 1777–1811. Michael Kohlhaas. 4. German literature—18th century—History and criticism. 5. German literature—19th century—History and criticism. 6. Violence in literature. I. Ronell, Avital, writer of preface. II. Title.
PT111.C47 2015
830.93552—dc23

2014036192

CONTENTS

ACKNOWLEDGMENTS

During work on this book I've been the beneficiary of an extraordinary group of demanding and rigorous scholars. To them I owe thanks not only for the living archive they have made accessible to me, for their own exemplary modeling of scholarly excellence and human expansiveness, for their seriousness as well as for the genuine capacity for play, but also for allowing me to flourish in the unwavering light of their support. My gratitude goes to my teachers and mentors: Peter-André Alt, Stanley Bates, Susan Bernstein, Andrea Dortmann, Murray Dry, Giuseppe Ferraro, Paul Fleming, Eckart Goebel, Ute Guzzoni, Werner Hamacher, Friedrich-Wilhelm von Herrmann, Carol Jacobs, Michael Jaeger, Marlies Janz, Horst Lange, Dennis Mahoney, Eva Meyer, Shireen Patell, Laurence Rickels, Zachary Sng, Allison Stanger, Friedrich Ulfers, and Martha Woodruff.

In addition, the following scholars offered generous guidance at important junctures of this project: Ulrich Baer, Zack Finch, Jeff High, Inka Mülder-Bach, Paul North, Christof Schöch, John H. Smith, and Kirk Wetters. I thank Hanna Dürholt for making the German language and its many literary and philosophical *Holzwege* an object of abiding love. My family (Robert, Mary Jo, and Jonathan Champlin) kept me on my toes and offered me the solid training one needs in order to engage the academic task with discipline and a modicum of pride. I thank them for their patient support and solicitude. I've also benefited from the kindness and consistent intelligence of my colleagues at Bard College. Roger Berkowitz has unwaveringly supported my research, fielded my questions, and broadened my horizons. I am grateful for Jonathan Becker's genuine intelligence and insight in pragmatic and theoretical aspects of university life. Tom Keenan, whose work I have admired from early on, has kept a guiding eye on my trajectories and sharpened my sense of literary and political engagement. I cannot fail to express gratitude for Jacques Derrida, who first introduced me to Hannah Arendt and his own inestimable inflections in the seminars he held at New York University in 2001–3.

Above all, I wish to thank Avital Ronell for her amazing interventions in the realms of literature and thought, for her fascinating seminars, and for her incisive comments on my research. Her rigorous teaching attuned me to the call of isolated and abandoned figures in German culture while at the same time instilling the deepest respect for the joyful science of Nietzschean philology.

An earlier version of part of the analysis of Hobbes in chapter 1 originally appeared in "Introduction," in *Terror and the Roots of Poetics* (New York: Atropos, 2013), 1–3. Portions of chapter 4 appeared previously in "Reading Terrorism in Kleist: The Violence and Mandates of *Michael Kohlhaas,*" *The German Quarterly* 85, no. 4 (Fall 2012): 439–54.

A ROGUE PREFACE

Avital Ronell

Irony never lets up. You think you've relinquished a familiar habit, even a cherished interlocutor, and suddenly they're waving a manuscript in your face, making a comeback. Jeffrey Champlin came around the bend *with a book*, pressing forward with a new set of existential propositions. Morphing by means of this evental turn, Jeffrey differentiates himself from himself, urging upon us a reflection of what it means in this day and age to create—or be created by—a book. Each new arrival logs a measure of labor and possible interiority, a regimen to which one has submitted with relentless application and teleological letdown. For his part, Jeffrey releases the book to our custody, offering no doubt a consequential way of reeling in an aggregate of newly minted readers, and also a surefire way of fixing—the attention of a shared discursive field, if not indeed my own sense of a history.

Such a delivery calls up memories of our training grounds; let me count the ways of our remembered encounters, their intradisciplinary probes and determining edges. I think of the drills that he endured: the ever-modified reading lists, inescapable test sites, the store and verve of delicate contestations and directed conversation on unique loops. There are other registers of remembrance that come to mind as well. One resuscitates the first daybreak moment: a paper submitted, shy and promising. One thinks back to the emergent classroom interventions—rhetorically reserved, cautious, quietly on point: the first time one saw his hand in the air, an inaugurating signal that says, "I'm in." Recalling segments of our history, I recap the early bursts of pride without hierarchical constraint—the smart outfits as papers are delivered around the country, in scattered university outposts and as part of the many conferences they host. I remember awaiting news from abroad, after a talk meets approval, in Berlin. Blips of exhaustion crackling over the telephone lines. I think of a particular afternoon a few years ago, during one of our many talking walks, picking up the pace as we stroll through cities where we may coincide. On that afternoon in 2010 we hooked a left near Brecht's house, taking in a visit to Hegel's grave, with Fichte sidling up to him in determined partnership.

For the long haul, beyond finitude's tickers. I was taken aback: can one decide on whom to R.I.P. with? Not anyone, but Fichte, along with Mrs. Fichte, tombstoned with the Hegels and all the incumbent ironies. If I were Jacques Derrida laced with Walter Benjamin I would not refrain from commenting on the allegorical if self-diminishing vignette, Jeff and I staring at the setup of legacies and their beyond-the-grave insinuations.

Back in New York, I stay aware of Jeffrey's trajectories, the increasing bulk of articles and teaching assignments, the pedagogies stirred by Bard and Middlebury colleges, staying tuned to Tom Keenan's Human Rights broadcasts. I recall the time put in during job searches tracking the movements of the young academic who logs in the fear factors of an extended travel plan. And even though everyone is pressed by the superegoical grid to bring up a book—somehow, without the proper support, or hours, or spiritual incentives—it strikes me as astounding when it happens. I befriend the book, dazed by its solemnity and discursive spring. The erstwhile student has become an authority, holding pace at a remove from the person I knew. He has now become an *author*, of another species and, if one can say so by taking current theories into account, his status becomes ambivalently calibrated, now that he's an author. Signed, sealed, archivizable, he turns up dead or alive—maybe, after all the effort and training, dead *and* alive.

✦

There were many beginnings and attendant eclipses, each time flagging a different punctuation of friendship. For Bataille, *reading* constitutes a sovereign act of friendship. This makes sense to me, and I have made it a practice to read my friends and friend my readings in a manner that does not simply follow a master plan or playbook of approval ratings. I have to suppose, though, that engaging another in this essential way, by reading closely, not only registers the shifting parameters of friendship, but can also wedge in remoteness, instituting hierarchy and complication. In some cases, the close-up of reading seals the deal of ambivalence or brings in an unexpected store of new proximities. In still other cases, it simply throws you off. Even the delighted reception can indicate some frequencies of traumatic intrusion. This level of strained receptivity may seem odd, if only because most readers are not so high-strung; they are perhaps less obsessed about what it means to read, or in the back of their minds they don't need to sum up the hours logged in, the manual labor implied, and the degree of exhaustion involved in preparing a book. I was trained differently, with relentless insistence placed on the responsibilities of reading, toned by the persistent demands of a hermeneutics of frustration: we were taught how *not* to call it a wrap, how to let the inexhaustible range of a text reopen its chasms, confound its questions, resist its areas of smugness. Keeping things open and intellectually vulnerable can be hard work. It would be easier to offer closure and certitude—to close it all down at one point, call it a day, nail a conclusion, or deliver a paraphrase. Instead, there are sleepless nocturnal communications tapping out responsibilities, as I said, and the cautious algorithms of responsiveness—of what is called for when coming in contact with texts, whether or not they are shy and recondite, up in your face, loudly distressed or handled with cautious pianissimo, part of an uncodified synchrony of thought.

✦

Rabbity and serious, I contemplated how best I could cope with the solemn task of accompanying the work at hand, without diverting from the major topoi and themes it addresses, the mood from which it emanates. I did not want to be involved in creating distractions or hijacking the sober style by which it is characterized: I wrestled with how, in short, to be *helpful*, rhetorically prudent—without pulling up short the carefully studied moments and tropologies of this compelling series of reflections. With my own work I can take certain risks, push back on a number of super-egoical pressures, let hell break loose on the syntactic registers of the exposition. When I say "my own work," I must immediately hit the pause button: I mean with works that bear my signature. I'm not sure I can convincingly speak of my *own* work, so overpopulated with teachers and students am I, riddled with stray shots, polydependencies, and purposeful appropriations. Faced with the efforts of a cherished younger colleague one could too easily disgrace—or over-authorize—oneself. Whether indulging inconsideration—or running narcissistically off the charts, one could be tempted to unclench, to take forbidden off-ramps to "see where this takes us." Still, it would be frivolous to experiment in such a way or to put my wildly idiomatic and stylistic stamp on the work of another; in some way, however, that is what I have been invited to do—to break open the work of Jeffrey Robert Champlin. Fortunately, I tell myself, the title and inflection of this subtle work gives me cover, for it speaks right off the bat of rogues and strays, and asks that we tap into the secret stores of meaning guarded by runaway brigands—the deviant undergrowth of which, in some way, I may be a part. There may well be a place for me here. I am beginning to settle into the work whose title puts out a call and traces, among other things, the making of a theorist.

("Rabbity," by the way, refers to Heidegger's pose of exemplary thinking: to listen with one's nervous little rabbit ears. I hope to live up to this standard of attunement, or at least to match prints with Walter Benjamin and Karl Kraus's "right of nerves," which also mobilize body responses, anxious quirks, in the effort to think, receive, respond, adopt, and work through.)

✦

Irony never lets up. What am I to Jeffrey Champlin? Normally, it wouldn't matter much, nor would we have answers to the unconscious portioning of such a question. Yet, the question has been cued up by the text at hand. Jeffrey, ever generous, attributes my passage through his life—in relation to the genesis of the book. In the conventional space of acknowledgment, Champlin thanks me for my "amazing interventions." We cannot know for certain if this locution refers to a felicitous place in his intellectual development or marks an unsettling disruption in his life, the place reserved for his life-and-works. For is it not the case that "amazing," as Nietzsche taught us, splits the returns among startling or intrusive violence, and unfigurable incursion, even connoting a beneficent upheaval? Or perhaps "amazing," when not qualifying an uplifting experience of another's approach, a moment of grace, opens the door to a welcome persecution of the sort Levinas might signal—or it can tip—toward Heidegger's fateful prod (*Stoß*). Maybe not so welcome, after all. "Amazing" does not necessarily mean anything that anyone can work with or call home about if one wants to score academically sanctioned points. Perhaps that is where Jeffrey is going, moving me out of the classroom, though this is not clear to me. To provoke amazement may not correspond to a teacherly disposition. Again, I'm not sure. Let me raise the stakes and situate the wayward mood to which Champlin refers us in this context. For "amazement" is philosophically charged, a highly invested suspension of mastery, a letting up on the stronghold of comprehension. To *amaze* may well mean to *disturb* the conditions that underlie understanding. Or it may also serve as the gateway drug to a truer understanding of complex and sensitive phenomena, with all the precautions and inescapable pitfalls that would need to be signaled here. In any case, I hope, despite its undecidability, that this quality, which is also a translation of philosophical awe at the outset—one is amazed by world, one starts out by being dumbstruck, according to the ancient Greeks—might guide aspects of the present intervention as well. I do not seek to "amaze," but one cannot deny the jitters and doubts that attend pedagogical scenes and acts of reading. The teaching body, when it somatizes or camouflages its angst, can create quite a spectacle. "Amazement" may be Jeffrey's way of translating another mood and modality by which I am regularly seized and perhaps put out there—anxiety. In Heideggerrian, *Sorge* is disclosive of understanding. That is the only hope I hold out, wishing for all this anxiety to amount to something. For I do not choose to be wracked by anxiety, but it does seem to function as a constant goad, one of Heidegger's severe prods. I suppose that if I haven't succeeded in underscoring the point emphatically enough, I should repeat how very anxious I feel about tagging the first major work of my young colleague. One might feel similarly wobbly when handed a newborn baby to hold when all familialisms are remote.

✦

Yet kinship there is, however ironically cast. The telltale indicators of kinship do not necessarily *show*, because the work is bound by the very rogue itineraries and inscribed deviations that it seeks to analyze. On a larger scale, the historical disruption that it seeks to contain requires the work to follow instructions of non-resemblance, which may circumscribe the only place where family resemblance emerges—the way we deviate from our teachers, marking parricidal routes that suddenly halt, or move forward, full force. I've seen it happen. I've also seen how the emergency brake is pulled when certain levels of anticipated collision become too intense. If it engages a target, this work addresses itself to a number of contiguous disciplines. By taking stealth pathways, initializing new texts and commentaries, Champlin upturns the protocols that steady ideological or thematic approaches to the study of literature and political theory. Despite the strict adherence to its sense of logic and argument, there is only very little in the way of domestication in this work that tends to stay off course as it interrogates questions of power and authority, sovereignty and violence. The sort of disruptive kinship that Champlin practices leads us to ask a more general question that attaches to academic and intellectual taxonomies and locators. How does a work establish a mark of belonging—or identify a specific idiom or lineage—by following a particular constellation or tonal habit, creating adherence to a determined syntactical schema and thematic choice, even as it de-programs traditional exegetics? Does a given interpretive *attitude* suffice to render a lineage recognizable, profiling what Husserl and Freud, on different registers, call *Einstellung*?

Jeffrey Champlin's attitude may not, in the first instance, bear much resemblance to my own set of vintage *Einstellungen*. Perhaps, though, it's sheerly a matter of taking a call, rather than tapping the lines for content or signified? Perhaps certain visitations with a number of persistent or clandestine motifs help create readable schools or groupuscules of commitment and practice? Of course there is the matter of shared reading lists and the trained ear of hermeneutic suspicion—not only *what* but also *how* you go after a given problem set, take up the referential authority knocked down or left intact, probe the rhetorical yield, or size the climate of resistance. For some textual interpreters, it's smooth sailing; things seem recognizable and one can deal with them accordingly. In more landbound terms, acts of constituting a hermeneutic dossier and identity often remain a matter of executing a confident pounce. Still others stay cautious and anxious, reachingly ungrounded, goaded on to analyze with care the jolt of motivating doubt. Jeffrey Champlin manages to combine qualities that come from all the sectors I provisionally set down, even though it may seem contradictory to be sure-footed and fragile at once.

✦

In this work we are invited to observe the way literature exemplarily takes down the fragile certitudes of political theories and sciences. The state of epistemic alert maps everywhere in and around this text. Champlin is committed to understanding the way language shores up on limits and points of non-knowledge and historical trauma. Incorporating a level of violence that cannot be assimilated by canonic narrative conventions, language leaves us stranded, referentially fragile. Schlegel and the romantics called the type of disruption that Champlin tracks *permanent parabasis*, indicating the outbursts and wounding breakage that meaning endures when historical accounts collapse in on themselves. In order to make room for such underdeveloped aspects of the narrative probe—be they historical or literary, referentially pitched or deliriously spun—Champlin pursues the representational break that ranges from Thomas Hobbes to Maurice Blanchot, where deactivated figures of sovereignty secretly broadcast their illegitimacy. He locates the historical fissures according to which representation falters and breaks apart when facing down obsolesced strongholds of power. Let me try to make the primary stakes of this study clearer.

Jeffrey Champlin leverages tropological breakdown to reflect the fundamental disunity of power that figures of terror introduce. He uniquely connects literary criticism and political theory for the purpose of interrogating disruption in the way things are recorded, remembered, incorporated, or disavowed. He sizes events of exclusion and containment that play out on referential and linguistic fields, stacking up the causal networks that lead to mutations or prevent the arrival of change. Besides the carefully set contiguities of insight for which this work is responsible, it monitors the influx of still other discursive areas. Champlin has a hold on political *desire*, which requires an understanding of the rhetorical undertow that regularly redefines the subtleties of historical movement as it accounts as well for the stagnations that still affect the way we think and live. The figure of the rogue serves to destabilize the interpretive grid by which we measure historical eventfulness, "open[ing] sovereignty itself to an unknown future." The rogue files through classical filters of literary inventiveness, but also disturbs any comforting grasp of how to tell or know a story, no matter how solidly documented or referentially framed it appears to be.

In the texts that Champlin has marshaled, there is a nearly libidinal, if not demonic surge of interference to contend with—something that washes out historical grounding at the moment history is in the making. Even at the most reasoned discursive juncture, sovereign intention is sideswiped by the abrupt irruption of accident, excess, and madness—by the upswing of obscenity, as in Goethe's case, and the libidinal giddiness that drives the protagonists of Schiller and Kleist beyond the pleasure principle. History writhes in the grip of antagonistic forces and contradictory mandates, clenched by perturbed aims that create unreadable legacies. The fateful encounter with unreadability is hosted by literature's acute sense of an event's secret holdings. Historians may try to render outcomes and their processes transparent, controlled, readably embedded by narrative appropriation. Literature, led by its alliance with unconscious invasions of sense and meaning, sets up alternative types of telling or *anahistory* and a host of new *unintelligibilities*, as Friedrich Schlegel would say. Or as Tom Cohen writes, the past also requires us to assume the work of "disinscription," effecting part of a pact that leans on history to yield other, more recalcitrant or underdeveloped aspects of meaning and occurrence.[1]

The work of casing the past, urging it to come forward in splendor or dejection, quietly or with a clamor, is one of the ways in which history comes at us from the future. Something else is happening or prevented from happening in a sweep that only literature, with its obsessive tracking record, knows how to bring to the table. The texts that Champlin rallies in order to document terrorist rage eye the rogue outbursts that tend to take shape as and in a *feminine intervention*—pulling in the excluded negativity of historical occurrence. Women do not traditionally hold posts in the making-of-history narrations. This does not mean that they fail to appear as sidekicks of genius in the *Goethezeit* or that they mismanage more eternalizing roles, such as those that Goethe himself later associates with the eternal feminine. They are simply not, for the most part, historical instaurators or situated in the major leagues of becoming. You always have to "cherchez la femme" to get a signal for some feminine instigation of historical note. In Hegel, women are squarely seen as the irony of the community, and as enemy. One has to get a close-up of irony to see how this statement can overturn on its own premises, but I am not going to strain myself today. The literature of the Sturm und Drang and *Goethezeit* distributes a different calling card to its women when it comes to the struggle of history. The feminine teams up with accidentality and contradiction to deal, in each case, a historical blow, if not a "rope-a-dope" facedown with the grand narratives to which these texts owe their constitution—and inherent deconstitution. In Goethe, as in Schiller and Kleist, feminine subterfuge builds up discreetly to take the whole house down, to topple the grandiose pose of the warriors that head up these texts. They belong to a secret police force hitherto undercover and, to an astonishing extent, unmarked yet capable of disabling aspects of telling.

✦

Champlin zones in on an invisible channel that delivers a pinch of significance, outpacing the isolated and abandoned figures that undergird political discourses of modernity. The stealth contamination of the feminine incursion sets off another story of historical eventfulness, so unimaginable that it has run circles around the first crew of rogues. A violence that cannot be incorporated, the feminine puts the fear in terror. She—or "it," since Kleist and Goethe especially knew how powerful a *force* the feminine invokes so that she belongs to or creates another order of being—accomplishes a destruction that rewrites and disinscribes history, scrambling the master codes and unhinging the way historical narrative feeds on the ego-pump of recounting. The feminine, Champlin argues, interrupts chronology and questions the very genre of history. She comes in from the side door, and, for Kleist, introduces the sideshow that upsets the carefully laid out blueprint of logical and legal determinations. Yet, by a subtle shift of focus, we learn that the feminine also manages to sidestep terror to the extent that, in the first place, she (or "it") never claimed to hold a membership in the house of reason. She was never in the sights, never figured as what needed to be contested or abolished—so short on consequence was the feminine for the big guns of the historical milestone. Maybe, though, she had something to do with the buildup of reason as a reactive defense mechanism, if in a greatly repressed way. Reason itself "follows from terror, exploding from within an extreme atmosphere of fear." The close collaboration of reason and its expunged other creates a standoff that paralyzes while "making" history. For the awful Nazi juror, Carl Schmitt, reason follows from terror, putting a clamp on what dredges up uncontrollable fear. For Foucault (to put this in provisional shorthand), reason is responsible for creating its opposing forces and lexicon of substitute aberrations. Reason regulates by placing adversarial terms, structures, outlook, in lockdown—hence the penitentiary and asylum operations that seek to isolate deviancy. The Age of Reason has performed these raids since the seventeenth century, rounding up what falls out of its provenance and program of checkpoints. In such momentous negotiations and apportionments of space and power the feminine is found, for the most part, to be neither here nor there. For large sectors of the *Goethezeit* the atopical flow of the feminine was itself a threat even as it evaded any conceptual grid. She rose up out of a poetic staggering of power, part of magical and alchemical concoctions that vaporized any possible phenomenology of mind. The feminine force that these works welcomed reinvented historical eventfulness by steadily leveling sovereignty. Whether or not these gendered alterities had their place in history, they speak for another history or they point at least to traumatic zones of historical understanding where something other than traditional intelligibility is called for and needed. They account for a smudge in the written pages of history, or a minoritized trace that rarely is handed the podium. But these texts clear the way for nearly unfathomable protocols and effects of uproar that deconstitute the solid ground on which we base our stories and from which we seek license to proceed or, in some cases, to depart. For the texts under study, the feminine spill can in some instances be traced back to the French source materials, of which these works try to rid themselves.

The feminine, curiously, operates in two dominant ways. In the first place, things are anchored according to a more credible logic than rationality or city politics relies on. One thinks of Antigone and the other law to which she adheres—sacred, unbearable, destructive of the polis. She at once upholds and repudiates law; Antigone stands and falls as a criminal who, as Derrida notes following Hegel, has committed no crime. In these contexts the feminine poses as something of an a priori criminal, a signpost for an *imaginary* crime scene that outrages the community. She terrorizes simply by standing up for mourning. Well, maybe not so simply, for the right to mourn puts up all sorts of contestatory scrambles. On the other hand, the feminine blows into historical proving grounds in order to disturb the solidity of human coexistence, bringing into play ungraspable vehemence—one thinks of the Furies, remastered—that threatens at each instance to topple institutions and household rules, as in Kleist. I cannot at this time commit to a roundup or triple-axis dialectical summation of the feminine shakedown to which these texts bear witness. I rely on the fine-tuned analyses of Jeffrey Champlin to prod and persuade, to discover the terror within, without, at the heels of the figures of terror that he puts up for examination. I'd like to think that this work allegorizes the making of a theorist, taking steps to analyze severe conditions of frustration and catachrestic abuse, linguistic injuries that help account for terroristic acts that spread to states and institutions, to small business bureaucracies and corporate deathtraps. But here I am stealing from Jeffrey's repertory and possibly redirecting his intention. What's a homegrown troublemaker to do?

✦

Oh. One more ironic twist that binds us—one more cut before I let go, or try earnestly to do so. For nothing says goodbye or binds you like a book. It's a toss-up: Does another's book take you in, offer you refuge? Or does it establish firm boundaries that put you firmly in your place? Maybe both; no doubt, there exist other interpretive options. Let us continue without deciding whether the book released at this time by Jeffrey is an aggression or a gift that bypasses me, an aneconomic occurrence, as my own teacher would counsel. In his breathtaking reading of Karl Moor, when seeking out the inassimilable violence to which this name has been historically attached, Jeffrey looks hard at a point of undecidability between the student and delinquent. The assertion points to a strategic drop in the abyssal structuring of this prefatory remark. Have I inadvertently treated the student as delinquent? Have I not identified my own trajectory and task as one that unavoidably brushes with delinquency—something mandated by language's close-ups? But this description is not about me, so I will unstick from the narcissistic annexation—a true temptation. In closing, then, let me just add a word of thanks for the jolting mesh of student and delinquent proffered by this and attendant passages. For it may help us understand why, at this time in our shared histories, the scholar is *at risk*. I think especially of the young scholar that cultural winds tend to fell these days, where scholars, materially undernourished and work-committed to a point of quiet fanaticism and serious world-fatigue—the structure of endless and hard study requires such a level of adherence, great solitude, unrelenting self-questioning—when young scholars are taken for rogues.

The Making of a Terrorist

Introduction

✦

The Making of a Terrorist

Three of the most highly revered and even *popular* works of eighteenth- and early nineteenth-century German literature, *Götz von Berlichingen, The Robbers*, and *Michael Kohlhaas*, recount scenes of extreme violence that have long fascinated readers, but have for the most part escaped genuine critical attention. Each text tells the story of a particular injustice and a tenacious commitment to resist the ruling powers that underwrite it. Yet the "heroes" of these texts (as they are often called by their legions of admirers in literary studies and beyond) quickly overstep the bounds of reason in their campaigns for what they see as right. While important research has allowed a better understanding of the political and philosophical background of these great works of Goethe, Schiller, and Kleist, their literary singularity seems to cause them to slip away from any given situating field.

The present investigation presses further into this singularity, to passages that make one want to look away: the moment when Götz von Berlichingen takes the leadership of a marauding band of rebellious farmers, when Karl Moor murders his lover Amalia in cold blood, and when Kohlhaas orders entire cities burned while their inhabitants sleep. If studies that draw on law, history, and political theory have not been able to circumscribe these acts, it is not for a lack of critical acumen but because these fields employ modes of knowledge that Goethe, Schiller, and Kleist push to their limit. Critics have done necessary work that approaches the perceptual border of violence, though they have rarely named it as such. Working at the limit, I argue that each of these texts confronts terrorism as extreme violence that causes power to approach its breaking point, a point where structures of political representation succumb to surprising non-dialectical shifts. In this sense, the so-called heroes appear as terroristic instigators.

The new readings that I propose of Goethe, Schiller, and Kleist arise from reconsidering these authors in light of the historical reemergence of terrorism as a central political and cultural problem following the attacks of September 11, 2001. At their heart, they struggle with an ethical question, in that they ask how to respond to the unique event of the terrorist attack. At the moment of truly extreme violence, at scenes of murder and fire, one instinctively turns away, unable to bear the sight. Political discourse responds to terrorism in an analogous manner, seeking to protect power by rejecting even the possibility that it may be fundamentally affected. The ethical demand of the victims of a terrorist attack, however, relates to the impact that the attack had on them and how they were enmeshed in the social order. At the extreme point, the demand I am formulating here approaches the impossible: it would compel us to look at the moment at which our very nature prevents us from looking, and it would ask our political discourse to open itself to extreme vulnerability at the moment when future danger appears most likely. In the greater arc of this book, I argue that literature stages this impossibility and takes a creative stand in confronting it. In so doing, Goethe, Schiller, and Kleist offer critical resources that are relevant in wider fields of thought, that are even potentially subject to deployment in the political sphere, if never simply mechanically applicable.

Under the title "The Making of a Terrorist" I propose newly inflected readings of *Götz von Berlichingen*, *The Robbers*, and *Michael Kohlhaas* that develop the implications of as-of-yet unexamined excessive violence in each text. These readings have two interrelated aspects, that of the rupture of violence and how to respond to it, each of which resonates with a different sense of my title. The first aspect hones in on the manner in which the incredible variety of definitions of "terrorism" in law and in the social sciences indicates an anxiety about containing the threat of extreme violence. Here my investigation traverses the ever-proliferating contemporary determinations of the term "terrorist." To privilege just one example as a point of entry, Title 22, Section 2656(f) of the United States Code states that "the term 'terrorism' means premeditated, politically motivated violence perpetrated against noncombatant targets by subnational groups or clandestine agents."[1] That Götz von Berlichingen, Karl Moor, and Michael Kohlhaas become terrorists in committing acts of this type alone requires a reevaluation of the reputations they have been awarded in literary criticism, which generally recognizes them primarily as warriors on behalf of freedom and justice.

My goal is not, however, to offer anachronistic interpretations of *Goethezeit* texts but to engage the crisis in the relationship between power and violence that they stage. In this respect, Götz von Berlichingen, Karl Moor, and Michael Kohlhaas are each made to be "terrorists" in that they are defined as specific objects of exclusion by a logic that attempts to cover up excessive violence. Each of the texts I examine establishes specific reading instructions, a precise hermeneutic apparatus that operates both at the level of form and content to immunize the depicted sovereign and sovereign reader. I open a field of literary analysis in which to examine and delineate procedures of systematic defense. In this regard, I employ "terrorism" not as a category that would allow identification, but as an indicator of a threat to political, aesthetic, and epistemological representation. In this light, the attacks in each text appear as true interruptions that demand reflection.

With a certain obscenity that emerges from the texts themselves (starting with *Götz von Berlichingen*), my title raises, in its second aspect, the question of what the terrorist *makes*. In the aftermath of a violent attack, surveying ruins and corpses, discussion of creation initially yields little sense. If anything, one's inherent impulse would be to rebuild as if the event were reversible. Yet while according to the logic of immunity upon which sovereignty generally operates, the terrorist could be said to make an even stronger and unified sovereignty, he also opens it to non-identity. The term "rogue" in my subtitle indicates an asymmetrical double of the terrorist, as a gambit to open a space prior to the specificities of the "terrorist" that does not immediately indicate an instrument of political discourse. The "rogue" would be first of all one whom the ruling power marks as excluded in preparation for containment. This does not simply mean that terrorism potentially opens the historical path for the institution of another sovereignty of the same or quantifiably different sort, as historians concerned with terrorism often suggest. Instead, it opens sovereignty itself to an unknown future that must create new, as-of-yet unimagined structures of representation.

Despite their best intention of staying with the facts, the social sciences and philosophy instinctively look backwards, seeking shelter in the knowledge of origins when confronted by violence. This makes it hard to perceive the rogue as such. Psychology, for example, seeks a model of aggression in the family or other past trauma, while political philosophy in the tradition of Hobbes explains away violence as the precondition of a social sphere that accepts rational limits on freedom. Literature, however, not only in specific tropes such as catachresis (which as Paul de Man notes, originates from the Greek word for "abuse") but in its broader insistence on the figural, opens a rupture between the literal and figural that is constitutive of signification in general. Through narrative it continually engages the fundamental fear of non-knowledge by telling the story of tropes that toss and turn between meaning and non-meaning. In the specific texts of Goethe, Schiller, and Kleist that I examine, close attention to rhetoric reveals the strain of efforts to contain violence at the most fundamental level of human speech.

Literary criticism may admire systematic philosophy for its rigor, but violence repels univocal interpretations and requires a criticism that moves with not only discipline but also a variety of methods. Conscious reflection on my approach will help to clarify the aspects of contemporary literary criticism that I employ and how my study contributes both to the refinement of criticism and the connection between literary criticism and political theory. The texts that I examine offer a striking deployment of rhetoric which, in general, organizes disruptions of meaning. In doing so it makes visible the detours language takes, detours that would escape an analysis that sought to reduce the form of speech to its content. Labeling certain phrases according to their structure (often drawing on the resources of Greek and Roman terminology) allows us to see the struggle of human attempts to produce meaning around violence while retaining the sense that these atttempts are fragile, not completely thought through, and at least partially unconscious. One could say the same of grammar, if one really looks at the hesitations and projections of specific uses of tense, subject, and so on as these texts demand. The important point is that in the very incompletion of linguistic organization, in the sense that at some level language always retains a measure of free play despite its potentially devastating impact, we see both patterns of language and the possibility of change through those patterns.

Language always steps away from its promised message but violence does more than make this distance apparent. It highlights gaps in meaning that demand we do something about it, we need to respond. The materiality of language thus intersects with contemporary efforts in political theory to think the fundamental disunity of power. For all its promise of rationally constituted unity, we will see that the social contract tradition from Hobbes to Hegel harbors a formalist and even potentially totalitarian threat that needs to be carefully confronted. When language slips out from ideals of meaning—in ways as simple as the multiple meanings of the same word, to the depths of etymologies, the surfaces of the homonymn, and even the levity of the pun—it offers ways of moving forward that connect to the past but reconstitute former outlines of power.

At moments of linguistic switchover such as Götz's sudden vulgar verbal attack on the Emperor's army, the rogue appears furtively and makes a provocation to reading to which certain privileged spectators respond. Each text not only marks a rupture of power in language, but also recounts a response to this rupture through surprising tropes offered by apparently minor characters. Or, in a more complicated vein, literature struggles to assure futurity knowing that the past remains in many ways elusive even to historians. Disinscribing the past as it tells the story of the past, literature must make way for the future. Götz's wife Elizabeth, Karl Moor's beloved Amalia, and the fortune-teller emerge as exemplary readers, those who, with little if any complicity in the violent acts they witness, see the heroes of each text as rogues rather than terrorists and propose new directions. I speak of my characters as "Classic German Rogues" in my title as an indication of the enduring capacity of these texts to provoke and offer new resources of thought (and with the hope that this sense of "classic" will not run into interference with the specific literary period of *Weimarer Klassik*, in which Goethe and Schiller adopt very different themes and poetics).

Situating my investigation in terms of Sturm und Drang scholarship allows a more precise description of its aesthetic and political stakes. Critics of this youthful and rebellious movement (whose first and last major dramas are at the core of my investigation) have traditionally focused on violence either as violence of style on the one hand, or as an instrument of political critique on the other. I both widen the scope of these analyses and connect them in a differently accented way.

Earlier responses saw Sturm und Drang as a movement that in the latter part of the eighteenth century opposed the rational principles of neoclassical aesthetics that guided drama during the greater part of the century. Here the immediate response to the movement focused on the violence of style over that of content. Indeed, proponents of the young German authors of the 1770s justified the former through an analogy with the latter: a young admirer of Goethe marvels that he breaks the constraints of poetic form just as Götz breaks through the lines of enemy knights.[2] The public applauded the rejection of the classical dictates of dramatic form as defended by Gottsched and saw the violence of the new generation of playwrights as a founding violence that creates a properly German drama free of French influence. I also pay close attention to formal questions, but in terms of aesthetics I broaden the array of techniques that mark disruption. In particular, I place a strong emphasis on the violence of rhetoric to show how Goethe, Schiller, and Kleist use classical literary tropes in unexpected ways, both as illuminating models for the political structures they engage and as stark challenges to knowledge and power hidden on the very surface of beautiful language.

More recently, scholars have argued that such an appeal to aesthetics can be explained by the fact that the older generation of contemporary critics largely agreed with the political direction of Sturm und Drang. Up to a certain point, rebels of this movement could be said to participate in a critique of traditional forms of social structuring and government as the Enlightenment extended its reach beyond the realms of art and science. Andreas Huyssen covers the shift in literary criticism since the 1960s and argues that Sturm und Drang radicalized, but did not break with, the Enlightenment project.[3] Such a conception has the virtue of emphasizing the political aspect of this movement against other aspects that might suggest it was merely a precursor of romanticism that opens an abyssal interiority (for which *Werther* can stand as shorthand).

While engaging the Enlightenment line of criticism, I argue that its interpretation succeeds only by ignoring the extreme nature of the violence in the texts I examine. Three of the greatest heroes of *Goethezeit* literature partake in violent attacks that go beyond aesthetic novelty or rational critique. As just one example, *Götz von Berlichingen* and *The Robbers* feature main characters who are responsible not only for attacks on the government, but for the killing of civilians. Although attacks on the government's representatives might be understood as staging an Enlightenment critique of tradition in that they resist corrupt rulers (albeit without the broad message of tolerance of such epochal texts as Lessing's *Nathan the Wise*), acts such as setting fire to an entire city can only be described as an accidental excess or madness from the point of view of the Enlightenment. The fact that such violence appears again and again, however, indicates that this excess plays an important role in these texts which needs to be addressed.[4] *Michael Kohlhaas*, which I read as a post-Sturm und Drang novella that confronts the age of the French Revolution with the unarticulated rage of pre-1789 Europe, leaves no doubt that the madness of attacks on civilians has become a premeditated method of pursuing a pathologically cast and personal goal.

Pivoting on this specific moment in history, my first chapter takes up political discourse and theory to trace the defense mechanisms that appropriate violence and assign it a function in the structure of sovereignty. I take my lead from a speech President George W. Bush gave on 9/11 announcing terrorism as a "test" but at the same time rhetorically disabling the true demand for inquiry that a test involves. In order to open a historical and theoretical field in which to situate my literary readings, I propose a selective mapping of the terms "terror" and "terrorist" in Hobbes, Robespierre, Hegel, and manifestos of the Red Army Faction that focuses on excessive violence. Ultimately, I suggest that Hannah Arendt offers a way to resist the strong tendency to appropriate violence in political theory and to instead perceive violence as truly disruptive.

Literature allows us to see the excessive aspect of violence that political theory seeks to hide while also offering examples of confrontations over the meaning of this violence. Chapter 2 begins with Götz von Berlichingen, who obscenely rejects the Emperor's effort to consolidate his territory by defining Götz as the leader of the rebellious knights and farmers. In the early scenes of the drama, Götz's supporters and enemies turn to him as the prosthetic supplement of their ideologies. Examining these moments establishes a turn and counter-turn that brings us, in the scene with Brother Martin, to the figure of apostrophe, which illuminates how the drama structures political desire by a detour through non-presence. I then examine the complex inner workings of the Emperor's ban of Götz through the work of Agamben and show that his attempt to consolidate the law depends upon a legal apostrophe that would constitute the knight as the outlaw. In a close reading of the end of act 3 we see that the knight does not resist but instead *insists* on his very absence, displaying his weakness as a form of strength, as a political and ontological gambit whose structure is revealed in the grammatical structure of the apotrope, the turn back, the turn to the rear and of the rear in language.

In my third chapter I examine the precise mechanisms that *The Robbers* employs to incorporate violence into its models of individual and social identity. In order to elucidate these psychic and social structures I mobilize the resources of Freud's death drive, which sees in repetition compulsion a structuring function: the traumatized individual organizes his life around a wound. In this light, Karl Moor's terrorism emerges as the clash between his actual violent acts and the drama's struggle to incorporate violence around the rhetorically projected figure of the "manly" right hand. When Karl announces his intention to sacrifice himself to the law at the end of the drama, he appears to simply repeat the structure of his oath in act 1 by figuring himself as a cast-off body that enables a greater logic of totality. Yet the violence that has come to the stage since then, culminating in his murder of Amalia, leads me to propose that the structuring power of violence be reconceived as reparation (to use Klein's term) emerging from an eternally compromised circuit that offers the potential of a new relation irreducible to a pre-set construct.

My final chapter examines the violence in *Michael Kohlhaas* in terms of a conjunction of the call and violence that cuts through the sovereign's authority over time. Kohlhaas sees himself responding to an appeal for action that in his acts of murder and arson becomes a call for revolution. Drawing on the work of Avital Ronell and Hannah Arendt, I argue that this appeal continues to reverberate even after he accepts Luther's appeal to lay down his arms. While he achieves his goal at the end, he is also put to death. According to the narrator this double outcome is not a threat to the history books, to which he sends the reader at the end of the novella. Yet careful attention to the fortune-teller story in light of the earlier violence in the novella reveals the problem of representing violence as a historical chronicle, a sequence of events. Instead, the eruption of the fantastic through the feminine hand of the fortune-teller interrupts this chronology, bringing into question the gender and genre of history.

Indeed, each text leverages its despair by introducing a counterforce to history and its upheavals. This counterforce appears in the guise of the woman—whether it be Götz's wife Elisabeth who urges him to write his biography of resistance, Amalia who forces the rupture of Karl Moor's economy of the wound, or the fortune-teller in *Kohlhaas*—that resignifies the narrative before us, opening the future of an alternative history. My conclusion returns to twentieth-century political theory, specifically the work of Benjamin and Arendt, to offer some new suggestions about how to respond to extreme violence based on the results of my literary investigations.

Literature may, in one of its modalities, offer an escape from affairs of the world to the pleasures of imagination. In this respect, classical works can be said to offer refuge in the events of the distant past and faraway places. Although I do not deny this valence, my investigation insists that German literature around 1800 opens an ethical field in which to examine questions of terrorism. With an insistence on showing the disaster even, indeed precisely, at moments when we want to look away, Goethe, Schiller, and Kleist force us to rethink key assumptions about politics, history, and knowledge that inform our response to extreme violence.

Chapter 1

✦

The Test of Terrorism

Retaking 1800

The ethical core of my investigation, the demand that violence be addressed as an interruption that requires original response rather than as an occasion to reinforce uninterrogated habits of thought, beckons as an intuition, as suspicion, as a sense of injustice. However, since epistemological roadblocks prevent its immediate articulation I need to begin by asking how we can even perceive violence in its excessive dimension. To show why we need to take the test of terrorism to German literature around 1800, I begin from political discourse much closer to the present. In George W. Bush's remarks on 9/11 I see a threat to power that, while disavowed by the president himself, deserves to be addressed as a serious question about the certainty of history in the eyes of the sovereign and the role of the spectator of violence.[1]

The following review of the history of the term "terrorism" suggests that it may indicate a value judgment rather than a description of a specific kind of violence. Instead of rejecting the term on these grounds, I propose a history of terrorism from Hobbes to Arendt that focuses on the excessive dimension of violence, staying close to that which prevents the closure of conceptual frames. Looking at terror in an arc from Hobbes to Robespierre allows a description from the point of view of the sovereign, who seeks to incorporate all violence as a sign of his power. This line of argument aligns with the first sense of "making" in my introduction. A second arc, from the German Red Army Faction to Arendt, suggests a temporary emergence of violence that would lead quickly to a new form of government, and then subtly points to a violence that cannot be incorporated. I read Arendt as engaging my second sense of "making" in a way that sends us to literature as a unique site of dramatic and narrative confrontation with challenges to aesthetics, epistemology, and political theory.

Terror as Test

In his public remarks from Barksdale Air Force Base in Louisiana on the afternoon of September 11, 2001, President George W. Bush began with a short but rhetorically intricate sentence that identified the victim of attack in a broad yet specific manner while introducing a placeholder for the attacker: "Freedom itself was attacked this morning by a faceless coward, and freedom will be defended."[2] Bush starts by substantializing an idea in a way that creates a complementary foe. The target of the attack was not specific buildings or people, but the freedom that they represent. He creates a body through this trope; it is almost a personification. On the other side, he unifies the agent of the attack, speaking of a single planner behind a series of hijackings and collisions. While freedom shines forth in Bush's rhetoric, the attacker recedes into a "faceless" obscurity that magnifies his threat.

Bush closed his remarks with words that seem to situate the hidden threat at least broadly in the precinct of the academy, where, in the true sense of examination, thought would confront the limit of its mastery: "The resolve of this great nation is being tested." Instead of pressing into the borderline of knowledge though, he escapes quickly to certainty and the divine: "But make no mistake: We will show the world that we will pass this test. God bless."[3] In warning the public against misunderstanding, Bush also makes it clear that he's taking a test where no errors are possible. As Avital Ronell demonstrates, Bush's remark instead cuts off the danger of inquiry in advance, imposing a simultaneity that closes the threat of non-knowledge at the same instant that it opens it: "the utterance subverts the condition of *being tested* by offering that, at the moment of its mention, the test has been passed."[4] Ronell goes on to explain how this preemptive closure has a clear political effect, since once Bush describes the test of terror in this manner it immediately produces meaning and places the president at the center of a historical task. That which potentially shakes the sovereign at his foundation becomes the very vehicle for his solidity and self-identity. The attack does not only fail to challenge accepted assumptions of strength and unity, but actually provides the opportunity to mobilize stockpiled defenses in the cultural, political, and military realms that prove not only that the state has not been wounded, but that it was whole in the first place.

A number of reasons could be offered to explain why Bush names the test of 9/11 but quickly closes down its disruptive question. First of all, if "freedom itself" suggests a stable, if vague, referent, the phrase "the resolve of this great nation" resists parsing. Who or what actually takes the test? Secondly, the test defies location. Specific sites were attacked but "we" Americans are all implicated. At the same time the challenge exceeds national limits since the entire world watches for our response. Thirdly, the question of the appropriate length of the test poses a threat. As we saw again later in this administration's decision to invade Iraq, time for reflection was second to the felt need for immediate action. Bush names terrorism as a test but forecloses arduous engagement with it.

As a response to the missed challenge, and considering the attacks of 9/11 as a traumatic blockage that needs to be engaged through detours and new vantage points, I will consider terrorism in literature. My inquiry takes seriously Bush's question of the audience of terrorism, the theater of war, and asks about "the world" that watches for a response.[5] Who are we acting for in a response to terrorism? Does the "the world" stand in for God? For History? Who would be the appropriate responder?

In order to interrogate these questions, I propose a move backward that lingers with violence rather than immediately looking forward as Bush's rhetoric proposes. Indeed, Bush appeals to an idea of history as judge even as he refuses to look back. The term "terrorist" arises in response to violence, and its trajectory allows us to more precisely describe the challenge to judgment that arises around extreme violence. Following closely on the heels of the liberatory event of the French Revolution, the Reign of Terror erupts violently from within what was supposedly a victory of reason. In French, *terroriste* first appeared in 1794, when opponents coined it to describe the recently deposed Robespierre and his fellow leaders, with German and English translations appearing in the foreign press shortly thereafter.[6] As a term with a specific political role, it attempted to frame the danger to the public realm that the most radical elements of the revolution continued to pose even after Robespierre's Reign of Terror ended. The word quickly entered the political vocabulary of Europe as a general term of vilification in the years leading up to the revolutions of 1848. Then it began to be employed more frequently as a description of specific groups opposed to the state, at first in reference to small, armed anti-government groups in Russia.

The *Oxford English Dictionary*'s general definition of "terrorist" follows this sense: "A person who uses and favors violent and intimidating methods of coercing a government or community."[7] Even this short sentence opens up a breadth of generality that also characterizes the legal definitions of the term today. Is a violent method always physically harmful? Can such a method ever fail to intimidate? Where does the line between private and public fall, and how does the phrase "government or community" gloss over this distinction? Importantly, this definition of terrorism does not tell us anything specific about the motivations or goals of the phenomena.

Social scientists who attempt to clarify the terms "terrorism" and "terrorist" have not been able to agree on a definition that gleans conceptual knowledge from the historical catalogue of instances in which the term has been employed. Even Rudolf Walter's patient and precise investigation of the term in the eminent reference work *Geschichtliche Grundbegriffe* (*Basic Historical Concepts*) fails to produce the minimum level of cohesion that the adjective "historical" in the title implies.[8] Rather than showing up in a limited number of situations and settling into common semantic boundaries, the term instead appears in practically every period of social upheaval and never congeals into more than a mere series of cases in which violence was used against a government. In moments of disciplinary self-critique though, social scientists do hone in on the problem that exceeds their methods and instruments of analysis. While also seeking distinctions and trends, Walter Laqueur, perhaps the most widely published contemporary scholar of terrorism, puts the problem bluntly: he admits that a definition of terrorism will not be found because there are simply too many variations of violence.[9] The political scientist Brynar Lia offers a subtler but more trenchant examination of the same question that shifts the historical problems of defining the word "terrorist" to the present. Lia begins his study of terrorism with a review of the use of the term in his discipline, noting the lack of empirical work and the preponderance of speculative accounts from a psychological or ideological point of view. Rather than establishing and questioning causality from a body of data that itself must be analyzed, such work tends simply to assign blame or argue for a future course of action. "Terrorism databases do exist, but they have been criticized for not being entirely scientifically coded."[10] Indeed, the problem turns out not to be merely one of further categorizing generally identified acts of terrorism, but of the very first determination. Terrorism resists empirical examination at the most basic level because social scientists are unable to agree on a definition that would allow them to constitute the object of empirical research.

Lia emphasizes the lack of criteria for clearly separating terrorist attacks from civil war operations as one of the main examples of such disagreement.[11] This specific aspect of the debate over the meaning of the term shows how the preferred methods of social scientists falter at the question of legitimacy, a question which circulates in all discussions about terrorism (at least in America since the 1980s) under the threatening reversibility of the terrorist and freedom fighter. In other words, is anti-state violence ever legitimate, and who judges this legitimacy? And of course an analogous inversion operates from the point of view of state and non-state violence: non-state terrorists have from the nineteenth century accused the state of prior terror.

Leviathan and Robespierre Go Rogue

The failure of social scientists to find a workable definition of "terrorism" might lead one to dismiss the term as a mere rhetorical label that adds nothing to the description of a violent attack other than an indication of the speaker's largely subjective and contingent evaluation of the event. In contrast, I see "terrorism" as a key part of political vocabulary precisely because of its inherent resistance to closure. Instead of seeking to end the debate over violence, I propose expanding it so that it breaks from automatically triggered accusations rooted in fixed ideologies. Classic German literature offers an occasion for such a widened discussion by staging violence that exceeds set frames of interpretation and then modeling reactions to violence from a number of different points of view. Even though literary narrative, be it in the drama or novella, tends to wrap things up at the end, my readings of Goethe, Schiller, and Kleist emphasize minority viewpoints that introduce productive structural fissures in apparently ossified arguments over the meaning of violence.

The literary texts that we will read offer a rich engagement with history as they look back from their own position to a time 300 years before. While their authors write in the years just before and after the French Revolution, they set their work in an earlier period of major change: the years when the decentralized feudal relations of the Middle Ages began to give way to a modern state that claims sole and ultimate authority. Moving from Hobbes (as the founding thinker of modern political thought) to Robespierre, I follow a link in political theory between acts and statements of "terror" and sovereignty's hidden desire to destroy the private realm that it claims to represent. To start, a close reading of Hobbes's text shows that the social contract does not provide the fully transparent and reversible conduit between the private and public that it promises, and that instead a subtle reference to "terror" serves as the power of the Leviathan to impose unity even in the face of dissent and model of agreement authorized by the social contract.

Responding to the civil strife that plagued England during his lifetime, Thomas Hobbes developed a theoretical justification of the sovereign that famously replaces tradition and divine guarantee with rational self-interest. While he was not the first to name the social contract, his articulation of this key conceptual document in the seventeenth century offered such promise that political theory has sought to resolve its many subtle inconsistencies ever since.[12] Speaking broadly in the language of political theory following Hobbes, the state of nature describes the sovereign state's other, a wild and violent place or time before people surrendered their individual right to violence to a ruler. On the standard view, terror plays a key role in the move to sovereignty in that the terror of the sovereign replaces an already existent terror in the state of nature. In his book on Hobbes's *Leviathan*, Carl Schmitt expresses this view of the pre-existence of terror with his customary deceptive clarity: "The terror [*Der Schrecken*] of the state of nature drives anguished individuals [*angsterfüllten Individuen*] to come together; their fear rises to an extreme; a spark of reason [*ratio*] flashes [*blitzt auf*]—and suddenly there stands in front of them a new god."[13] In this formulation, Schmitt speaks of terror as an extreme state of anxiety. As our investigation begins, we can bracket the trenchant analyses of "Angst" from Kierkegaard to Heidegger and understand it as worry about one's immediate safety. However, such fundamental and primal worry will continue to exert existential pressure on the unfolding discussion of political motifs and themes.

In the state of nature, one breathes terror as the total pervasiveness of concern for defense from attack. One can never escape from its reach, but in its very totality it acquires the force of compulsion, a structuring power that brings people together. Indeed, terror itself reigns supreme, acting both from without (the location of the threat) and within (full of anxiety, the individual has no space for reflection). Surprisingly, according to Schmitt even reason itself follows from terror, exploding necessarily from within an extreme atmosphere of fear.

The apparent simplicity of Schmitt's description, however, elides Hobbes's own intricate use of the term "terror," specifically in relation to "fear." Working out this distinction will help us focus on the moment when the sovereign appears, a famously problematic transition that Schmitt's dash inadvertently highlights. On the one hand, we might suppose that his description of a sudden flash (*Blitz*) means that reason exists in the state of nature, at least in a basic form that allows it to burst out at the highest moment of threat. On the other hand, Schmitt's phrasing opens the possibility that reason comes out of nowhere, striking unexpectedly like lightening (also *Blitz* in German) from within the highly charged atmosphere of fear. The undecidability of Schmitt's description points to two contradictory models of representation in the *Leviathan* that will allow me to describe a moment within sovereignty that resists sovereignty.

Hobbes's *Leviathan* proceeds to its renowned political discussions after a lesser known preparatory section on the basic characteristics of the individuals that will form the sovereign. Hobbes, the great nominalist, provides precise definitions of "the passions" which he refers to later in the part of his treatise that focuses on the theory of the state. In this section he defines "fear" as "Aversion, with opinion of Hurt from the object."[14] His definition grounds a subject by defining him in his attempt to avoid an object that nonetheless remains a constant point of reference. The phrase "opinion of Hurt" retains some minimal sense of knowledge and indicates at least a basic moment of judgment. Further down the list, Hobbes precisely defines "Terror," as a subtraction from fear that arises from the absence of this object: "Fear, without the apprehension of why, or what" (Hobbes, *Leviathan* 45). In a break from its point of reference, the subject comes unanchored. A longer note of what seems to be commentary on this first definition runs: "whereas in truth there is always in him that so feareth, first, some apprehension of the cause, though the rest run away by example; every one supposing his fellow to know why" (45). This explanation revolves around an opposition between the one who fears and the ones who follow him. This first person actually fears, in that he still has a relation to the object. His flight from this object, however, induces a kind of contagion, and the others mechanically follow him. From an epistemological point of view, there has been a transfer of knowledge, but it occurs automatically, without the pause needed for reflection and without precision. The followers assume that the first person has a legitimate connection to the feared object and conclude that they should fear this object too despite the fact that this conduit does not actively reveal the object to them.

On my reading "fear," while characterized as an emotion, allows a space for considered decision, while terror causes a sudden jump that does not. When Hobbes describes the move from the state of nature to the Leviathan in chapter 13, he remains faithful to his earlier definition when he speaks of fear as a determinant, but one consistent with rational decision. At the start of the process, he famously describes life in the state of nature as "solitary, poor, nasty, brutish, and short" (Hobbes, *Leviathan* 113). One remains alone, always responsible first and foremost for one's own survival. The constant threat to security leaves time for little else, hence the condition of poverty. And clearly a life of this sort cannot be expected to last very long, since one faces threats at all times from all directions and existence, in any case, has a relatively short shelf life. The adjective "brutish" sends man back to the animals, an important aspect of Hobbes's negative conception of nature and a point to which we will return in more detail later, especially in the metaphorical descriptions of Götz the wolf, Karl the bear, and Kohlhaas the foaming horse—metamorphoses that Derrida has described as part of the crucial metaphorological dimension of sovereignty in crisis.[15] In the sentence just before this one, however, the thing that Hobbes terms "worst of all" in the state of nature is the "continuall feare, and danger of violent death" (113). Thinking of this "fear" in terms of his earlier definition of the term, we see that it has a clear "object." Since humans are effectively equal in physical and mental strength, each can challenge each when a particular good is scarce. "Terror" would not apply here because one knows the "what" and "why."

In order to escape this condition of the state of nature, people decide to establish a social contract (called by Hobbes a "covenant") that provides security at the price of individual freedom. Hobbes describes this decision in rational terms that imply objectivity. People weigh the advantages of security and relinquish their original freedom. It makes sense to do so because the gain in safety is real, but the loss of freedom is not a real loss. Instead, the individual transfers power to a representative. As Hobbes writes later, men "confer all their power and strength upon one man, or upon one assembly of men, that may reduce all their wills, by plurality of voices, unto one will" who is "to bear their person" (Hobbes, *Leviathan* 157). Hobbes's political theory relies on a complex process of representation in which the wills of the private person appear again in the will of the leader. The process appears to be a simple exchange but instead marks a transformation that depends on a careful rhetorical formulation. Hobbes identifies the medium of the transformation from private to public in terms of an equal physical force (of "power and strength") that then allows the reduction of mental force (of "wills") that parallels a reduction in number. One might expect this reduction to result in a loss but on the contrary, in a picture of perfect clarity and pure speculation, authority spreads out at the same moment that it draws into a center.[16] Each person should "acknowledge himself to be author of whatsoever he that so beareth their person, shall act, or cause to be acted" (157–58). The people look at the ruler and see themselves, a relation that implies knowledge ("acknowledge"). Further, the ruler, who "beareth their person" according to this metaphor, bears them, carries them and carries out their will. Intention, in the form of an authorship that moves to authority, starts outside of the leader.

From the point of view of the individual, Hobbes's description of the move from individual to sovereign works as a smooth and rational transfer. According to the model of clear reciprocity that this transfer implies, one would expect his later description of this relationship from the point of view of the sovereign that follows shortly thereafter to simply restate this move in reverse. A subtle terminological shift, however, indicates a theoretical fault line and asymmetry: "For by this authority, given him by every particular man in the commonwealth, he hath the use of so much power and strength conferred on him, that by terror thereof, he is enabled to form the wills of them all, to peace at home, and mutual aid against their enemies abroad" (158). According to the definitions set forth earlier in *Leviathan*, "fear" would seem to be the correct term here instead of "terror," in that a specific object can be identified, namely, the "strength" that the people had previously "conferred" on the sovereign. The Leviathan would seem to rule by fear to the extent that the individual must avoid him as the composite power of the state.

By choosing the word "terror," Hobbes points to a change in quality that takes place after the institution of the Leviathan. The power of the state results not simply from a shift from many people to one, but in a jump to a totality of strength because once power has been given away, representation assumes a unity that cannot be re-divided. The sovereign has the creative and framing power, he can "form the wills" of the people once they form him. The passage explicitly says that this does not only offer protection from without, but "peace" within the state. In other words, the unity that has been established may not be reversed. The point of view of the sovereign depends on a proleptic logic: the terror that he acquires from the people's unity allows the creation of this unity in the first place. Thus, the people both recognize and do not recognize themselves in the Leviathan. What appears to be a smooth and transparent transition becomes a hard block when one looks back.[17]

In the quote above "terror" at first seems to be used in a different, more general sense than Hobbes's specific definition requires. Only attention to the specific epistemological threat of the term reveals its surprising accuracy: the self-positing sovereign withdraws as an object for the people, and to this extent their relation to him is indeed one of fear of the unknown, one of terror.[18]

This is the key to the state's temporal stability, as a short passage earlier demonstrates. Discussing the artificial condition of the covenant, as opposed to the natural modes in which animals (such as bees) associate, Hobbes writes that "it is no wonder if there be somewhat else required (besides Covenant) to make their Agreement constant and lasting, which is a Common Power, to keep them in awe, and to direct their actions to the Common Benefit." In a political theory supposedly centered on the rational agreement of the social contract, the contract (covenant) is not enough. A society that relies on the contract alone creates a hypothetically pure horizontal relationship in which each citizen makes an agreement with every other. Beyond the impracticality of such an arrangement lies a serious theoretical problem: unity, even if it were once achieved, would immediately be in jeopardy. It would be anarchy in the strict sense of a society without ruling principle. For Hobbes, consistency requires that one man be invested with more power than the sum of all the others. "Keeping them in awe" indicates a move from the rational relation of speculation to one in which the language of emotion takes over. "Awe" aligns with "Terror" and marks a loss of knowledge that Hobbes's sovereign needs to hide the process of its creation and maintain its unity. The sovereign cannot act as a unified representation and enact the process of unification at the same time.

Another parallel might be drawn with the definition of "terror" in the section on the passions, in terms of fear through another person who knows the object of the threat. As privileged example, the sovereign can be seen to take over the role of the subject supposed to fear (to allude, if only in passing to Lacan's description of transference in terms of "the subject supposed to know": the patient needs to see the analyst as an ideal that can understand the symptoms he describes). In this light, the sovereign bears the person whom he represents by taking over his fear of violent death.[19] This individual becomes a political subject in losing *this* fear. For the relationship to the Leviathan to operate, it must not be a relationship of fear, one that connects to a specific object that can be broken down into composite parts. Instead, a distortion must arise in the creation of political representation that ensures its solidity.

For Hobbes then, "terror" functions as the marker of a paradoxical instrument of power that enables formation of the sovereign by both acknowledging and denying reference. The sovereign splits and operates on two theoretical models. Meanwhile, the individual seems to have been expelled from the state. In the wake of the French Revolution, this expulsion finds its historical instantiation. "Terror" entered political discourse in the speeches of Robespierre, who, with the fellow members of the Committee of Public Safety, was called "terrorist" in the French press shortly after his fall in 1794. With his careful dialectical motion, Hegel's concise reading of the Reign of Terror in his *Vorlesungen über die Philosophie der Weltgeschichte* (*Lectures on the Philosophy of World History*) will help identify a point of breakdown in terror's role in establishing sovereignty and indicate a turn within this breakdown which creates the subject that not only seeks to withdraw from the social contract, but turns the sovereign's claim to total power against it.

Hegel picks up on the Law of Suspects, officially "The Decree of September 17th Relating to Suspect Persons" ("Le décret du 17 septembre 1793 relatif aux gens suspects"), as a pivotal point in the aftermath of the French Revolution. The law infamously inverted the standard presumption of innocence that the citizen assumes when accused of wrongdoing. For a time, one was guilty until proven innocent. At this point in history, Hegel says that "virtue [*Tugend*]" (Robespierre's *virtu*) operates as the standard of deciding who belongs in society: "Here, virtue is a simple principle which merely distinguishes [*unterscheidet*] between those who are virtuously disposed and those who are not. But disposition [*Die Gesinnung*] can only be recognized and judged by disposition."[20] Virtue works as a sharp instrument, cutting (as the *scheiden* in *unterscheiden* suggests) a line between those who belong to the revolutionary society and those who do not. It creates an original division between the inside and the outside. The diacritical power of this instrument faces a problem of judgment in that it does not have an external standard of measure.

Hegel describes the implications of the law in terms of "disposition [*Gesinnung*]," which he employs as a broad term of belonging that we can align with Hobbes's formalism. The German term resists exact translation but one may provisionally think of it as "attitude" as well, especially to the extent that both "disposition" and "attitude" suggest the difficulty of linking up with a definite external referent. More specifically, Hegel uses the term at this point in his work in the sense of "the right frame of mind," to indicate the formal aspect of the public realm.

Even when one reads "Gesinnung" as ethos (another of its definitions) the problem remains: it must both exclude and justify itself as a totality. When it attempts to do so, Hegel sees a paradigmatic moment of dialectical inversion. The assumption of power turns into downfall: "Consequently, suspicion rules [*herrscht*]; but as soon as virtue comes under suspicion, it is already condemned [*verurteilt*]."[21] "Suspicion rules," as in "suspicion is everywhere," but also more literally in the sense that suspicion has the power. Virtue as purity and unity does not have a chance to pass the test of suspicion. The judgment that it hoped to mete out turns against itself in that in failing to institute a division that would create identity, it shows itself to be non-unified, no more than an originary dispersion. *Beurteilen* collapses into *Ur-teile* in the literal sense, and from here the entire attempt is itself judged (*verurteilen*).

At this point terror emerges in Hegel's exegesis: "Suspicion acquired terrible power [*eine fürchterliche Gewalt*] and brought the monarch . . . to the scaffold."[22] Terrible violence marks not the success of judgment but its failure. The following line begins with specific reference to Robespierre's speech of February 5, 1794: "Now *virtue* [*Tugend*] and *terror* [*Schrecken*] prevailed; for subjective virtue, whose rule is based purely on disposition, brings the most terrible tyranny in its train. It exercises its power without legal forms, and the penalty it imposes is equally simple, namely death."[23] Rule "based purely on disposition" fails to achieve the objective form of law. The form of governance that it leads to lacks mediation in the sense of legality for its punishment, and the death penalty gives evidence of a failure to distinguish. Execution exemplifies simple negation of that which does not belong to the state; it demonstrates the failure of the state to reach the basic point of unity that would permit representation.

A comparison between "terror" in Hobbes's description of the Leviathan's emergence and Hegel's account of the French Revolution reveals a key difference for my investigation. The thousands of individual killings at that point, leading up to the execution of the former king, only *attempt* to create the unified representational structure that Hobbes describes. The audiences around the guillotine should be read as the state's attempt to create the impression of absolute power, while the fact that the executions lead to ever more executions reveals the failure of its operation. Seen from the perspective of Hobbes, Hegel's phrase "*virtue* and *terror*" indicates a disjunction rather than the correct connection. For Hobbes, the sovereign rules *through* terror; his power induces awe. Robespierre's reign of terror demonstrates instead the *separation* of terror and power. My close reading of Karl Moor's final monologue in chapter 3 in which he imagines his own execution will provide an opportunity to more carefully examine this relation between sovereign power and the criminal's body. For now, let us say that the people never sufficiently stand in awe of Robespierre in the manner that Hobbes requires for the state to be pointed in a certain direction. Instead there are, if not merely executions, executions that merely fail to represent.

Continuing with the combined logic of political and aesthetic philosophy that Hegel has developed, we need to ask why political representation goes wrong in the case of the French Revolution, and what this tells us about its representation more generally.[24] One might take a historical route to explain why certain groups continued to engage in civil attacks, or even to show that the government itself caused the problem by not assuming power and stopping the executions. Such an approach obscures the underlying structural problem though, which is that power needs to make its own rules for ruling. It needs to assume its authority but showing how it does so necessarily works against its intent. We have reached an impassible point, an aporia of representation. The following chapters trace engagements with this aporia in the literature around the time that it emerges in political theory, not to examine *why* political representation goes wrong, but *how* it goes wrong in specific instances. These encounters show how each failure leads to displacements of power that are hard to perceive within a model that seeks to do away with subtle deceptive gestures of representative construction.

Before moving on to my literary readings, however, I wish to complete the arc from the excluded subject of sovereignty to this subject's turn against the sovereignty that excluded him. Hegel concludes his section on the French Revolution with a famous move in which world history goes forward by seeming to go backwards, leaving France for Reformation Germany and freedom of conscience. Our reading of Hobbes suggests that the threat of the private cannot simply be reduced to a specific stage in the history of government, but instead constantly endangers it. The Reformation, from this point of view, would be another attempt to refigure the private threat to the public, though not a solution to the fundamental antagonism.

Maurice Blanchot develops precisely this generality of the threat of the private in a passage which, while opening with a reference to Hegel's reading of the Law of Suspects, brings us back to the sleight of hand at the heart of political representation. In his inquiry into the seemingly innocuous idea of the "everyday," in the *Infinite Conversation*, Blanchot begins by pushing it out of its usual private realm and into the public by considering the moment of revolution. Moving quickly from an explicit paraphrase of Hegel to his own exposition, he writes: "The suspect is this fleeting [*fuyante*] presence that does not allow recognition [*ne se laisse pas reconnaître*], and through the part always held back [*toujours réservée*] that he figures forth, he tends not only to interfere with the work of the State, but also to place it under accusation."[25] Far from being easily identified and picked out from the lineup, the suspect challenges state knowledge, the "connaître" within "reconnaître." He gets in the way of the state and can't be circumvented. Instead, he turns around the accusation.

We'll want to follow the variations on this turn, starting with Götz von Berlichingen's rhetorical turn of the backside to the Emperor's troops. At the moments of resistance that I will read, the terrorist is first a rogue, "fleeting" in the words of Blanchot, but at the same time stubbornly in the way. In their singularity, in their unique persecutions, the literary figures I follow reveal something more than an unwanted remainder in a model of political unity. Indeed, like the suspect in Blanchot they become the figure for the individual as such in relation to the state: "From such a perspective each governed is suspect; yet each suspect accuses the one who governs and prepares him to be at fault since he who governs must one day recognize that he does not represent the whole, but a still particular will that only usurps the appearance of the universal."[26] In this sense the suspect signals an obstacle to the ruler, something that he will not be able to accept in the time of his rule. He will eventually recognize that he is not able to totally recognize and represent, falling from the position of awe and terror that Hobbes awarded him. The "still particular will" implies but resists, in the "still," a transformation into a "general will" of the sort that Rousseau proposed in the *Social Contract* (in a development of the Hobbesian conception of the ruler who wills for the people).[27] While Blanchot had opened his reading with a gesture to the public nature of private life in moments of revolution, his analysis ultimately demonstrates a crisis on the public/private split as a danger that must be temporarily and temporally contained with subterfuge. The ruler never truly governs legitimately; he is always an impostor, one who "usurps" the totality.

At this point we seem to have gone off track, to have swerved away from the question at hand both in terms of terminology and discipline. The French Revolution and the "suspect" have hijacked and diverted an investigation into "terror" in political philosophy from Hobbes to Hegel. I want to hold on to this swerve by connecting what Blanchot calls the "suspect" with a mechanism that turns against the common meaning that imposes itself. To do so I conclude this section by mobilizing the figure of the "rogue" in order to twist open a conceptual space from which the "terrorist" will emerge as one who makes a specific kind of accusation with the violence that he employs.

In the logic of the representational break that I have described from Hobbes to Blanchot, sovereignty, in its very insecurity and inability to establish itself, produces the figure that broadcasts its illegitimacy.[28] Expanding this investigation by articulating the place of the rogue in a logic of sovereign power prepares us to see this logic from another point of view—ultimately one that the sovereign no longer controls. In *Rogues*, Derrida sets his sights on the "rogue state" and its relation to democracy, picking up on a phrase that had been recently thrust into the center of political discourse by President George W. Bush. In order to work up to Bush's bellicose speech act, he starts with specific definitions, individual rogues that he summons or beckons, drawing them out from their hiding places. While Derrida wants to open the semantic field of a term that has been put to specific political use, I wish to stay, for the most part, at this preliminary stage, highlighting a few of the evasive figures that gather under the name "rogue."

The word appears in the middle of the sixteenth century in the sense of "an idle vagrant, a vagabond." Its etymology is uncertain, but it probably derives from the Latin *rogare*, meaning "to beg." From the very beginning, it relates to a drain or non-productive withdrawal from an established economy. The *Oxford English Dictionary* notes that it may have a nearer relative in "roger," a slang term from the sixteenth century referring to "a begging vagrant pretending to be a poor Oxford or Cambridge scholar," a definition that points to the rogue's reliance on the mask (and perhaps a point of undecidability between the student and the delinquent—Karl Moor). The term's meaning expands by the end of the century to "a dishonest, unprincipled person; a rascal." Here we can note the negative prefixes, the "dis-" and the "un-" as indicators of the rogue's negative force.

In the nineteenth century the term branched out from the realm of the human to that of the vegetable, referring to a non-standard variant of a plant, as well as to the animal realm, particularly elephants and horses. Derrida emphasizes the connection to the animal, noting that the terms *voyou* and *Schurke* that are used to translated "rogue" into French and German apply only to humans.[29] The blinkers of the horse are referred to as "a rogue badge," which Derrida sees as significant in that it marks and sets the rogue apart. In fact, it does more than set apart, it prepares a more active persecution, it is a "mark of infamy" that "discriminates by means of first banishing or exclusion which then leads to a bringing before the law."[30] The broadest metaphorical sense of the word developed in the twentieth century: "Inexplicably aberrant, faulty, or defective; misplaced, occurring (esp. in isolation) at an unexpected place or time; uncontrolled, undisciplined, irresponsible." I see the fact that the failure to conform cannot be explained as an indication of the rogue's expulsion from the common regime of language, of his exclusion at the most basic level.

"Terrorism" in the reading I have been developing would then not be a category that allows identification but an indicator of a threat to representation that is at once political, aesthetic, and epistemological. In his reading of the terrorist attacks of 9/11 published shortly after *Rogues*, Derrida points to the difficult logic of this threat in a manner that I wish to distill in order to further specify the stakes of my investigation and develop the approach that my readings of Goethe, Schiller, and Kleist will follow. In his formulation, on 9/11 the very system that allowed the attack to be identified itself suffered a blow. He describes a "double *crash*" of 9/11 which impacted both particular individuals, buildings, and symbols and the very "hermeneutic apparatus that might have allowed one to see coming, to comprehend, interpret, describe, speak of and name 'September 11.' "[31] Italicized for emphasis, the "*crash*" suffers typographically the injury it should signify. It cannot quite stand up and instead appears to lean into the space of the characters surrounding it, a typographical displacement that points to a future that evades predictability. The second part of his list in this quote descends from a broad question to successively narrower threats. Turning it around, one sees a model for the creation of knowledge of Kantian precision: the "hermeneutic apparatus" would build meaning on the foundation of the name that would allow fuller verbal description, then work on the meaning of what was described such that ultimately one reaches predictive understanding.

The "double *crash*" of the terrorist attack brings out the excess of violence, that which cannot be contained or limited to a circumscribable wound. Perhaps this excess defines violence as such, but if this is the case the "hermeneutic apparatus" generally reins it in. Anticipating an objection, Derrida admits that this may appear to reduce the problem of the attacks "to a question of knowledge; it is as if I were in fact content to say that what is terrible about 'September 11,' what remains 'infinite' in this wound, is that we do not *know* what it is. . . . And that is in fact what I am saying."[32] Derrida figures the "terrible," that which aligns with terror, as an epistemological threat; he sees the injury as one to what can be known. He may be "content" with this formulation, but not in the sense of simple satisfaction. He still has more to do to show "that this horizon of nonknowledge, this nonhorizon of knowledge . . . is anything but abstract and idealist."[33] A problem that appears first to be one of epistemology will be seen to have important political ramifications. Work on the "nonhorizon" depends on the horizon that imposes itself as the first ordering system. It backs away from the latter in a manner similar to that of phenomenology, successively bracketing out parts of the hermeneutic apparatus.

While Derrida turns to readings of contemporary political events within the context of the Cold War, I propose a connection between the "double *crash*" and the "nonhorizon of knowledge" that guides patient close readings in the literary field. This slowdown is necessary because, despite the years that have passed since 9/11, there has been little in the way of working-through. The first task is to admit the problem at all. In the rush to recuperate, rebuild, and go to wars that now pass for normal, we do not even know what happened. Terrorism as excessive violence requires an examination of thinking that does not merely confirm what one knows nor identify a measurable quantity of non-knowledge. Instead it challenges the very basis of knowledge by damaging the standard by which such a measure would be taken. Here the excess of violence points beyond social self-identity and in doing so attends to a call for a difficult reconception of the governmental and legal structures that constitute society. In other words, a reading of terror must attempt to engage the very unreadability of violence since this resistance to meaning indicates a demand, something which cannot be expressed within the dominant structuring language of power.

Derrida works out the way the naming of a "rogue" serves sovereign power: it "casts a normative, indeed performative, evaluation, a disdainful or threatening insult, an appellation that initiates an inquiry and prepares prosecution before the law."[34] Here we have the basic strategy of challenged sovereignty that we saw in Hegel and Blanchot's reading of the Law of Suspects: one names that which does not submit in order to incorporate it. My literary analyses will show that this naming also opens a point at which challenges to political power must be acknowledged. The name that should contain also threatens the power of naming, and here a shift in responsibility becomes visible.

Violence as Part and Apart

Before moving to literature though, we need to further specify the second sense of the "making" of a terrorist and articulate the limit of political theory that requires a shift in terrain. If Hobbes explicates a strict theory of incorporating all violence within the purview of the sovereign, later political movements that subscribe to a dynamic view of history after Hegel tend to give violence an important, if only transitional, place. Bringing my review of terrorism into the twentieth century, I now examine an exemplary manifesto of the German terrorist group the Red Army Faction (RAF). The RAF still had hopes that violence could be used as an instrument of historical progress on the model of Hegel and Marx, but its manifestos also reveal a loss of faith in the automatic progress of society. Jumping ahead historically from Hegel to the RAF thus allows us to see violence escaping the intention of its author.[35] Carl Schmitt and Hannah Arendt provide additional conceptual precision in this regard when they explain the view that terrorism is an early stage that leads to greater civil war and thus revolution. Arendt, however, also points to a kind of violence that would be a true interruption of history, and that is where I see a call for literature.

The Enlightenment tradition of thought following Hegel and the French Revolution has a distinct place for violence that stands out most clearly when contrasted with the alternative mode of reasoned debate associated with Kant. As a contemporary defender of this Enlightenment tradition, Jürgen Habermas seeks to exclude violence from his influential conception of the public sphere. With a clear emphasis on rational discourse in the mode of the Enlightenment, he writes that "mutual understanding and intended agreement manifestly rely on the force of more or less good reasons as the only alernative to overt or covert violence."[36] Habermas positions his conception of the public sphere between the purely private realm and the formal power of legal authorities. In this sphere, people discuss pressing issues under the assumptions that, in principle, each participant is equal, shares a common purpose, and seeks to voice the concerns of the whole society. The ideas that they work out, paradigmatically in the meetings in coffee houses but later in the broad field of publishing (especially in newspapers), indirectly reach legislators and thereby can change laws.

Responding to criticisms of his idea that see it as defending the status quo, Habermas writes that

> the question is not that these people are just interested in keeping order, in the sense of keeping a blind order; the question is how can we best institutionalize procedures that presumably have those characteristics, at least until somebody convinces us, in light of the same procedures, that the very implantations are highly selective and repressive. So keeping order is not the issue here; rather it is solving problems of action and coordination with as little violence as possible.[37]

While denying that the public sphere merely ossifies into a defense of one mode of organization, Habermas defends the stability of method. He insists that changes in procedure only occur through certain specific channels, namely "the same procedures" that currently operate. For the purposes of dealing with violence, then, Habermas operates under a logic of self-assumption analogous to the one we have analyzed in Hobbes. The problem here is not so much that the public sphere excludes violence as that it offers strictly limited resources for dealing with its occurrence. The *Goethezeit* texts that I will read raise the question of changes to procedure that result in violence precisely *because* the basic rules for handling a disagreement falter.

Switching back to the Hegelian and Marxist line of the Enlightenment, the RAF's obsession with manifestos speaks to the struggle between language and violence, of the group's difficulty and determination in describing the function of their attacks. The volume *Red Army Faction:*

Texts and Materials on the History of the RAF (*Rote Armee Fraktion: Texte und Materialien zur Geschichte der RAF*) includes sixty-five manifestos from 1970 to 1996. Among these, the text "On Armed Struggle in Western Europe" (dated May 1971) both demonstrates in broad terms the RAF's commitment to a definite tradition of alternative political thought and, more narrowly, explicitly addresses the question of terrorism as a problematic instrument of revolution.[38] In its project of grafting terrorism to Marxist revolution, we learn how the RAF itself saw violence as part of a social progress, while in its critical isolation of the individual violent actor we begin to perceive an inappropriable violence in a form that will be at least a starting point for my literary readings.

"On Armed Struggle in Western Europe" was originally signed "RAF Collective," but, unlike most other manifestos of the group, was later declared to be the work of one person, Horst Mahler. It takes its lead from Mao and Lenin, both of whom Mahler cites at length. In terms of theory, the manifesto develops a Maoist reading of Lenin that argues for the central position of the latter's lesser known writings on terrorism. The section "Terror Against the Ruling Apparatus—A Necessary Element of Mass Struggles" ("Terror gegen den Herrschaftsapparat—ein notwendiges Element der Massenkämpfe") gets to its point quickly. It addresses criticisms of terrorism that appeal to the authority of Lenin's harsh critique of adherents of the anarchistic Narodnaja Wolja (People's Will) party, whose attacks on tsarist Russia ended with the assassination of Alexander II in 1881. In these writings Lenin argues against the anarchist belief that attacks of this type would cause the people to rise up against their oppressors spontaneously. Instead, he insisted on the revolutionary party as a necessary intermediary.

The RAF text then develops an alternate position through reference to texts by Lenin, which, around 1905, explicitly sanction terror as long as it accepts a tie to the party organization. When the manifesto cites Lenin's assertion that "terror must actually fuse [*verschmelzen*] with the mass movement" (*Rote Armee Faction* 80), it speaks to the wish for getting rid of terror as an independent force, even while the RAF still condones it as a temporary means. Although the manifesto emphasizes the differences between the anarchist and communist interpretations of terrorism, from the point of view of violence's signifying structure it is clear that the two methods agree on their goal, at least along the general lines of a rebellion of the people who would then take power and start a better society. The attacks of the anarchist, like those of the Marxist, reach forward to a set result.[39] From this point of view, special attention must be paid to the RAF text's specific emphasis on Lenin's positive response to the communist party resolution in 1906 which recommended "terrorist partisan actions against the representatives of regimes of violence" (*Rote Armee Faction* 81). The conjunction of the partisan and terrorist suggests a path of inquiry in which we can maintain the future-oriented perspective of the Hegelian tradition but recognize severe challenges to its ideas of automatic development and final result.

In *Theory of the Partisan*, Carl Schmitt opens a space between the soldier and the criminal that allows a further disassociation of terrorist from an end goal. His conceptual description applies to the Cold War partisan, whom Schmitt primarily had in mind when he wrote this book in 1962. At the same time, his description also indicates a way of approaching terrorism after the Cold War. Schmitt insists that the partisan is a part of something and by dismantling this structure to reveal a desire, if not achievement, of meaning, we come closer to a method for approaching the singular act of excessive violence. He roots his investigation in the Spanish guerrilla war of 1808 against Napoleon and emphasizes the irregular fighting employed in this war. Schmitt's explication under the heading "Partisan: Word and Concept" works between the two poles of soldier and criminal.[40] He defines the modern partisan as an irregular fighter, who, unlike the uniformed soldier, does not openly display his weapon. He also distinguishes the partisan from the common criminal in that the "partisan" maintains a connection to a "party" and thereby to the political. These distinctions allow Schmitt to produce a positive definition of the partisan as "the tie to a fighting, belligerent, or politically active part or group" (*Theory of the Partisan* 15). The exact constitution of this connection depends on the particular configuration:

> The word *partisan* means one who follows a party, and what that means concretely is very different at different times. This also is true with respect to the party or the front someone belongs to, and also with respect to following [*Mitgehen*], fellow-travelling [*Mitlaufen*], fighting-with, and eventually, to becoming fellow-captives. (15, translation modified)

With an emphasis on motion and action, Schmitt himself makes a number of loops around the partisan. His appeal to "different times" suggests a potential historical catalogue of partisans based on the specifics of the party to which they belong. Each type of partisan attempts to further his reach in a different way and even has his own unique mode of surrender. The partisan works in between; he is *bound to* the party in the sense of an origin and, as Schmitt's use of "gehen" and "laufen" suggests, *bound for* the party. Above all, his following or "going-with" refers to his essential tie to the regular army. Schmitt cites Che Guevara on this point: "it is obvious that guerrilla warfare is a preliminary step, unable to win a war all by itself" (*Theory of the Partisan* 17). In other words, the partisan always looks to a victory whose terms are defined by the army and political power that follows.

At the end of this section, Schmitt considers the extended uses of the term "partisan" in contemporary novels and historical treatments. At the extreme, there is a danger of "dissolution of the concept." Here the term can be used for any "individualist or non-conformist . . . without any consideration as to whether he would even think of taking up arms" (18). Two additional minimum conditions are thus implied: that the partisan be connected to a weapon (and thus violence) and that the party be comprised of more than one person. Schmitt emphasizes that a party of one makes no sense; it cannot provide the military and political frame for violent acts.

Schmitt's description of the partisan applies to the discourses of the German terrorist groups that I have discussed above in that they continually speak of themselves as part of a greater historical movement. I wish to retain the idea of the "first step" that Schmitt cites from Guevara while confronting it with the "individualist or non-conformist" as dramatized in German literature. In each case, the characters in question are more than a party of one, in that they attract followers of varying devotion. Beyond these followers, however, they also attract observers who offer novel interpretations of their acts that do not rely on the pre-set views of a formal political party.

In *On Violence* Hannah Arendt approaches the rhetoric of political violence during the late 1960s not in terms of political or tactical criticism, but as a sign of the decline in the belief in a capacity for action in her specific sense of the ability of people to come together to create something new. Like the RAF's "On Armed Struggle in Western Europe" and Schmitt's *Theory of the Partisan*, *On Violence* addresses the idea that violence pushes forward. In Arendt's view, however, the preachers of violence have misunderstood its function in Hegel and Marx.

On Violence originally appeared in *The New Yorker* magazine in 1968 before being reprinted in book form, and is marked by the energy of thinking from within a specific time and place, of a pure attempt to combine journalism and the Western intellectual tradition.[41] One of the most fascinating aspects of the text is the varied voices and sources that it cites, including students in newspapers, journalists commenting in magazines, and American, French, and German theorists who respond to contemporary events. On the one hand, Arendt might be seen here to attempt to impose a hierarchical relation between actual student voices and philosophy through the layout of her book since she sends discussion of student acts down to the footnotes, or, in the case of their worse offenses, to an appendix in the back. On the other hand, her struggle to even name the object of her investigation attests to her fidelity to the difficulty of representing the violence in question. Verbally feeling her way through the field, she attempts a number of appellations: "the New Left" (*On Violence* 11), "the new militants" (15), "the new preachers of violence" (22), "the students" (15), "the student movement" (18), and "student rebellion" (28). Each of these names marks a different contextualization and relation: for example "preachers" emphasizes speech and attempts to convince, "movement" suggests direction, and "rebellion" implies dominating force. The students are unruly even in their names, and this multiplicity already testifies to Arendt's attunement to the difficulty of finding an origin or subject for the violence.

In the face of this multitude of voices, and perhaps in reaction to its overwhelming nature, Arendt sets up a speaker system to propose possible readings of student violence. First she cites Mao's statement "Power grows out of the barrel of a gun" (*On Violence* 9) and attacks it as condoning the belief that violence creates power. Such a position diametrically opposes her own theory. Then, against Mao, Arendt explains the problem of violence in relation to newness through the philosophical tradition of Hegel and Marx. She insists that for these thinkers violence accompanies but does not cause historical progress. For Marx, she claims: "The emergence of a new society was preceded, but not caused, by violent outbreaks, which he likened to the labor pangs that precede, but of course do not cause, the event of organic birth" (11). Arendt works around a simile. Violence serves as a signal; it accompanies the new, but does not bring it about. For Marx, the cause is elsewhere, as Arendt reminds us in referring to "Marx's idea, borrowed from Hegel, that every old society harbors the seeds of its successors in the same way every living organism harbors the seeds of its offspring" (26). Compared to Mao's, she finds Marx's theory more plausible, even if it is ultimately wrong.[42]

At the end of this section, Arendt herself suddenly becomes the one who can speak for the students. Her reading emphasizes interruption as the non-organic, as that which breaks with inevitable growth: "If we look on history in terms of a continuous chronological process, whose progress, moreover, is inevitable, violence in the shape of war and revolution may appear to constitute the only interruption" (*On Violence* 30). Arendt employs "interruption" in a positive sense, since the "progress" she names here is really just more of the same. The true problem raised by her statement concerns the ability to decide if violence was a qualitative break or not. Precisely in the terms of Marx's theory as described above, violence *would* be readable as the sign of contradictions in the previous society. Arendt insists on a different kind of dislocation. The etymological resources of the word "interruption" help us think about this in that they indicate both mediation and failure, "inter," which means "between," and "rupture," meaning "break." A relation and the disruption of relation, the term runs parallel to Arendt's quotation of Mao, which equates the empty hole of the gun and the living growth of power.[43] Arendt intervenes in the concept of continuity and then, in a parenthetical note, continues with her own interruption: "(Theoretically, as far as I know, the point was never made, but it seems to me incontestable that the disruptive student activities in the last few years are actually based on this conviction)" (30). How are we to read the parenthesis? After her long critique of those who supposedly speak for the students, Arendt finally arrives at their real intention. She does not boldly announce her discovery though but typographically shields it, perhaps to justify her failure to defend the proposal. It may be that the parentheses themselves give birth to something new, but if this is the case, we have to ask how this insertion functions and how it maintains a unique position. Perhaps they guard the "conviction" that she notes, which convicts the students of a fixed intention. "Conviction" marks a return, a return that in the context of my reading would be classified as a regression to an interiority that had evaded Arendt's critical tracking system up to this point. She speaks for the students and for violence.

Ultimately, Arendt objects to the claim that *only* violence can interrupt, and argues that in fact all action has this function. Provocatively, she implies here that violence is related to action or at least shares something important with action. In terms of her broader philosophy this idea demands serious attention, but for now I wish to stay with the interruption. Seeing violence as a break in history aligns well with the rhetoric of German terrorists of the 1960s and 1970s. It also indirectly counteracts the structurally similar certainty of George W. Bush's rhetoric after 9/11, the certainty that violence tests society in a way that it knows it can withstand in advance. By focusing on the interruption of violence as such, Arendt opens a point from which to see a key and unexpected change in perspective. Now neither the point of view of the agent of violence or the sovereign who reacts can claim dominance. When power is knocked out and "in the street" (49) as Arendt writes later in *On Violence*, unexpected interpretations may emerge.

In the context of *On Violence*, Arendt's sudden naming of abandoned power remains a provocative idea that she does not further develop. I return to the phrase in more details in chapter 4 and my "Conclusion" but for now wish to highlight that she hits a limit of political theory here, pointing to power in its dispersion, which would ultimately be its absence. After all, power emerges for Arendt only when people act together and this reference to "the street" is prior to action. In the following chapters, Goethe, Schiller, and Kleist provide specific models of how to envision and discuss this dispersion of power and how to move through it. I begin my literary examination of the rogue with Goethe's first dramatic success, *Götz von Berlichingen*. We have already seen that Derrida argues that naming one a rogue operates on the register of the insult. He also emphasizes the rogue's failure to adhere to the standard norms of linguistic politesse: "One begins acting like a rogue as soon as one begins uttering 'profanities.'"[44] Götz's vulgar rejection of the Emperor's troops and tropes will be my focus.

Chapter 2

✦

Turning One's Back on the Sovereign

Götz von Berlichingen

Götz von Berlichingen founds the proud tradition of Sturm und Drang drama with a violent energy tied to both formal and linguistic obscenity. This unleashing of obscenity is not, however, merely an excess that could be done away with. On the contrary, by staging that which should remain offstage, by bringing the ob-scene on scene, this work not only delineates its own aesthetics but also enacts a critique of sovereignty. Attention to the rhetoric of the drama reveals a logic of political representation that works not by identifying preestablished links between groups and leaders, but instead by outlining ideological desires through intricate performative circuits. While early scenes describe a specific modality of projection through the apostrophe, its central concern is the self-positing effort of the sovereign to establish power through the legal act of the ban, an effort that the drama exposes through its temporary failure in Götz's resistance. As a new legal regime emerges despite violent resistance, alternate modes of political organization disappear into the past. The drama marks the memory of this other possibility and of the possibility of another order as such, in writing.

The knight Götz von Berlichingen serves from the very beginning as the pivot point of aspirational projections, with the monk Brother Martin introducing him as "this man hated by princes, and to whom the oppressed turn" (7, translation modified).[1] The drama takes place in the early sixteenth century, when the coherence of the Holy Roman Empire depended on the Emperor's ability to draw support from two opposed groups: the militarily essential free knights (a group that includes Götz) and the wealthy princes. Influenced by the Bishop of Bamberg, Götz's childhood friend Weislingen betrays him and convinces the Emperor to order his capture. One expects a straightforward declaration of war in response, but instead Götz mobilizes a paradoxical assertion that proclaims his faith to the Emperor at the very moment he denies the authority of the troops who attempt to enforce his order. Captured shortly thereafter, Götz agrees to endure house arrest, which he then breaks in act 5 when rebelling peasants demand that he serve as their leader. Condemned to death for this act, but ultimately forgiven, Götz dies in old age with his wife and servant Lerse bemoaning the future that has no place for their hero.

This chapter begins with the turn of the rogue, with the way that Götz von Berlichingen's refusal to present himself compels the creation of political hopes for both the peasants and the Emperor expressed through apostrophe. The image of Götz as the active and ultimately violent hero, an image so enthusiastically praised at the time of the drama's first performances and so eloquently lauded as a moral model by Lenz, contextually stems from a projection established in a number of scenes in which both his admirers and enemies turn away from their immediate discussion and address him while or as if physically absent. After showing how power structures are formed around his absence, I examine the obscene staging of the *Götz Quote* (Götz's reply to the army facing him, which shocked the public with its obscenity and became part of the German vernacular). Here Götz does finally confront his enemies, but only by insisting on his very turn away through an *apotrope*, a type of phrase that has its origin in defensive magic.[2] In the textual center of the drama, Götz infamously responds to the imperial army captain's demand for surrender with the *Quote,* which idiomatically translates as: "He can kiss my ass." This defiant saying, a rhetorical turn of the rear which has its roots in superstitions intended to ward off evil, demands that one attend to a logic of the turn that threatens aesthetic, political, and epistemological structures, ultimately exploding in the incendiary violence of the peasant uprising with Götz as its leader.

The King Reads Goethe

The stakes of the drama's intervention at the juncture of linguistics, aesthetics, and politics emerge clearly in an early critique authored by King Frederick II of Prussia. His attack on Goethe can be seen to reveal an anxiety that disrupts his own sovereign equilibrium. Moreover, it offers the prototype for the future critical stabilization of the knight Götz as a center of strength that close reading of his obscene exclamation challenges. Written in French, *De la littérature allemande* (1780; *On German Literature*) performs on the most literal level an adherence to the French authority whose aesthetic rules it defends. He immediately couches his critique in the language of sovereignty by addressing the "little taste that rules to this day in Germany."[3] The first example of this lack of aesthetic sensitivity involves the popularity of Shakespeare's dramas in Germany. It is a question of "rule," and these dramas break the classical unities which, Friedrich insists, are not arbitrary, but in fact guaranteed by the solid authority of Aristotle. The authority of the philosopher dissolves along with that of his centralizing rules. Among the reasons for this upheaval, Frederick notes Goethe's disregard for the unity of time, his depiction of years on stage. Furthermore, the social classes are no longer isolated: the drama mixes "gravediggers" and "princes" in what Frederick terms "a bizarre mixture of baseness and grandeur." This social contamination infiltrates aesthetic categories; the mixture (*mélange*) also combines low and high art, "buffoonery and the tragic." Aspects of genre that should be kept separate mingle so that the seriousness and wisdom of tragedy can no longer maintain a safe distance from the lightness and, as one gathers from Frederick's tone, stupidity, of comedy.

In an act of critical sovereignty, Frederick grants Shakespeare amnesty for such scenes but only because they were written before the advent of the more aesthetically advanced French drama. *Götz von Berlichingen* is, on the other hand, untimely, if not grotesque and mimetically depleting: "But see yet again a Goetz of Berlichingen, who appears on the scene, a detestable imitation of these poor English plays, and the parterre applauds and enthusiastically demands the repetition of these disgusting platitudes." Goethe's drama allows something that should have been forgotten to suddenly reappear. It is not the quality of imitation that poses the problem but the fact that the drama imitates Shakespeare in a time when he should be left behind. Frederick, who proudly accepted the role of enlightened monarch, here takes a stance on art in line with his view that political rights should develop modestly as the times change. The "yet again" of *Götz von Berlichingen* threatens the very notion of progress that Frederick calls on in his critique, not only in terms of its atavistic return, but in the endless loop of the applause that demands this regression be staged again and again. The approving audience comes from below (*le parterre*, literally "by the earth"), demanding a repetition of low speech, of "disgusting platitudes." The privative "little taste" of a few sentences earlier now becomes the strongly negative "disgust." While these "platitudes" could refer to what Frederick sees as a boring narrative, they also indicate a reference to the language of the drama, which reaches its disgusting nadir in the critically infamous *Götz Quote*. Frederick II thus identifies the obscene threat of this drama in language that threatens all hierarchy through an endless demand from below.

Indeed, the words of the *Quote*, often shortened (through censorship or politeness) from "he can kiss my ass [*er kann mich im Arsch lecken*]" to "he can kiss my [*er kann mich*] . . ." drew an uproar of cheers and applause in German theaters at least as late as the second half of the twentieth century.[4] The enthusiasm for Götz's rebellion provides an index for the drama's central provocation: that it urges cultural rebirth through rejection of sovereignty. In his first great drama, Goethe responds to Herder's call for a literature free from French and Latin formal influences that would contribute to the rebirth of German culture as a whole. Upon reading the first version of the drama Herder (whom Goethe met in Strasbourg in 1770) was less than supportive. In fact, he famously criticized his younger disciple for relying too heavily on another national tradition. While Herder's letter no longer exists, Goethe's reply quotes one specific objection: "Shakespeare has completely spoiled you."[5] According to the recollections of *From My Life: Poetry and Truth* (which, begun in 1811, recounted his life up to 1775), Goethe took this potentially crushing assessment in stride, not seeing himself (or his work) as ruined or spoiled, but instead rethinking the unity of the drama. He had drawn the basic outline of events from the sixteenth-century source *Autobiography of the Knight Götz von Berlichingen with the Iron Hand* of the actual Götz von Berlichingen and decided that the story he wished to tell could not be contained by the classical unities (to which Frederick II refers).

Following Herder's criticism regarding Shakespeare's influence, one might expect that the problem with the drama was that it had too many scenes (fifty-nine in the first version), covered too much time (many years), or depicted battles of such a scale that they could never be brought to the stage. In all of these cases realism challenges the form of the drama in that, from the point of view of the classical rules of French aesthetics, it tries to portray too much. Goethe does not shy away from admitting the difficulties of staging of the drama. The *Lesedrama* (reading drama) genre offers a hybrid description that would seem to accommodate the aspects of the tale that he thought important, but his goal of a "higher unity" could not find satisfying refuge in this form.[6] More importantly though, the character of Adelheid posed a different kind of challenge, one that affected the very path of the narrative composition.

In his account of his revision of the drama, Goethe does not abstractly describe shortcomings of plot, but instead speaks affectively, claiming that he had fallen under the spell of one of his own characters: "especially towards the end, a strange passion ravished [*riß . . . hin*] me unconsciously. I had, while aspiring to describe *Adelheid* lovably, fallen in love with her myself."[7] He employs violent language, talking of a rip (*riß*), or pull that threatens the drama through an excessively well-written character. As an author, Goethe attempted a portrayal that would evoke love in the reader but in so doing causes the space between author and his text to collapse. He fell in love with his own character such that he lost the perspective needed for narrative tension and development. Goethe was *too* successful in his description, and this success damaged narrative form. Looking back though, he says that he was able to notice this unconscious detour. In the revision process he saw something in the text of which he had not been aware.

A few lines later in his account, he describes more precisely how he focused his revision: "I now had, instead of the autobiography and German antiquity, my own work in mind and wanted to give more and more historical and national content to it and delete that which was only a fable or just passionate."[8] Goethe opens with an apparent contraction, claiming that he had to leave the historical source behind in order to add more historical content. He employs history against the threat of the "fable" and the "merely passionate." The latter phrase refers back to the "strange passion" that drew him to Adelheid. This pull brings the drama to a halt because it does not inform the whole but remains *merely* passionate. The "fable" connects to the feminine, and Goethe takes specific steps to address this threat, not only reducing Adelheid's role in act 5, but shortening the scenes with the fortune-teller in that act and replacing Adelheid with Götz in key scenes. Acknowledging this composition history, my reading holds on to the question of unity that Goethe raises by looking at what kind of hole the expulsion of Adelheid actually produces.

In other remarks in the same section of *From My Life: Poetry and Truth*, Goethe describes the fundamental problem of the drama's structure in another way that suggests that Adelheid may indicate a greater structural problem. At the end of the drama, Götz is out of action and only pulled back for an unhappy participation in the Peasants' War. Placing Götz more firmly in the center of the last act only orients it around an inactive hero. But is Götz *ever* really active? Through its roots in the work of Lenz and Hegel, *Götz* scholarship defends this proposition well into the twentieth century. Or is the drama about his failure to act, about the way he is acted upon and resists action? Goethe identified an important threat to representation in Adelheid but wrote the threat of violence to presentation *into* the drama rather than simply excluding it in the new version. I will follow this threat to presentation, returning to it at the end of the chapter where a trace of the feminine still inflects the relation between history and violence. The composition history of *Götz von Berlichingen* sets us on the path of representational questions in the final version of the text that have gone unnoticed, though they were there all along.

Götz scholarship has traditionally sought to stabilize this challenge to representation through a fixed view of either Götz as hero or history as the frame of his life. The original publication of *Götz von Berlichingen* in 1773 created a sensation that divided its readers into those, like Frederick II, who condemned the drama for its failure to adhere to classical rules of composition, and others who looked past this supposed lack of style to celebrate the nobility and exuberance of its main character. Lenz articulates the latter tendency, famously writing: "see, there is the whole man, always productive, active, warming and doing good like the sun, but also so scalding as fire, when one comes too close to him."[9] He sees Götz in terms of a masculine and productive totality. In a corollary motion, Lenz also routes aesthetics through morality in a manner that would later come to be associated with Schiller, seeing Götz as a model for life. The drama should be praised because of the "worth" (*Wert*, also meaning "value") of its hero.

Later critics test this vision but have never succeeded in fully freeing themselves from it. By the early nineteenth century, criticism of *Götz* based on its failure to adhere to the rules of French aesthetics had faded. While interest in the character of the knight would continue, a historical reading of the drama began to shift the boundaries of his supposed self-sufficiency, albeit by transferring critical concern for totality to the temporal field. In the first volume of the *Lectures on Aesthetics*, Hegel begins this line of research, seeing in *Götz* the collision of two historical periods, the Middle Ages and modernity: "the new order of things brings Götz himself into wrong and destroys him."[10] The historical and legal ground shifts beneath the feet of the heroes of the drama and Goethe brilliantly highlights this acute transition. Earlier emphasis on Götz's independence gives way to a mere *desire* to act independently. While he may have the needed personal characteristics, he does not have the power to implement these virtues on a large scale.

In the same paragraph, Hegel sharpens this shift by writing that the knight's adherence to the old order leads to the laughter of Don Quixote. The rebel who attacks the modern law risks becoming a fool because this law has achieved an independent existence that a single person can no longer challenge. I wish to hold on to the fine line between the outrage of the *Götz Quote* and the dissipation of force in the burst of laughter. The border emerges more clearly in the second volume of the *Lectures on Aesthetics*, where Hegel writes that *Götz*, like all modern drama, focuses on subjective particularity rather than the external force of fate. Despite this downgrade within the broader history of aesthetics, the failure of Götz's rebellion receives a positive evaluation. Like Wallenstein "Götz von Berlichingen too attacks an existent and firmly established political order and therefore perishes."[11] While grasping ("greif[en]") is too proactive, I nonetheless wish to focus on Götz's engagement, how he shifts the substance of political life, if only for a moment.[12] If Schiller's Wallenstein acts desperately after a devastating hesitation, Götz will transform the fundamental untimeliness of his rebellion into a powerful accusation.

In light of Hegel's emphasis on Götz's failure, the work of contemporary critic Rainer Nägele stands out for the way it reconfigures traditional interpretations by focusing on the motif of the iron hand itself as a sign of dismemberment.[13] According to Nägele, the hand does not form a central image of strength but circulates broadly throughout the language of the drama and haunts its action. Specifically, Goethe describes Weislingen as the missing hand on which Götz depends, and this lack sets up a chain of metonymic substitutions that completely enmeshes him. History cannot orient this decentered subject because the drama presents it in a contradictory manner, "vacillating between backwards-oriented historical pessimism and forward-looking utopia, between rebellious social criticism and conservative anxiety."[14] History swings to the point of epistemological blurring; one cannot decide where it is headed. The drama proposes a historical unpredictability that develops in Sturm und Drang from within the Enlightenment.

Nägele can thus be seen to look back on *Götz* criticism to interpretations first proposed by Lenz and Hegel, critiquing the received view of the knight as *Kraftkerl* (strong man) while at the same time relating this critique to the work's rejection of dialectical and teleological models of history. I situate my own investigation within this critical tradition. I focus, however, on Götz's forceful but ultimately futile resistance to sovereignty and how this resistance brings the preconditions of this sovereignty to the stage. I begin by examining scenes where Götz's supporters and enemies turn to him as the prosthetic supplement of their ideologies. In each case, Götz refuses to co-sign, responding only by turning away. I then follow the text to the Emperor's ban of Götz and, returning to questions opened in my first chapter, read this ban as a critique of sovereignty as conceived by the tradition of social contract theory. Only with this background will the radical nature of Götz's later rejection of the Emperor achieve its true contours.

O Götz! Apostrophe at Work

The constant return of critics to Lenz's interpretation (up to the eminent Germanists Heinrich Meyer-Benfey and Emil Staiger) of Götz as great man, even if only to critique this idea, indicates its seductive power.[15] My reading of the drama begins by holding on to this attraction in order to investigate its poetic mechanism. From the very start, Goethe carefully positions Götz as the center of all hopes, dreams, and desires. One expects such grandeur from the genres of the history drama and chivalric romance. One does not, however, expect the hero to rigorously deny the central place attributed to him as Götz does. Examining the opening scenes of the drama will establish this turn and counter-turn, bringing us, in the scene with Brother Martin, to the trope of apostrophe, which (in turn) will allow a preliminary formalization of the way the drama structures political desire by a detour through non-presence.

In the very first scene of the drama, the characters that will later lead the farmer uprising introduce Götz von Berlichingen in his absence. Sitting in a tavern, Sievers requests another drink and Metzler demands another story: "Tell me again about Berlichingen!" (2). Metzler prefigures and programs the reaction of the audience that Frederick II later condemns, installing a limitless appetite for tales of Götz by asking that the story be repeated. Metzler opens the particular case: "Since when has Goetz been having difficulty [*Händel*] with the Bishop of Bamberg again? The report was that everything had been worked out and smoothed over [*vertragen und geschlichtet*]." The "Händel" refers to an argument (the plural form marks this sense) and "trade." The linguistic multivalence indicates an indecision at the heart of the relationship between Götz and the Bishop. They were connected through a mode of exchange that has now been disrupted. That they were getting along before indicates an agreement of some sort, even if it was not formalized, *vertragen*, if not *Vertrag* (contract). It may have been one that was recognized only by rumor, things were said to be "smoothed over [*geschlichtet*]," suggesting that routes were open between the negative to the positive sense of "Händel." This word relates etymologically to "Hand," making it an early reference to the body part hand anticipating the handshake between Götz and the Bishop that starts their feud.[16]

Sievers responds to Metzler's question regarding the problems between Götz and the Bishop with a short narrative, the first of many attempts to organize the disagreement through storytelling:

> When the Bishop saw he was getting nowhere and always coming up short, he started to crawl to the cross and bargain for a truce. And

> unbelievably, honest Berlichingen gave in, as he always does when he's got the advantage [*Vorteil*]. (2, translation modified)

The Bishop was missing the mark, failing to enforce the power that he assumes as a high official of the church. Siever's choice of the expression "crawl to the cross" not only tells what the Bishop did (ask for forgiveness) but also suggests that the Bishop's hypocrisy goes well beyond this particular matter, that his relation to the cross might only be a figurative one. In contrast to the Bishop's drive for wholeness, Götz renounces the extra part, his "Vorteil," refusing to capitalize on the situation when he has the chance. The peasants associate his refusal to capitalize on the situation with moral worth. His "giving in" gives back. Metzler responds with the exclamation: "An upright Lord! [*Ein rechtschaffener Herr*]!" *Rechtschaffen*, a composite word, includes law or right (*Recht*) and creation (*schaffen*). Most frequently translated by the English words "honest" and "upright," it foreshadows the rhetoric of posture that will be central to act 3.

Metzler and Sievers create a laudatory picture or projection of Götz in their stories. As the scene comes to a close though, they encounter actual knights in Götz's service. These knights ask Metzler about the location of Götz's former friend and current enemy Weislingen, and he helps them by providing the important information that he is with the Bishop of Bamberg. When Metzler asks in return for assistance fighting the Bishop's men (who have attacked him and are still in the bar) the knights refuse. The *Rechtschaffenheit* that Metzler and Sievers so praise inspires in them the belief that Götz would help them with specific problems. They draw a lesson from his past behavior that the knights in his service disappoint for reasons that are not clear. Perhaps they are being fair or perhaps they just do not want to help. Either way, the response of Götz's men stages an asymmetrical relation. Metzler and Sievers establish an expectation of aid with their praise of Götz that the knights in his service fail to fulfill.

Even when Götz sets foot on stage he remains elusive, and language steps in again to fill the space. After meeting Brother Martin in the forest, Götz refuses to give his name, substituting instead the extension of his left hand: "My right, although not unusable in war, is insensitive to the clasp of affection, it's one with its glove, you see, it is iron" (7). The hand can be used to hit but cannot feel. A dead point in the affective politics of Sturm und Drang, it puts a cold stop to the warmth of sentiment. His right hand is always a weapon; it cannot be extended in a handshake that, at least to one theory of the convention, originally demonstrated that the hand was empty. Unable to offer the customary greeting and the hospitality that would follow from it, Götz reroutes his gesture, indicating the name that he initially withheld by taking a detour through his left hand.

Moving by synecdoche from hand to person, Martin now names Götz. Instead of satisfaction though, the directness of his realization seems to be too much for him. In an apostrophe he suddenly turns to address God, thanking him for the meeting: "So you are Götz von Berlichingen! Thanks be to God, that He has allowed me to see him, this man hated by princes, and to whom the oppressed turn" (7, translation modified). After the rhetorical turn to God, a description of how both the princes and the oppressed are moved by Götz follows. The feelings of the former are moved, in that they hate. The latter move in a less clearly defined manner, one described in terms of direction.

Götz has a tropic effect on the people, a "trope" being linked essentially to a "turn." In rhetoric a trope indicates a deviation from the literal signification of a word. Then to which meaning do the oppressed turn exactly? *Apostrophe*, a rhetorical figure that comprises one of the central techniques of lyric poetry, always indicates a detour, an interruption of communication between two subjects in favor of establishing a circuit with the inanimate, the abstract, or the absent. At least on one level, Martin's turn to the divine provides a perfect example of the smooth functioning of the apostrophe in that he briefly turns away from Götz himself to God as the transcendent ground of communication. This limited moment of recognition would then only strengthen the exchange between Martin and Götz that follows. Instead of a return, however, Martin doubles his trope, turning once again, this time in an apostrophe to Götz's hand itself: "Thou, more valuable than a reliquary hand, through which the most sacred blood has flowed, dead instrument enlivened through the noblest spirit's trust in God" (7). This example of Sturm und Drang pathos indicates more than a simple hyperbolic, subjective feeling. The relic, from the verb *reliquare* in Latin, refers to something left behind, and Martin focuses on Götz's hand as a mere tool that, he implies, would therefore be all the more active and alive. He does so with a prosthetic rhetorical act. The saint's hand takes a place in a pair of synecdoches: it refers to the entire saint and the saint refers to God. This chain of substitutions fills the relic hand with a divine life that replaces its lost worldly life. The same is true, for Martin, of Götz's hand. It comes back to life, no longer a "dead instrument," but "enlivened" through the spirit of Götz, which by analogy would also be divine.

Susan E. Gustafson points out that in fact the iron hand distinguishes itself precisely by the fact that it lacks circulating blood: "It is what Lacan would call the phallic signifier, the great mask, the 'stand-in' for that which is absent. The knight's injured body reveals that the phallic signifier is a sham."[17] While Gustafson focuses on the importance of this figure for the dynamic of male desire in the drama, her insight has broader significance. Within my reading in terms of the apostrophe, this break in circulation appears as an interruption of what should be a circular motion. One should turn away only to re-turn.

In parsing the turn as re-turn, however, we may fall prey to a temptation to emphasize narrative over apostrophe, when, they are, in Jonathan Culler's reading, opposing forces. In fact, strictly speaking, according to Culler, lyric poetry, with its emphasis on the move to transcendent meaning, can be seen to thrive on the power of the apostrophe alone. It can turn directly towards a higher realm of significance without an intervening temporality. In another twist though, this trope that should make the most direct and natural connection to meaning appears at the same time as completely artificial within the formal vocabulary of the poem: "the high calling of poetry must not depend on a trope, an O."[18] In Culler's analysis the vocative marker of the "O" functions as an undecidable zero point of signification, both providing passage to a higher realm and keeping one tied to the ground level of the signifier. Götz highlights this disruptive aspect of the apostrophe by withdrawing in response to Martin's panegyric: "*Götz puts on his helmet and takes his lance*" (7). He refuses to acknowledge the role attributed to him; he refuses to co-sign. In fact, in preparing to leave, he also arms himself against Brother Martin's description.

Martin, only drawn in further by this retreat and fortification, recounts the story of how Götz's arm was shot off in battle. He feels overwhelmed now not by Götz's presence, but by the story he had heard of him. He talks to himself (and thus of course to the audience), using the third person to refer to Götz, repeating the story as if he were there himself. His description places the wound in a religious framework in that the missing hand, the wound, opens the way for a fiction of spiritual wholeness. Götz spoke "with noblest and truest trust in God" (8, translation modified) in response to his injury. Martin sees the loss of the hand as simply referring to its opposite, an inner fullness associated with divine unity.

By turning away from Götz to speak of him, Martin employs the apostrophe in its purest function. He addresses the knight not as an empirical subject but as an idea, as a transcendent object. In its very purity, however, this use of the trope exposes its disruptive force, the way it splits Götz in two without the guarantee of future reunification. Indeed, rather than connect the ideal with the so-called real Götz, Metzler, Sievers, and Martin link the ideal to their own desires. In a difference that marks the malleability of Götz as political cipher, Martin takes another tack, seeing a faith in God rather than a concern for worldly fairness.

Götz himself neither legitimates nor acknowledges either interpretation in these two scenes. In his evasion he reveals the inner mechanism of the apostrophic logic at work in the words of his admirers: the address in the stubborn absence of the supposed subject of address foregrounds the speaker's own desire. Continuing his development of the fundamental tension between narrative and apostrophe, Culler explains the potential victory of the latter as follows: "Apostrophe is not the representation of an event: if it works it produces a fictive, discursive event."[19] As *Götz von Berlichingen* continues, it repeatedly stages this attempt of the apostrophe to work, attempts that repeatedly prove unsuccessful to the extent that they never result in the desired totality. Close attention to the failure of the drama's turns toward transcendent meaning will reveal the actual political investments of its characters.

In a fascinating symmetrical fashion, Götz's enemies also employ the logic of the apostrophe in an attempt to solidify their power. Perhaps unexpectedly, a close reading of how they do so demonstrates that this symmetry does not produce a balance but rather instigates a clash over a discursive event with political stakes. Both sides evoke a totality in rhetoric that demands the participation of Götz for its realization, something that he will expressly, and obscenely, deny. At the beginning of act 3 Weislingen has traveled to Augsburg to convince the Emperor to take action against Götz. As they walk together, merchants from Nürnberg approach the Emperor. They explain that as allies of the Bishop of Bamberg they were attacked by Götz. The Emperor complains about the problems he faces:

> EMPEROR: Still more troubles! They proliferate like heads of Hydra.
> WEISLINGEN: And will not be eliminated but by fire and sword, and by resolute action. (39)

The Emperor faces an unstoppable injury, decapitation that only exhausts the attacker through regeneration. He faces problems of the same origin again and again, problems that resist his power to solve them. Weislingen advocates a course of action that will prevent the wound from continuing to be productive, a course of action that makes sense within the Emperor's metaphor. After all, Heracles ultimately defeated Hydra (the mythological beast who grew two heads for each one that was cut off) by burning the stub of his neck. This amputation does not, however, aim at mere negation, as the Emperor's implicit equation of himself with the slayer of the monster suggests. Instead of being a simple obstacle to his rule, the knights offer a different model of rule. In order for his own power to be effective, it must produce a body to which it can attach.

Weislingen develops this separation and its correlative promise of unity more fully as he continues:

> It is by no means all of Germany that complains of unrest. Only Franconia and Swabia still glow from the embers of civil war and its internal destruction [*glimmt noch von den Resten des innerlichen verderblichen Bürgerkriegs*]. And even there many of the nobles and the freeborn yearn for peace and quiet. If we only could get rid of this Sickingen, this Selbitz—this Berlichingen, the rest would soon collapse of its own accord. Those are the ones whose spirit drives the rebellious crowd [*Denn sie sind's, deren Geist die aufrührische Menge belebt*]. (39)

Weislingen draws the Emperor's attention to a smoldering remainder. In doing so, he mobilizes an undecidable point, picking up on a glow which would seem to be on its way out, but exists and threatens for the moment. Whereas the Bishop had described the knights as causing damage that affected the whole empire, Weislingen first describes their power as quite limited. The general threat to the political body ("all of Germany") has been reduced to small embers, a mere "remainder [*Rest*]," a strictly circumscribed leftover. Many of those that still challenge the Emperor's rule have already given up to the extent that they wish for peace. The danger that remains can be located not only geographically, in the regions of Franconia and Swabia, but even corporally, in three knights. However, at the same time this very limitation poses an outsized threat to the totality. The knights are not merely three men but the "spirit [*Geist*]" that brings to life the body of the mob. This life moves against those who want peace and stillness. The embers may yet start a new fire. Weislingen participates in the logic (if not the rhetorical form) of the apostrophe that I have explicated above when he moves from the merchant's complaint against Götz and Selbitz to an image of Götz and Selbitz as the spiritual leaders of a mob that threatens the country.[20]

This logic implies that by interrupting the circuit, by removing the knights, the Emperor can become the spirit of the people in the place of Götz and his allies. The Emperor hesitates to accept this advice, since he depends on the knights for his campaigns. Weislingen repeats his arguments, emphasizing that the pawns, so to speak, are on the side of the knights:

> [The followers of Götz and Selbitz] will not be checked until we have reduced them to nothing in the eyes of the world and have cut them off

> completely from all hope for the future [*ihnen alle Hoffnung, jemals wieder emporzukommen, völlig abgeschnitten haben*]. (39, translation modified)

The phrase "in the eyes of the world" recalls Götz's words to Weislingen in act 1: "I am a thorn in your eye, as small as I am" (16, translation modified). This common German phrase arises from a picture of a rose that is spoiled by the presence of an ugly thorn in the frame. "Eye" serves as a metonym for "the scene viewed by the eye." Weislingen uses this trope again, saying, in short, that the thorn has to be removed from the picture. This will prevent the ones who depend on Götz from holding onto any hope of coming back to life, of climbing back out of their low social position (*emporkommen*, connected to the earlier adjective "rebellious [*aufrührische*]"). The smoldering remainder, Weislingen recognizes, poses at once a deadly threat and the glow of hope.

Weislingen continues with the rhetoric of decapitation, initiated in the metaphor of the hydra: Götz and his friends have to be cut "off completely." The Emperor again refuses to consent to such harsh action but in his alternative nonetheless accepts his logic. Rather than cutting Götz out, he makes his own plan in which he orders that he and Selbitz be captured and made to swear an oath to restrain from attacks and remain within their own territory. He will force Götz to submit, but the instrument for doing so, the ban, can only function by first acknowledging the knight's exclusion and rupturing the link to the totality that the rhetoric of the apostrophe, however tenuously, maintained.

The Time of the Ban

The Emperor's exercise of sovereignty will thus establish sovereignty itself: he orders that Götz be dealt with to free the Empire from the threat of the rebellious mob. The complex inner workings of the Emperor's ban require a close reading showing that his attempt to consolidate the law depends upon a legal apostrophe that would constitute Götz as the outlaw. This reading will complicate the relationship between violence and the social contract that I opened in my first chapter. The drama's deployment of the ban reveals not just a particular punishment but a fundamental political structure.

Götz receives the order from the Emperor in the form of a letter. He declares to Sickingen: "Banned! There, read the edifying letter. The Emperor has ordered the ban to be executed against me [*hat Exekution gegen mich verordnet*], the ban that says to carve up my flesh to feed the birds beneath the sky and the beasts upon the field" (41). The editor of Götz's *Autobiography* of 1731 noted the official wording of the ban: "we divide [*zuteilen*] your body and your flesh out among the animals in the woods, the birds in the air, and the fish in the water."[21] This full citation shows that the Emperor rhetorically dismembers the person whom the ban targets. The "edifying letter" to which Götz ironically refers in fact has a dispersive rather than constructive character. The text distributes him into nature, depriving him of cultural protection, and, in a parallel movement, reduces him from the "spirit [*Geist*]" of the mob (in Weislingen's formulation) to mere pieces of a body. The "Exekution" refers to the *Reichsexecution*, authorization of the army to confront him. At the same time, the term suggests an execution in the more common sense of the term of a state-ordered killing.

How does the image of flesh being cut off the skeleton relate to the Emperor's stated goal, which is really to exclude Götz only to include him again after forcing him to swear the oath? The letter speaks of an expulsion to nature but in fact will be a means affecting civilization by stabilizing the legal realm. The passage to stabilization, however, will be one of conflict, the struggle of sovereignty to ground itself. In his reading of *Götz von Berlichingen*, Horst Lange shows that this transition, which seems like a progression to a modern state, actually opens a question of legitimacy: "the play seems to ask whether the modern state's challenge to the legality of the medieval feud could not be answered with Götz's counter challenge to the legitimacy of the modern state."[22] Lange thus ties into Hegel and Korff's focus on history but relates this to a key question of political theory. Focusing on a metaphorical association to the natural world, he points out that Götz is continually associated with the wolf and that this opens a connection to Hobbes's *homo homini lupus*, that "man is a wolf to man" in the state of nature. According to Lange, however, the famous "state of nature" should not be seen as a mythical period of complete human independence, but rather as a different "state"; one in which family and clan bonds organize society. In other words, Lange argues that Hobbes's account of the move from the state of nature to the commonwealth should not be seen merely as a heuristic tale. Instead, it has a specific historical reference point, corresponding to the medieval society that was replaced by the modern state.

Following this understanding of Hobbes, *Götz von Berlichingen* stages the transition from medieval to modern society and in so doing exposes objections to the concept of the social contract that provide a key justification of this transition in political theory. It also brings into question a progressive reading of the social contract, one that sees it as a step forward from a violent state of affairs to a peaceful one. Continuing to combine Hobbes's work with precise episodes in history, Lange focuses in on the Ewige Landfrieden (a law implemented in 1495 by Maximilian I that outlawed feuds) as the founding social contract in the historical context of *Götz von Berlichingen*. He points out that Götz did not himself sign this law (though in the drama he tells of how he was present at its institution as an observer), which raises the question of how Hobbes's theory accounts for the state's legitimacy with regard to those who did not agree to its founding. Lange identifies two responses of the sovereign to the person who objects in this manner. Both are violent: the sovereign can force the person to sign the contract or expel the dissenter from the protection of the law. In the latter case the outlaw can then be killed, in Hobbes's words "without injustice."[23] This implies that the sovereign completely defines justice, that the conceptual territory beyond his reach is not governed by an alternative system of justice: "Hobbesian social contract theory found it necessary on the one hand to construe the state of nature as a society modeled on the Middle Ages, but on the other hand to wrongly deny it the status of a law-governed society."[24] Lange's reading of Götz's resistance shows that social contract theory collapses into a pure positivism in which the legal and legitimate are the same.

The sovereign, however, ultimately fails to hide the violence upon which authority depends.[25] Lange sees it as Goethe's virtue to have presented a society in transition, to have shown both sides in such a manner that neither can be said to be correct. He presents the violence of the outlaw simultaneously with the violence of the sovereign, and while from the point of view of the sovereign the outlaw (Götz) seems to be in the wrong, the sovereign's own insecure position cannot ensure the reader's sympathy. Lange sees the drama as "presenting the trade-off" between one form of society and another; it shows the "tragic loss of alternatives." This loss, however, seems to be necessary in Lange's view, the loss that occurs in the course of historical change.

Rephrasing Lange's conclusion, one could say that when Götz breaks the *Landfrieden* he exposes the fiction of legitimacy that Hobbes's social contract intends to establish. This contract can present itself as legitimate only by projecting violence onto the past to justify its own violence. It claims to argue against a lawless state of nature, when, even according to Hobbes's own depiction, this society was not devoid of social bonds.

If we continue to consider the drama in terms of the social contract as Lange suggests, we see that the Emperor in effect excludes Götz from society and leaves him in the state of nature. Heeding Weislingen's advice, the Emperor sends the letter of the ban to Götz that attempts to cut him off from society. The argument proceeds throughout as a process for establishing peace. However, if the concept of the state of nature actually serves as a theoretical instrument to disguise the sovereign's use of violence, the strict opposition between the outlaw and the sovereign no longer holds. While Lange clearly describes the manner in which social contract theory creates the outside that it then uses to define itself, he leaves open the question of how to conceptualize an alternative to this theory. Giorgio Agamben offers such an alternative when he proposes the ban as a model for understanding sovereignty. Agamben's use of the word "ban" originates in the work of Jean-Luc Nancy and draws on both of its definitions, "exclusion from the community and the command and insignia of the sovereign."[26] The one who is banned is not simply excluded from the realm of the sovereign, but rather "exposed and threatened" at the borderline of the law.

To clarify the significance of the ban, one might be tempted to call it a negative relation to the law. Indeed, Agamben says that the ban "has no positive content" and that its form is "the simple positing of relation with the non-relational." A dialectic seems to be established here, at least to the extent that the two terms are related only through privation. Agamben does not go the Hegelian route though and insists instead on a critique of "the very form of relation" itself, putting one on guard against the philosophical concept of negativity.[27] Rather than a negative space that gives rise to positive significance, the ban is more correctly understood as the condition of possibility of sovereignty. While Agamben argues that the ban itself is non-dialectical, the structure of sovereignty does depend on it since it "makes possible every localization and territorialization."[28] If the ban does not establish the ground for power it has a transcendental function in the Kantian sense as the a priori condition of power.

Agamben chooses the Roman legal figure *Homo Sacer* (minimally defined as one who can be killed but not sacrificed) as his primary example of the target of the ban. The outlaw offers another, closely related model. Agamben picks up on the eminent nineteenth-century jurist Rudolf von Jhering's indication of the etymology of "outlaw" from *wargus, vargr*, meaning "wolf" and sees the outlaw as a wolf-man. He is neither fully human, in that he is banned from the city, nor is he fully reduced to the status of an animal (who would belong to the forest) in that the city declares that he can be killed at any time.[29] Götz, figured repeatedly as the wolf, stands on this borderline. From his reading of the outlaw as werewolf, Agamben moves to Hobbes's description of the state of nature as a condition of *homo homini lupus*.[30] He argues that this description does not describe a purely natural state but rather a "zone of indistinction" between the natural and cultural that comes to light in the outlaw. The city does not simply exclude the state of nature, as the progressive interpretation of the social contract suggests. Instead it incorporates it in the person of the sovereign as its founding exception. To support this argument, Agamben refers to passages in the *Leviathan* that indicate that people do not simply give up their right to violence freely to form a social contract. Instead, the ones who are to become citizens of the state give up their right to violence, leaving only the sovereign with this right. This description suggests that the establishment of the sovereign in social contract theory does not occur without coercion. The sovereign decision "refers immediately to the life (and not the free will) of the citizens."[31] It is in this sense that the sovereign himself rules as the wolf-man within the city.

Agamben bases his critique of the state of nature on the role it plays in the temporality of sovereignty, that it is thought of as "an event achieved once and for all" in the transition to the state.[32] Violence would thus be left behind as well. Reading the myth of the werewolf through Pliny's *Natural History*, Agamben emphasizes that the transformation into the wolf occurs only for a limited amount of time, after which the person returns to his human form: "The transformation into a werewolf corresponds perfectly to the state of exception, during which (necessarily limited) time the city is dissolved and men enter into a zone in which they are no longer distinct from beasts."[33] The "state of exception," a constant concern of Agamben's, here points to the violence "beneath" the rule of law that can suspend it at any time. In a key innovation, Agamben puts the "necessarily limited" nature of this transformation into conceptual as well as typographical parenthesis. His account indicates the "threshold of passage" rather than presenting an allegory of a move from the outside to the inside and from the past to the present.[34] The ban indicates a complex structure of sovereignty in which the State is "always already non-State and pseudo-nature."[35]

Götz von Berlichingen relates the execution of a specific ban in a literary-historical account that illustrates the paradox of sovereignty as articulated by Agamben's theoretical use of the term "ban." In Goethe's drama the Emperor very specifically issues his ban to strengthen his sovereignty but in so doing for a moment reveals the violent and tenuous nature of this sovereignty. *Temporarily* removing the law's protection from Götz would enable him to strengthen the law in the long run. In other words, the drama stages in time the theoretical structure that Agamben always sees active in sovereignty. Rather than offering a simple story of sovereign self-support though, Götz disrupts the process of auto-authority—at least for a moment. The infamous scene of act 3 stages a breakdown of the sovereign structure that shows the ban to be not only the condition of its possibility but also the condition of its impossibility.

Sovereignty and Obscenity: "He Can Kiss My . . ."

"He can kiss my ass!" Götz's infamous declaration has traditionally been considered an example of Sturm und Drang rhetorical excess, mere youthful bravado on the part of its precocious author. At the most it would demonstrate the emotional fidelity of the text, pointing the way to the romantic celebration of the subject. Reading this outburst in the context of the structure of the ban as explicated in the previous section, however, will reveal its serious implications for the concept of sovereignty. Götz, who, as we have seen, consistently refuses to present himself, has now been cast out from the protection of the law by a ban that doubles on the level of the law the projection of the rhetorical figure of apostrophe. A general appeal rings through the drama, an *O Götz!* that positions the knight out there rather than here, as the "O" of opening and absence, as zero, as null point in the desiring economies of his friends and foes. In a close reading of the end of act 3 we will see the knight insist on this very absence, displaying his weakness as a form of strength, a political and ontological gambit that the grammatical structure of the apotrope embodies.

The confrontation in question takes place during an attack on Götz's castle by the imperial army that wishes to arrest him on the Emperor's orders. Götz scores a preliminary victory but Selbitz falls and Götz takes him back to his castle to await the next attack. At this point, barricaded in his castle, only words can enter. Götz's page Georg reports that he was up in the tower and saw the flashing weapons of the army in the distance. Götz then takes over and reports the approach of the herald, which also occurs off stage: "Aha! Some redcoated scoundrel, to put the question to us [*der uns die Frage vorlegen wird*], whether we want to be dog food" (52, translation modified). There are a number of possible explanations for the employment of the theatrical device of *teichoscopy* (the reporting of events offstage) at this point in the drama. Most obviously, the physical scale of events demanded here could not be presented on stage; galloping armies are better reported than brought into the theater. In this particular case it also allows the action offstage to be portrayed through Götz's eyes. We do not see a simple soldier in a red uniform, instead we hear of a "redcoated scoundrel," a phrase that conveys a judgment as well as a description. From Götz's point of view, the outlaws are those advancing to his castle. He stands above in the castle looking out a window and presumably down on the herald. Götz predicts that the question will be literally "laid down [*vorlegen*]," and this implies that he will be expected to lean over to pick it up or respond to it.[36]

Not only does what occur offstage need to be described visually, it also needs to be parsed audibly. From the stage directions the audience only hears something but cannot make out the precise words: "*Talk is heard in the distance*" (52). We must rely on Götz's citation, which the text marks: "'An insult to his Majesty!'—A priest put up that challenge" (52). The charge originates in the Bishop, a necessarily corrupt source in Götz's eyes. What does it mean to insult the majesty? Lèse majesté, as it is now knows, has its origin in the treason laws of the Roman Empire. These laws originally prohibited only acts of rebellion, but were employed for verbal attacks as well starting with Emperor Augustus.[37] Götz's insult at first occurs as action (in that he physically resists capture) but quickly shifts to the verbal field without thereby losing any of its force. Teichoscopy plays an important role in this displacement. It also allows one to avoid presenting something onstage that would go against the taste of the public, such as violent acts. Here presentational evasions are even more complex though, since Götz responds to what occurs off the stage with an obscenity onstage. The quotation marks fall away and Götz continues with paraphrase rather than direct citation:

> GOETZ (*answers*): I should surrender! Unconditionally! Who are you talking to! Am I some robber! Tell your Captain: To his Imperial Majesty, as ever, I offer all due respect. But as for him, you tell him he can kiss my ass! [*Sag deinem Hauptmann: Vor Ihro Kaiserliche Majestät hab ich, wie immer, schuldigen Respekt. Er aber, sag's ihm, er kann mich im Arsch lecken*]! (*He slams the window shut*) (52, translation modified)

Götz gradually stops transcribing and finally formulates a response, as the stage directions indicate. While we do not know if the herald posed a direct question, Götz's answer emerges from broken, amputated, speech. The passage begins with four exclamations. The first two sentences are incomplete, missing both subject and verb. He only repeats what should be done, and then says in what way it should happen. The third and fourth sentences are grammatically correct, but end with exclamation points rather than the expected question marks. They are apparent openings that are then slammed shut, as if to indicate that Götz does not want a response. The words and sentiments that he reflects back on the herald show his refusal to accept the message, to sign for the descriptions that are imposed upon him.

The fourth sentence demands specific attention. The word "robber" has appeared twice in the drama so far, both times in reference to Götz but not originating from him. The first time Adelheid used it in her attempt to persuade Weislingen to do her bidding: "Companion to a robber! You, Weislingen with your gentle soul!" (31, translation modified). The second occasion was the farmer's wedding, where the peasants recounted the assessor's exuberant fees. Selbitz reacted with *antiphrasis* (a single ironic word): "Goetz! *We're* supposed to be the robbers!" (37, translation modified). Here Götz repeats Selbitz's incredulous cry, the soldier's words cannot reach their destination because they have the wrong addressee. The exclamation mark shields him from the accusation with a forceful break in speech, and lends the repetition a tone of sarcastic mimicking that dilutes the force of power.

After all these broken phrases that show us how Götz has been charged with being one who insults, he now really does produce an insult. Though rarely mentioned in recent criticism, the history of this saying (commonly referred to as the *Götz Quote* [*Götz-Zitat*] in order to avoid repeating and extending its obscenity) has in fact been thoroughly researched.[38] Attention to its rhetorical form and anthropological background will put us on the track of the logic of the insult at work in the drama as a turn that repels sovereignty. Maximilian Müller-Jabusch shows that this phrase, which today is considered simply an insult, in fact has its origin in apotropaism, magic believed to ward off evil.[39] The *Oxford English Dictionary* defines apotropaic as "intended to avert evil influence; considered to have power to avert evil influence or ill luck," and notes that the term has its origin in the Greek *apotrepein*, "turn away."[40] Müller-Jabusch attends to this turn by first citing numerous examples from anthropological research into European folk beliefs. In one story the devil was said to travel through the night with goods and money. Showing him your behind would make him drop what he had and you could pick it up. In other examples such sayings are used to stop storms or prevent fields from failing to grow.

Searching to explain these diverse instances of the same gesture, Müller-Jabusch draws on the work of the archaeologist and philologist Otto Jahn, who relates these sayings to superstitious belief in the evil eye. According to Jahn, this superstition refers to the eye of the god looking upon the person who forgets the divine origin of his good fortune.

In his pride he falls into debt with the god, who will then take back what he has given. Jahn reports that one can draw attention to oneself by speaking proudly, or the god's wrath can be drawn by another person who expresses praise. Obscene sayings are meant to cause the eye to turn away: "When that which generally passes for immodest becomes visible, one involuntarily turns one's look away and that is what should be achieved in the jealous one, which is why one confronts him with it."[41] The revelation of the improper causes a reaction that cuts off the will of the viewer by being automatic and unintentional. The repulsion is double and mechanistic, since in self-defense one impels the aggressor to turn in self-defense.

Let us linger for a moment on this obscenity, interrupting the swiftness of its action to examine it in more detail. To begin with, the model of the evil eye imposes a specific economy. It is not, as one might expect, a question of having too much. Instead, one errs by not remembering, and thus not recognizing the origin and guarantor of wealth. The god appears when one forgets him, and his appearance functions both to punish the offender within the system and to remind him of the origin of the system.[42] This origin calls for a certain decency, a humble attitude. The Emperor's order to arrest Götz functions according to this logic of the evil eye in that the knight has forgotten the origin of his position. In act 1, Götz had employed this very language to describe the Emperor's power. He acknowledged his disruption, saying, "I am a thorn in your eye, as small as I am" (16, translation modified). Later Weislingen named the public arena as the "eyes of the world" (39, translation modified) that need to witness the knight's submission. Now the forces of the Emperor come to punish Götz and remind him of their power. Shockingly, Götz refuses to bow in recognition but instead rhetorically forces the bow on his addressee. In relation to Götz's insult, the adjective *unanständig*, usually translated as "improper" or "indecent," has a literal connotation through the etymological resonance of that which does not stand (by means of the root *stehen*). When he addresses the captain with the words "he can kiss my ass," Götz stages the head of the Captain (*Hauptmann* includes the word *Haupt*, meaning "head") down and behind him.[43] The *unanständige* aspect of his insult stages the captain not as standing, but as bent.

Rather than accepting the founding power that should be consolidated, Götz opens the question of its origin and implementation through a precise intervention. It would seem that Götz faces the Emperor (reading the *vor* in the phrase "Vor Ihro Kaiserliche Majestät" as itself a rhetorical staging through the location "before" rather than "to") while turning his back on the captain. Götz tells the first intermediary, the herald, to tell the second intermediary, the captain, that he will not obey him. He refuses to admit that he targets the Emperor, aiming his words at the captain, the head of the army. In a clear contradiction, Götz proclaims his loyalty to the Emperor but will not obey his orders. He confirms his debt (*Schuld*) to the Emperor, but challenges the relationship that this debt should found. Götz's insult affirms authority at the same time that it attacks it.

In the poem "Prometheus," written in the early 1770s but published only a decade later, Goethe offers another paradigmatic vision of Sturm und Drang rebellion that mirrors the challenge to authority in *Götz von Berlichingen*. He conjures an emaciated divinity, describing gods that need men more than men need them: "I know of nothing more wretched / Under the sun than you gods! / Meagerly you nourish [*Ihr nähret kümmerlich*] / Your majesty / On dues of sacrifice."[44] Still, in a mode that Hölderlin and then Rilke radicalize, the very pathos of his address reveals a strong desire for connection to the divine that the content of the text explicitly questions. The *Götz Quote* works in analogous manner, but in its longer narrative arc *Götz von Berlichingen* also offers a way out, or at least a way through, this clash of faith and doubt.[45]

A rhetorical parallel in the language of the drama further brings out the paradox of Götz's simultaneous submission and non-submission. The first of Götz's two sentences includes an expletive, a short phrase that intensifies the message. He respects the emperor "as ever," emphasizing the unchanging, eternal aspect of Götz's position and intensifying the manner in which he presents himself "before" the Emperor. The following sentence has a parallel structure: "But as for him, you tell him he can kiss my ass." Perhaps the "you tell him" should be read as an expletive as well, emphasizing Götz's own sending of the message, the fact that he talks rather than listens. In this case the expletive marks a kind of stuttering, etching a verbal resistance that parallels Götz's physical resistance to the Captain's order. In both cases two small words that seem to modify the sentences in question are themselves the essence of the sentences. They become the center, emphasized and graphically separated by commas in the German. Read in a parallel manner, they indicate that Götz eternally addresses the Emperor, but in so doing challenges his power.

Götz employs the *unanständig* as that which refers to a founding moment in an oblique way, but at the same time avoids simply opposing that which is "proper [*anständig*]." As such it resists dialectics, the pick up or pick-me-up of the sublation (*Aufhebung*). In *Glas*, Derrida develops an important paradox of the apotrope that will allow us to more precisely explicate this resistance. Derrida's intervention takes place in a reading of

Hegel's interpretation of the biblical story of Abraham that focuses on the role of castration. Circumcision provides the physical mark of this break, which Abraham repeats when he demonstrates his willingness to sacrifice Isaac. In cutting himself off from "his only love [*die einzige Liebe*]," Abraham ensured the survival of his family. Derrida reads both circumcision and the Isaac story in terms of a "simulacrum of castration."[46] The "simulacrum," the fact that the sacrifice does not really occur but still has the significance of proving Abraham's devotion, offers a specific way to gesture to power without being crushed by it. Like the circumcision, the interrupted sacrifice marks the exposure to a threat but then provides protection against this very threat. It shows a relation that emerges after one survives a wound. From this point forward, Abraham, his family, and his nation will be the favorite of God. Through the not-quite-sacrifice that proves his faith, he both accepts subordination as the favorite slave of God and masters the threat of the infinite, acquiring the ultimate power of negating all of his enemies. Once the injury and subordination to God have been transmuted into a source of meaning and energy, it can be employed as a weapon: "He exhibits his castration as an erection that defies the other."[47] An inversion, a sublimation, an *Aufhebung*, seems to work here, turning threat into power.

With his apotropaic exclamation Götz stages the logic of the ban which I have read in the previous section. He brings it out in the open and forces us to see how it works, which undermines its secret mechanism. The Emperor attempts to consolidate his power precisely by first giving it up, thereby removing the law's claim on Götz. The ban thus participates in what Derrida calls "the logical paradox of the apotropaic: castrating oneself already, always already, in order to be able to castrate and repress the threat of castration, renouncing life and mastery in order to secure them." With his verbal resistance however, Götz linguistically mirrors the logic of the ban as an apotropaic logic and in doing so reveals the danger or obscene secret of the apotrope: that this gesture of negation does not necessarily succeed in producing the mastery that is its goal. The linguistic obscenity thus marks a political obscenity. Götz says what should be hidden; he exposes the illegitimacy of the sovereign by insisting on serving as his double. He articulates his position both inside the law (respect for the Emperor) and outside the law (refusing to obey his orders). As an outlaw, expelled from society but within it, he is the inverse of the sovereign who marks the state of nature within the society.

A young admirer of the drama, Gottfried August Bürger, suggested that the *Quote* be addressed to critics of the time.[48] Goethe's work can defend itself from those who do not recognize its brilliance by telling them to kiss its ass. The words said to the herald, intended for the captain and not for the Emperor, pierce the frame that should hold them. Götz also turns to the reader in a *parabasis*, a trope classically understood in the theory of drama as a move from the speech within the fictional world of the stage to speech to the audience. Here, parabasis confronts the sovereign procedures of reading itself. Suspending the laws of interpretation that would reduce a text to pre-given principles, reading opens a kind of ban in which the mere relation of text and its unfolding comes to the fore. The localization of a specific interpretation relies on closing this ban, but may not be able to force it.

The exchange ends with the slamming of the window, cutting off the lines of exchange and communication. Götz does not wait for a response. This can certainly be seen as an extreme reaction of the Sturm und Drang individual against the abstract and leveling power of the law. The gesture goes further though, allowing the law itself to be reconfigured. Barricaded in his castle, Götz claims a territory outside the conceptual and physical reach of the law, while being topographically located within it.[49]

Susan Bernstein's work on "Goethe's Architectonic" allows us to venture a reading of this scene in terms of a political topology that resists metaphors of attempted internalization. In the context of a groundbreaking project that rethinks the relationship between the external and internal in architecture, literature, and philosophy, Bernstein analyzes Goethe's early and late texts, both titled "On German Architecture." The first essay, written in the early 1770s (like *Götz von Berlichingen*), exhibits what Bernstein calls "a certain extravagance" in both the ornamentation it describes and its own rhetoric.[50] Goethe claims to overcome the strangeness of the Strasbourg Cathedral, recounting his move from an enjoyment of the structure in its immediacy to a mediated understanding of its totality. This unifying process operates according to a logic that opposes the outside to the inside—a logic that also governs the relation between the earlier and later text in Goethe's 1823 account. Bernstein shows, however, that the specific terms of this second account suggest an alternate reading in which "repeated readings and editions" elucidate a horizontal model of edification aligned with writing.[51]

The castle window in act 3 of *Götz von Berlichingen* serves as a mediating point that structurally enables the intrusion of the Emperor's troops and the incorporation of the rebellious knight. In other instances, the drama's many interior scenes offer resistance to the unitary aspirations of the Empire. Indeed, Götz's speech describing his political utopia at the end of act 3 testifies to a fundamental dislocation that will keep history open even as he himself succumbs to capture.

Writing, Revolting

While the obscenity of the *Götz-Quote* marked *Götz von Berlichingen* as a scandal in the years immediately following its publication, the obscenity of the final act took longer to become an object of critical attention and remains a matter of intense debate to this day. Broadly speaking, scholars still tend to assume that Götz only succumbs to the deceit of the rebelling peasants and remains free of any responsibility for the violence that takes place under his leadership. According to the logic of the text that I have been following, the knight would *not* appear to evade this guilt, since apparently the apostrophe finally does work and the peasants produce the leader they so desire in Götz. Perhaps more significantly, this guilt would be rightly assumed as part of a legitimate power struggle. The drama seems to be on the verge of producing historical meaning in the form of revolution in which the people accept a new leader to represent them.

If this were the case, the violence of war would be a momentary disruption that allowed the transition from one regime to another. Instead of following through on this transition though, the drama merely announces it before recalling it. In doing so it leaves violence uncoded and a challenge for reading. In this final section I follow the difficult path of Götz's leadership before turning back to a scene in act 4 that, when read with the last line of the drama, may not explain the violence that bursts forth, but does attune the reader to a new inflection of its resistance to significance.

Violence heads act 5. We see it right away in the stage directions: "*Peasant's war / Tumult in a village and plundering. / Women and old men with children and baggage. / Flight*" (67). These words situate the scene both in the broad historical terms of the Peasants' War and then as a certain place ("a village"), and two actions that have no agent. Anonymous history appears to be on the move, with the "tumult" (related to the Latin term *tumor*, meaning "swelling") indicating another refusal of submission. Within the logic of the drama, the Peasants' War erupts in the space opened by the ban and maintained by Götz's refusal to submit to force. The sovereign's claim has been rejected not only by Götz but by the mass of peasants as well. Indeed, it seems that Weislingen's warning about the faith of the masses in Götz has come true as a result of their very attempt to eliminate him. As we saw earlier, he argued: "Those are the ones whose spirit [*Geist*] drives the rebellious crowd" (39). This time the "spirit" indicates the active principle again, but also a spectral force, a threat that haunts the Empire. It cannot be precisely measured or located but has a power inestimably larger than that of the actual number of people that form it and reaches well beyond their local territory. As the threat separates from its empirical foundation we gain insight into the way it challenges the framing efficacy of power structures.

A conflict between the rebelling peasants Metzler and Wild both shows the way to new leadership and its spectacular failure. The violent and directionless body politic comes to the stage when the other peasant leader Link asks where to find the "main force [*groß[e] Haufen*]" (68). Now the people are more than "Volk," which already takes the "people" in a political, or at least pre-political, direction. The "Haufen" is first of all only a "heap," "pile," or a "mass," and only through leadership and organization could it be considered a "force" with some sort of directionality, if not exactly agency. Metzler identifies the problem of a lack of order and control: "They're lacking a commander that all the people [*Volk*] would respect. We're only their own kind, they sense that and get difficult" (68). Metzler wants someone to unify the peasants, someone to produce a representable "people" by giving them someone to look up to.

Metzler seems to have his own motives, but they are never stated in a univocal manner. He wants to lead, but recognizes the structural reasons why this cannot work: he and the other leaders are on the same level. Only distance can create "respect," a term that recalls Götz's reply to the Herald in act 3. I noted in that context that the word's etymology indicates a looking back, and thus a turning away that appears to conflict with its literal meaning. According to Metzler, the people need someone they can turn to, and Link has his preference: "That would be good—give the whole business some polish [*Schein*] if Goetz would do it; he always counted as an upright knight" (68). The oppressed would turn to Götz if they had the chance. *Schein* indicates not only "polish" or "shine" but also "appearance" and this formulation implies that *only* the appearance would change and that this would allow a certain manipulation. Link repeats Metzler's proclamation to Sievers in the opening scene of the drama that described Götz as an "upright [*rechtschaffnen*] lord" (2). He can stand up, taking the mass of rioting farmers with him.

This "upstanding" nature, however, must be instrumentalized. Metzler and Link want a head without a head. They want to unify the rebelling farmers through a leader that stands above them while keeping control of the power created by this new formation. The paradox of this structure announces in advance the failure of the alliance between Götz and the farmers. In an early indication of the detours this circuit will open, Wild and Kohl, rather than the decision makers Metzler and Link, approach Götz and negotiate the agreement with him:

> KOHL: You are to be our commander.
>
> GOETZ: Am I to break my knightly word to the Emperor and leave my ban?
>
> WILD: That is no excuse.
>
> GOETZ: And if I were totally free and you continued to behave as you did at Weinsberg toward the nobles and the lords and carry on this way, so that the country round about burns and bleeds, and I was meant to assist you in this shameful, raging business—you'd have to beat me to death like a mad dog before I'd become your chief! (69)

Götz replies with a question of his own, but Wild refuses to accept it. Rather than arguing this point, Götz accepts it, hypothetically imagining that he were "totally free," a phrase which recalls the term *vogelfrei* (literally, "bird free") as synonym for the ban. As he thinks aloud, he structures his reply through the figure of *polysyndeton*, repeating four clauses introduced with the conjunction "and." He tries to add up the situation but arrives only at a paratactic list rather than an ordering principle. He cannot even reach a position of rule and domination within the free realm of the imagination. A dash interrupts this line of thought and Götz, who identifies with the wolf, announces that he would become instead a mad dog if forced into this position. He seems to face the fact that things just do not add up: if he were free and he were helping a murderous mob, how would he be free? The farmers are also described in terms of their "raging business," and Götz would react to madness with madness, becoming a "mad dog." This figure of the "mad dog," of the domesticated pet that violates domestication, resonates with the figure of the wolf-man that I examined in Agamben above. It has a place in the household of power that it refuses to relinquish but also runs wild in a way that prevents it from being peacefully integrated.

When the peasants threaten him, Götz begins to be more sympathetic to their demands. Faced with an impossible decision, he succumbs to the logic of the apostrophe. He projects a clear referent: "Why did you set out? To get back your rights and freedom?" (69). The rebellion should be subsumed as a means to an end, the people should act to reclaim lost rights and freedom. They should accept this goal and restrict their frenzy, forming not a "Haufen" but a group free from the violent depths of confusion. They should behave "as responsible men [*Leute*] who know what they want" (69, translation modified). By producing a target and knowledge, they would transform themselves from a mob to a respectable alliance. In other words, Götz here gives in to the idea that the rebels should present themselves clearly and properly, which would already tame their spectral threat.

Surprisingly, Wild does not answer Götz's questions directly. Instead he resists the knight's attempt to subdue violence and non-knowledge: "What happened, happened in the first heat of it, and we don't need you to prevent it in the future" (70). His reference to the future leads to a discussion about the length of time Götz will lead them, which is a perplexing specification. They agree *only* on this point, and it is the essential point because in accepting this circumscription, Wild evades the attribution of meaning suggested by Götz. The puzzling written contract that Götz demands to mark the agreement here has often attracted the attention of critics, since Götz has otherwise been a strong defender of the spoken promise. Having broken his word to the Emperor by becoming the leader of the band, Götz does not accept Wild's "word"; his request for Götz's hand must be supplemented by the contract.[52]

Götz gives in when confronted with the mob's resistance to signification in all of its madness. That he demands to sign a contract with them is a sign of despair, as if writing could fix that which shows no sign of being tied down. Caught up in this non-referential mass, he signs a document that makes him a rebel. Shortly thereafter, abandoned by Wild and Kohl, Metzler (whose name itself refers to butchering) announces his intention of burning Miltenberg. When Götz sees what has happened he exclaims: "This is the way they keep a contract? Ride there and give them a piece of my mind. Murderous arsonists! I declare myself free of them" (72). At the moment of dismissal, Götz implicitly references his tie to these deeds, that he has been a murderous arsonist. Through this insight, he decides to end his alliance.

The rogue overlaps with the terrorist at this point. Götz's twists and turns lock him up just long enough to align him with representation as it clashes with the undirected violence of the Peasants' War. Instead of engaging in further arguments regarding Götz's guilt or innocence, however, I wish to focus on how this clash puts us on the track of reading violence. Although *Götz von Berlichingen* does not come to terms with violence, it does attune us to the historical register of its semantic challenge in a scene in act 4 that adds resonance to the drama's final line. Götz's wife Elisabeth urges him, while confined to house arrest, to write. Here she assumes responsibility for a lineage, setting up the future by programming a line of descendants.[53] When Götz complains about the narrowness of his confinement, Elisabeth points to the openness of history:

> ELISABETH: So keep on writing the history [*Geschichte*] of your life which you've started. Put the evidence into the hands of your friends, with which to shame your enemies; create for a noble posterity [*Nachkommenschaft*] the pleasure of not misunderstanding you [*dich nicht zu verkennen*]. (65)

One might read this as two senses of *Geschichte* merging: the sense of *Geschichte* as personal story would become a part of history as Götz writes it down. In allowing those who come later to know of him, to know his account of his rebellion, he not only provides additional knowledge, but creates an alternative point of view. In writing, though, Götz does not so much accept his place in history as turn away from the present. A brief return to critics who developed Hegel's historical reading of the drama allows us to specify the importance of Elisabeth's command "so keep on writing the history" and Götz's response. H. A. Korff's *Geist der Goethezeit* (*Spirit of the Age of Goethe*) appropriates the historical insights of the previous century while criticizing the teleological drive of that period. Korff begins by following the general contours that Hegel puts forth. Götz acts "as if there were neither a political or legal order to which he had to submit."[54] He also questions the habit of simply accepting the new order as in fact better than the old one, noting that the *Landfrieden* and introduction of Roman law are used by corrupt rulers for their own ends. Thus, rather than seeing the drama as exemplifying a moment in historical progress, Korff sees it as staging "undisolvable antinomy" between the rights of the individual and the right of the society.[55]

Unlike the eponymous hero of Goethe's drama *Egmont*, then, Götz will not be able to offer a rallying cry at the end of his life. Influenced by Weimar classicism's reputation for balance and harmony, critics frequently underemphasize the structural power of *Egmont*'s return to the theme of rebellion. In fact, the drama's measured language smuggles the earlier theme of prosthetic resistance through stylistic checkpoints while giving up little of its force. After all, like Götz, Egmont responds to the influences of the people rather than leading them through a strong will. Despite his passivity, his last words in prision appear to proclaim an exemplary failure: "Protect your property! And to preserve your dearest ones, gladly fall as my example shows you."[56] The historical context of the drama makes it quite clear what it means to "gladly fall," since Egmont's death inspired popular uprisings that ultimately freed the Netherlands from Spain. Schiller's Karl Moor and Kleist's Michael Kohlhaas "gladly fall" as well, though, as I will show in my next chapters, the response of the viewers of their acts problematize their optimisim. In contrast, Götz falls with resignation and sadness. Ultimately though, the context of his defeat will be much more important than his mood.

In more recent criticism, Kenneth Weisinger develops with greater specificity the challenges to political and historical concepts that *Götz von Berlichingen* poses. He defends it as historical, but argues that in contrast to Enlightenment and baroque drama, it lacks a didactic purpose. Instead, "Goethe has dramatized a historical dead end."[57] The work does not seek to teach a specific lesson about political change but instead imparts a sense of historical contingency from Götz's demise and his relation to writing. A "new Götz" emerges at the end of the drama that accepts the demise of the "old Götz" and makes a place for him in history by authoring a text. [58] In other words, Weisinger opens Korff's antinomy towards the future.

My reading accepts the importance of Götz's writing scene as proposed by Weisinger but diverges from his interpretation by seeing Götz as still evasive, rather than self-creative, in his writing. He responds to his wife's suggestion (or command) with reluctance: "When I write about what I have done, I get angry about the loss of the time when I could still do something" (65). In terms of his resolute commitment to evasion, we can read this as indicating he does not simply lose time, but writes of the loss of time as he stands against it. This negative inscription does not promise a consolidation around Götz. We do not even so much see the loss of historical alternatives (that of the feudal age) but the loss as such of political structure in a non-reconcilable confrontation with violence. Still, this perception, this orientation toward tracing loss, opens the way to the temporal displacement of power structures that will play a greater role in my following chapters.

In popular critical memory, Götz has the last word of the drama, with a final, moving call to freedom. In fact, however, there are three more lines, the final one spoken by Lerse, who repeats Elisabeth's words in the writing scene with a twist: "Woe to the coming generations that fail to understand you [*Wehe der Nachkommenschaft, die dich verkennt*]!" (82). Pity on those that do not appreciate your greatness, those who do not recognize you, on those who, even with the aid of your own testimony, fail to stabilize your evasions. With his writing, Götz has produced a lineage of readers, but not one that can be assured of understanding his textual and historical intervention.

In chapter 4 we will carefully examine the repercussions of Michael Kohlhaas's rebellion on the future of the ruling family of Dresden. First though, we move to one of Götz's heirs, Karl Moor. We see that he begins how Götz ends, looking to a book, but sets it aside for the sword. Götz has prepared us to examine an exclamation that seems to be merely obscene in terms of political resistance, and reading Karl's apparently irrational outbursts and attacks through the unconscious will show that it is a realm that threatens not only the consolidation of the ego but political and legal consistency.

Chapter 3

✦

The Law of the Death Drive

Swearing on Corpses in *The Robbers*

Karl Moor's murder of his beloved Amalia in the final pages of *The Robbers* marks a scandal that critics have been too quick to explain away in their attempts to maintain a positive view of Schiller's hero. In this chapter I examine the mechanisms that the drama employs to incorporate violence into its models of individual and social identity. In order to elucidate these psychic and social structures I mobilize the resources of Freud's death drive, which sees in repetition compulsion a structuring function: the traumatized individual organizes his life around a wound. In this light Karl Moor's terrorism emerges as the clash between his actual violent acts and the drama's struggle to incorporate violence around the rhetorically projected figure of the "manly" right hand. While this potent masculine referent should organize the social group of the robbers and establish an interpretive grid for their violence, the drama eventually reveals a wound of paternal abandonment.

When Karl announces his intention to sacrifice himself to the law at the end of the drama, he appears to simply repeat the structure of his oath in act 1 by figuring himself as a cast-off body that enables a greater logic of totality. Yet while the drama appears to make use of Amalia's murder by establishing the law as the ultimate organizer of violence in Karl's final monologue, I argue that this crime in fact trips up the economic flow. Melanie Klein's insistence on the aggressive aspect of the death drive allows me to conclude by casting violence in the drama in a different light: Klein's reparation is not a mere repetition of the same but the creation of a new relation irreducible to a pre-set construct.

As we approach Freud, or rather return to him, I wish to acknowledge the necessary variation of my theoretical models and indicate their connection. These models are not always harmonious, but they offer the depth of resources that a study of violence in its errancy requires. Götz loses his political (social) future to those destined to misunderstand him, just as Karl confronts the collapse of his psychic model of intentionality when faced with Amalia's corpse. Agamben's notion of the ban and Freud's death drive allow us to see these disruptions. Later, in my reading of Kleist, Arendt's work on violence will help describe the non-dialectical mode of responding to violence employed by the fortune-teller in *Michael Kohlhaas*. As different as the thinking of Freud, Agamben, and Arendt (to name just three main interlocutors) may be in their structural detail and positive approach, they all, at certain moments, help us perceive the problem in a new way and thus provide the preconditions for further thinking. None of these writers are fully up to the task of terrorism, and indeed it would be folly to look for any one system that could help us. Instead, Goethe, Schiller, and Kleist help us at a point in history when new tools need to be gathered.

The Robbers opens with Karl Moor's plea for reconciliation and recounts his violent campaign in the face of rejection. Karl, the eldest and favorite son, decides to abandon his hedonistic life of idleness and gambling and to ask his father Maximilian for forgiveness. He wishes only to return to his home and to his fiancée Amalia. Fueled by resentment, his younger brother Franz intercepts his letter of repentance and inverts its message, convincing their father that Karl has disgraced the family name and that he should be disinherited. Karl, filled with outrage and cursing humanity upon receiving this judgment, then accepts the plan of his libertine friends to form a gang of robbers. With a vow to freedom he declares himself above the law. While Karl maintains what seems to be a concern for justice in his life of crime, his robber group shows little devotion to such ideals. They set fire to an entire city to free one of their comrades, despite knowing that it is not empty as Karl thinks. This results in the death of the sick and weak who were unable to escape. After a surprising victory against a local army, Karl must choose between the sanctity of his oath to his group and return to the arms of his beloved Amalia. Instead of coming down at an expected resolution, be it bittersweet or adventurous, the drama concludes with an incomprehensibly violent sequence. Karl murders his fiancée, leaves the robbers, and finally renounces the path he has taken and submits to a sovereign figure that combines God and the law.

Critics have not wholly ignored the violence that repeatedly punctures the narrative line of *The Robbers*, but they have sought to anchor it by returning time and again to the question of the motivations of Karl and his brother Franz. A brief review of the coordinates of this debate shows that it operates at the juncture of the personal and the political while pointing to an excess of violence in the drama that has not yet been accounted for. Emil Staiger pioneered such work, and indeed he explicitly compares Götz von Berlichingen with Karl Moor on the question of terror: "Above all, Götz is not at all ready to ride with iron and fire over the beautiful German land and exercise the terror to which Schiller's hero largely decides to commit—despite a few measures of caution and considerations of his creator."[1] Staiger offers a subtle but clear contrast: Götz drew a line at the irresponsible violence of the Peasants' War while Karl knows no such limits. Götz stays on the safe side of terror's excess while Karl's hesitations and second thoughts do not change his behavior in time. In an article that addresses Piscator's staging of Schiller's drama, Michael Patterson develops the main thrust of Staiger's insight: "*The Robbers*, over two centuries old, might make a fair claim to being the first in world theater to deal with the subject of terrorism."[2] In developing this claim, Patterson describes Karl Moor as fundamentally violent, seeking to destroy the powerful, and committed to a political ideology. As he interrogates this claim he comes to focus on the third part of the description, ultimately concluding that Karl's drive arises from personal rather than political considerations.

Friedrich Engels's often overlooked assessment takes the opposite route, positing a consistent ideological application: "We know that the first true socialist in the Bohemian woods was Karl Moor. He was unable to bring his work of regeneration to the end, his time did not understand him, and he delivered himself to justice."[3] For Engels, Karl does not just destroy but works for something new. The message that he sought to deliver could not be comprehended, which necessitated his ultimate surrender. This position has been developed more thoroughly in Engels's wake, particularly, but not exclusively, by authors of the former German Democratic Republic. Seeing progress and history at work, these authors frequently claim to represent a later audience that understands Karl better than his fellow robbers, who are unable to fathom the higher value of his actions.

H. A. Korff attempts to hold on to both the personal (as Staiger) and political (as Engels) sides of Karl's motivation. While recognizing the importance of his supposed rejection by his father, Korff argues that "this pure psychological motivation of Moor's leadership of the robbers is really not sufficient [for Schiller]. The rebellious attitude of the hero has to be ideologically grounded, the crime morally grounded."[4] This lack of explanatory sufficiency calls for investigation. On the side of madness, it opens to something more, something fascinating, even fantastic, not only in Schiller the author, as Korff claims, but in the character of Karl himself. This remains the case, indeed assumes even greater dimensions, if we are unable to grant the author of the drama the power of bridging the personal and political realms. Karl's actions exceed psychological explanation while at the same time falling short of the political justification that supposedly opposes them.[5]

This debate over the question of the origin of Karl's actions both testifies to the difficulty of producing a justification for his actions and at the same time distracts attention from the severity of these actions as such. For while Karl does attack specific wealthy and corrupt members of society, at the end of the drama he also murders his childhood love Amalia in cold blood. Violence in the drama consistently exceeds instrumentalization and intent, even as it produces a seductive rhythm that appears to organize this excess.

The drama swings repeatedly between strong commitments to violence and severe disavowals of it. A brief outline of the main moments of this to and fro movement indicates the contours of my reading: in act 1 Karl commits himself to life as the head of the robbers but after learning of the devastating effects of the attack on the city to free Roller in act 2 he renounces violence. Surprisingly, when the priest announces the arrival of a local army later in the same act and confronts Karl, he explicitly accepts his murders and again swears eternal allegiance to the group. In act 3 he then expresses a wish to leave his life of crime for Amalia, but these two desires prove irreconcilable and he kills her in act 5 without warning. He then announces his submission to the law and sets off to turn himself in.

"By This Manly Right": Swearing Obliquely

Karl does not begin the play as a terrorist; he begins it as a student.[6] When he puts his book aside he emerges to speak from his own position on the side. In the course of act 1, scene 2 he reacts to two texts. The first, Plutarch, evokes "disgust" when compared to the contemporary world. The second is the letter he receives, written by Franz but with the signature of his father. This betrayal evokes a rage that his friends eventually direct to make him the head of the robber band. I begin by examining how this rage erupts through the lens of Lacanian theory. This leads the way to a discussion of the drives (as explicated by Freud) that potentially organize Karl's movement from the book to the sword.

The first time we encounter Karl and his friends they have fled Leipzig to escape their debts and, according to the stage directions, now find themselves on the border of Saxony. These directions also specify that

Karl is "deep in a book" (35) and before he says his opening words he lays the book aside.[7] The criticism that follows addresses the world he lives in rather than the book and expresses the powerful sense of disjunction between ideals and reality that will drive the drama. Karl exclaims: "This century of scribblers disgusts me, when I can pick up my Plutarch and read of great men. [*Mir ekelt vor diesem tintenklecksenden Säkulum, wenn ich in meinem Plutarch lese von großen Menschen*]" (35, translation modified). Karl stops reading his book, but only to read the current condition of the word with his stomach. "Disgust" indicates an extreme reaction that takes a path through the body.[8] It points inward and thus takes a route in the vicinity of subjectivity but ultimately blurs the line between subject and object. As a seemingly immediate and overpowering reaction, this feeling of illness appears only to negate. Karl's rhetoric, however, provides critical direction. This physical feeling of illness links the book and the world in a manner that indicates a critique of some kind, but one that has not yet been articulated.

The rich figure of the "century of scribblers [*tintenklecksenden Säkulum*]" adds precision through a complex movement. It not only employs the flow of ink metaphorically but itself has fluid contours. "Century [*Säkulum*]" literally indicates a specific time period, and "tintenklecksenden" refers to a specific action, ink staining. It soon becomes apparent, however, that the terms have a metonymic function; the "century" refers to the people of the century and "ink staining" refers to their writing. Karl complains of the contemporary commentators of ancient texts, condemning them as unworthy of the heroes and concepts they expound upon. Their "ink staining" would be what they write about these great men. They are unworthy of being critics because their weakness and frailty contrast with the strength of the men they study.

Karl explicitly takes the side of the great men of history, but his weakness as a reader (his "disgust") sets him in the vicinity of the commentators he rebukes. His education has taught him of great heroes, but he finds them condemned by (and to) the very institution which has delivered them to him: "A fine reward for your valor on the battlefield, to live on in the grammar-school, and be dragged around immortal in a schoolboy's satchel" (36). The "sweat" in this sentence and the "blood" mentioned in the next one are bodily fluids that deserve to make better marks. They deserve a higher memorial; the "ink staining" of current writers is not an adequate substitution.

Karl then expands his criticism from academics to the society of the day more generally. The century itself seems to not be only "ink staining" but itself an ink stain, a garbled image. The phrase "mir ekelt vor diesem tintenklecksenden Säkulum" could be translated as "this age makes me disgusted," or more literally as "I get ill from this age." Going further and zooming in on the preposition "vor" suggests "in front of this age." Drawing on this resonance, Karl appears to set himself in a particular double position, both in his book *and* before the age. Considering this scene more precisely in terms of *anamorphosis,* the visual phenomenon of an artwork distorted to require viewing from a marginal viewpoint, allows the use of spatial terms to preliminarily map out Karl's "disgust." Describing how Karl looks from the side highlights the psychic and social disjunction that will explode later in the drama. In *Four Fundamental Concepts of Psychoanalysis*, Jacques Lacan draws the attention of his seminar to Holbein's painting *The Ambassadors* (1533) as a privileged example of the distortion inherent in the structure of subjectivity. For the most part a realistic depiction of two wealthy men surrounded by symbols of arts and science (such as a globe, books, and a lute), this painting contains a strange, unfocused oval blob in the center of its foreground. Only when one looks at the painting from the side does this blob take the shape of a skull, which thereby marks death as the limit of earthly life.

Importantly, this limit cannot be recognized directly within earthly life itself. Lacan sees the distortion of the anamorphosis as "something symbolic of the function of the lack, of the appearance of the phallic ghost."[9] The lack, that which prevents the subject from being present to himself, can be symbolized if not immediately identified. Digging deeper into Lacan's use of the phrase "phallic ghost" reveals a powerful multivalence: it both indicates and resists the power of the symbol by employing the psychoanalytic concept of the phallus as an adjective that modifies the figure of the "ghost." While the concept should in principle allow stability, this formulation relegates it to a dependent position. In its double movement of authority that cannot consolidate itself, this pseudo-concept will allow us to follow the intricate formulations of Karl's oath later in the drama.

In his specific reading of Holbein's painting, Lacan continues to say that it shows us "the subject as annihilated—annihilated in the form . . . of castration, which, for us, centers the whole organization of the desires through the framework of fundamental drives." In his initial outburst, looking at the world from the perspective of his book, Karl Moor suffers an annihilation that has a least two sides. He not only condemns the world ("an age of Eunuchs" [36]) but also implicitly excludes himself at the same time. Continuing to read act 1, scene 2 with the expectation of an "organization of the desires" in the wake of this annihilation points both to a hope for liberation and a commitment to violence. More fundamentally, the annihilation that Karl Moor inflicts and suffers will structure the drama but at the same time push the theory of centering destruction to its breaking point.

In a sense the position of exclusion and marginality that fuels Karl's rage seems to open the possibility of a better world. His particular social circumstances reinforce the exclusion that he stated after putting down Plutarch. He can move to a general attack on hypocrisy because he himself has been pushed to the side of society, forced to flee to the border to escape his creditors. He recounts how he beseeched them to forgive him but his pleading human hand was rejected. Following this rejection from society, Karl in turn rejects the law: "The law never yet made a great man" (36). He laments the loss of potential of some sort but it is not clear what Karl wants when he speaks of a greatness. The description at first provides no positive content. He wishes for negative freedom, freedom from the restraint of the law. The passage continues:

> Oh, if only Arminius's spirit still glowed in the ashes!—Put me in front of an army of fellows like me to command, and I'll turn Germany into a republic that will make Rome and Sparta look like nunneries. (*Tosses his sword on the table and stands up*) (37, translation modified)

Karl wishes to see Arminius's spirit in the ashes of the present, to synthesize his time with the time of Arminius just as Plutarch brings together the heroism of the Romans and Greeks. These "ashes" offer another figure for the stain of the current age. He then imagines another position for himself, in front of ("vor" once again) a group of men. The reference to a "republic" here is perhaps the most frequently cited proof of Karl's liberatory aspirations.[10] Surprisingly, he does not mention Athens, the obvious example of a democratic state. Thus Karl's use of the term "republic" may refer to its later sense of "a government without a monarch" or its earlier and more general sense of "a state."[11] His political motivations are strongly worded but press forward to contradictory results rather than a single goal, especially since his reference to Rome could be a model of citizen rule but also one of dictatorship (especially when one notes that he pairs it with Athens's great rival Sparta).

Even if he does not really know where it is going, Karl's fit of rhetorical passion appears to be pushing towards action but then ends with an ambiguous gesture. Karl's tirade begins after setting a book aside and apparently leads him to pick up a sword. The text fails to mention this weapon before, and indeed it seems to be a product of his rhetoric, a tool that arose from his desire to lead an army. Throwing down this potential symbol of power at the end could be read as a challenge, but must be an ambiguous one. It leaves Karl without the weapon he would need to act in the world, and the force of speech remains without explicit instrument or destiny.

At this point Karl's friend and rival Spiegelberg steps in with a proposal that redirects the energy of his friend's words and in effect challenges him to pick up the sword again. He attempts to instrumentalize Karl's insight and draw him into a life of action, recalling how the people readily followed him in a prank he played at one point. In response, Karl reveals that he has asked his father for forgiveness a week ago. From the point of view of this request, Karl's emergence from his book in this scene takes on the character of a final exam in ruling ideology. His monologues would in this sense be evidence that he has been successfully socialized by his education: he has learned from the great heroes of the past, from the corruption of the present day, and the impossibility of acting against this condition. The solution would be to retreat to a position which would protect him from his insight into hypocrisy and the restrictions and illegitimacy of the law for the individual. He wishes to take refuge: "In the shady groves of my father's home, in my Amalia's arms a nobler pleasure waits for me" (41). This idyllic scene of presence would allow the decentering effect of Plutarch to be contained. Spiegelberg's stories of their student pranks would also be safely disarmed from this position. After all, Karl belongs to the nobility and is thus entitled to all the enjoyment of the "nobler pleasure" that high social standing offers. His psychic split would be no more than a passing episode.

Karl is mistaken, however, to believe that the pranks are over just because he says they are. He receives a letter not from his father, as expected, but in the hand of his brother Franz. In his famous speech upon his return to the stage after reading the letter in act 1, scene 2 Karl storms up and down the room, ranting to himself.[12] Now he provides no description of his reaction (such as the disgust that he named before) but instead lashes out. He can find no place for mankind, screaming as if before a terrible picture:

> Men—men! False [*falsche*] breed of hypocrites [*heuchlerische*] and crocodiles! Their eyes water, but their hearts are of iron! Kisses [*Küsse*] on their lips, but swords [*Schwerter*] in their bosom! Lions and leopards feed their young, ravens take their chicks to feast on corpses, and *he, he*—Wickedness I have learnt to endure. I can smile when my arch-enemy is drinking my heart's blood [*Herzblut*]; but

> when blood kinship [*Blutliebe*] turns traitor, when a father's love becomes a raging fury; oh, then catch fire, manly resignation, be as a raving tiger, gentle lamb, and let every fiber stiffen to hatred and destruction! (48, translation modified)

Karl's outburst employs a long list of stylistic measures that include antithesis (*Küsse / Schwerter*), the accumulation of traits (different animals named), repetition (*Blut / Blut, Liebe / Liebe*), alliteration, and assonance (*falsche, heuchlerische*).[13] Each of the nine sentences ends with an exclamation mark. Disengaged from normal language, this rant formally parallels Karl's vain attempt to describe the lost referent man. Humanity has withdrawn into a tautology walled in by an exclamation mark: "Men—men!" He receives his father's rejection as the rejection of society as a whole, a terrible stain that throws him into a rage marked by the failure of figurative language to connect with its object. He begins by condemning men as animals, then proceeds to rank them less than animals, who at least respect the relation of parent and child. Then Karl stutters again; the fury of his language can find no point of contact, only anacoluthon, tautology, collision with a dash. He hangs up on language within language, clinging to fragments of articulation.

Karl's outrage, as expressed in broken language, works on the model of Lacanian anamorphosis described above. In an explication of this concept Slavoj Žižek relates it to Kant's insight that subjectivity is "*ontologically constitutive*." The thing-in-itself is excluded not because the subject is finite in an infinite world, but rather because his own structure presents everything he can perceive about the world. Seen from within this ordering grid, the fact of structuring itself needs to be distorted in order to create the basic distance needed for reference. Žižek emphasizes that when the skull in the painting becomes clear, this occurs at the expense of the rest of the picture:

> The black space of the Thing-in-itself is therefore something extremely dangerous to approach, for if one gets too close to it, "world" loses its ontological consistency, like the anamorphotic stain on Holbein's *Ambassadors*, where, when we shift our perspective and perceive it "as it is" (as a skull), *all remaining reality loses its consistency and turns into an amorphous stain.*[14]

Suddenly cut off from his family, and thereby his position in society, Karl suffers precisely this sort of breakdown.[15] His position has changed now; the nobility that offered a peaceful and easy integration with society has been withdrawn. Whereas before "disgust" marked his reaction to contemporary society when seen from the point of view of Plutarch, Karl now loses the anchor of the other position and sees all of society as a stain with no connection to meaning. What Žižek describes in terms of "ontological consistency," that is, the stability of relations in the word that produces a sense of trustworthy reality, appears in Karl's unfinished sentences as a loss of linguistic consistency. Things just will not hold together in speech.

At first Karl cannot focus his rage, even when it gets beyond expressive curses. He calls for total negation: "repentance, and no forgiveness! Oh, would that I might poison the ocean, that they might drink death from every spring!" (48). Having repented and been denied mercy by his father, he now denies mercy to the race. The failure of the mechanism of forgiveness means for him the break in the tie between father and son, as well as the loss of his place in society. His friends ask him to listen three times (48), but he certainly does not appear to consider their offer very carefully: "[*foaming, stamping on the ground*] ha! he who should put a sword in my hand, to deal a deadly blow to this generation of vipers! he who should say to me: if I can pierce the heart of its life, crush it, strangle it—that man shall be my friend, my angel, my god—I will worship him!" (48–49). Foaming at the lips and stomping on the ground (a description than will tie Karl to Kohlhaas, as we will see later), Karl transforms himself into one of the animals that he has rhetorically called upon.

Once he hits this bestial zero point of reference his language begins to cool. He has a hand that would allow him to act, if he were appropriately employed. Here his friends jump in, turning mere rhetoric into action. The sword he threw onto the table now reappears in another figurative sense, one that will lead to new social cohesion.[16] Karl's famous lines at the end of the scene deserve to be quoted more extensively than they traditionally are in order to expand the rhetorical field in which his rejection of the law takes place:

> My spirit thirsts for deeds, my lungs for freedom—murders, robbers! at that word I trample the law beneath my feet—men showed me no humanity, when to humanity I appealed; so let me forget sympathy and human feeling! I no longer have a father, I no longer have any love, and blood and death shall teach me to forget that I ever held anything dear! (49)

Karl does not even connect deeds and freedom here as he did at the start of the scene. Instead he rejects the law in general. The call to humanity was rejected, but the robbers have answered Karl's appeal. Still, the lines of this call remain tangled. His father has been lost, but the memory of the paternal link remains a troublesome remainder. With the exclamation "I no longer have a father," Karl proclaims himself as an orphan, related to the father only by negation. In the drama this "no father" will be one of the ruling figures, imprisoned beneath the earth but still psychically controlling both Karl and Franz in ways they only ever partially understand.[17]

Karl's call to humanity as family in both the narrower and wider senses has been refused and he now reroutes it into both a curse (above) and an oath. These two speech acts appear at first to be diametrically opposed, but *The Robbers* leads one to consider their interrelation and the extent to which they can be exchanged. Both are related to the promise. One might assume that the curse excludes, cuts off, ends, while the oath includes, binds, and founds. Such an opposition is deceptive, though, since this curse also opens, if only through a commitment to a future of violence, while the oath has a protective function that excludes most of humanity:

> Oh, my amusement shall be the terrible dispersion [*fürchterliche Zerstreuung*]—it is agreed, I shall be your captain! and good fortune to the champion among you who lights the fiercest fires, who does the foulest murders, for I say to you, he shall have a kingly reward! Gather round me every one, and swear loyalty and obedience till death! Swear by this manly right of mine [*bei dieser männlichen Rechte*]! (49, translation modified)

The "terrible dispersion [*fürchterliche Zerstreuung*]" replaces the productive dissemination that would have linked Karl in a family chain. He offers no suggestion of a noble ideal leading this group. In fact he appropriates his friends as weapons for his own wish to destroy, promising them rewards. Ironically though, the very promise of destruction founds a substitute family when Karl steps out from his student friends to become the father of the group, allowing not only himself but them as well to consider themselves adults. He refers to his hand as the referent of the oath, its body. This referent, however, only comes into being with the oath itself. With the oath the robbers proclaim themselves men who can then swear on the "manly right [*männlichen Rechte*]."[18] The gendered language here plays a key role in establishing Karl as one who challenges paternal power and also attunes us to the feminine threat to this power that Amalia will pose. The German phrase, which omits the actual body part—he means "this manly right hand"—actually highlights the absent center that the hand will become through this ellipsis. Moreover, the nominalization "Rechte" places the right hand in the vicinity of law, justice, and right through the legal sense of *Recht*.

By announcing the hand as guarantor of the oath, Karl produces a symbol that covers over the loss of meaning caused by his brother's letter. It does not, however, fully sublimate the destructive desires that Karl spoke of earlier in the scene. Instead the oath only reroutes violence, holding off Karl's psychic dissolution by continually attacking others. In his commitment to a future of violence, the back-and-forth motion that I described above in terms of the two points of view of the anamorphosis shifts from a spatial to a temporal model. One way of following this shift in the drama would be through the "temporal anamorphosis," which Žižek defines in another commentary on Lacan as follows: "the Object is attainable only by way of an incessant postponement, as its absent point of reference."[19] This "temporal anamorphosis" swings between the two points of view on a painting such as *The Ambassadors* in which one at first faces an incomprehensible loss that one then manages to symbolize by moving to another position. Only the movement between the points of view provides the entire picture; it is never accessible at one single moment. The unity of the group of robbers contains a stain at its center, the hand, which is only recognizable outside of the group in attacks on others.

In order to more clearly explicate this rhythm as a potential method of organizing the violence in which the robbers engage, I begin the next section by describing the oath according to the *fort/da* structure that Freud describes in *Beyond the Pleasure Principle*. With this theoretical background I then turn to close readings of passages in the second act of *The Robbers* in which Karl Moor hears the results of an attack he ordered and recounts the murders that he has committed himself.

Fort/Da? The Structure of the Death Drive

While the violence of *The Robbers* ultimately disrupts all economies, the structuring power of Karl Moor's oath provides a seductive model for the production of meaning according to at least one Freudian register. In *Beyond the Pleasure Principle* Freud discusses a challenge to his theory of the pleasure principle that has arisen from new analytic observations. Broadly speaking, these observations threaten the system of signification that Freud developed throughout his career by carefully mapping necessary detours through the unconscious. In a review of this earlier work he emphasizes that the general economy of the pleasure principle functions through a buildup and release of pressure with the aim of keeping the amount of excitation "as low as possible or at least constant."[20] The intervention of the reality principle alters, but does not fundamentally disrupt this economy: it merely installs a series of delays in the path to pleasure.

The new evidence that absorbs Freud's attention relates to trauma, specifically war trauma. He reports that soldiers frequently dream repeatedly of the war injury that they tend to not think about during the day. This disruption of the usual functioning of the dream as wish fulfillment leads Freud to ask why the body wishes to put itself back into the traumatic situation. He connects the repetition of traumatic dreams with the famous *fort/da* episode in which he witnessed a child playing a game with a wooden reel tied to a piece of string. The child would throw the reel over the edge of his bed, making it disappear, then pull the string so that it came back. "That was then the complete game, disappearance and return."[21] The first action was accompanied by the sound "o-o-o-o" which Freud interprets as "fort," meaning "gone," "away," or "lost." With the second action the child said "da," meaning "there." Freud sees the game as the "great cultural achievement of the child" in that it stages the absence and return of the mother and through this staging gives up his instinct (the reference is to "Triebverzicht") to protest when his mother leaves.[22] The drive has been suppressed and thus satisfied, resulting in pleasure. As a symbolization of loss, this suppression allows the child to master his situation.

Looking closely at this privileged example allows us to see the important Freudian concept of repetition compulsion as a reenactment of violence that follows a double course through symbolization. In its outward aspect, the child's violence against the mother does not address her directly but shifts to the reel that he casts away. At the same time, the violence that the child commits against himself by imposing this absence of the mother no longer poses an essential threat because the child sees himself as the author and master of the absence. In the previous section I linked Karl's violent rhetorical outbursts in act 1 with the vow that he makes at the end of the act by describing this vow as what Žižek calls a "temporal anamorphosis." As my reading of the drama continues, we will see that while this vow does create order, it faces repeated threats and thus must be repeatedly reinforced. To better describe this troublesome rhythm of the vow as *The Robbers* presents it, I suggest that it be considered as functioning according to a *fort/da* logic. The vow allows symbolization and the creation of identity but does so by displacing violence. Karl's crimes always do more than he says they do, and their errant significations lead to the greater question: to what extent can the death drive be reduced to a structuring principle at all?

In act 2, scene 3 the attacks that Karl promised in the scene of the oath become the main topic.[23] The robbers have set up camp in the woods and recount their crimes. Roller, one of the robbers, had been captured and the others freed him in an attack on a town. As another robber named Schweizer recounts this episode the extent of their violence sends Karl Moor into a fit of renunciation, which, while later withdrawn, begins to articulate the threat to authority that he has grounded in the oath. This threat routes its way through the figure of the hand (which Karl set up as the elided center of his oath's power) explicitly at the end of the scene, and as it does so it figures a danger to the group of robbers and the outside world.

The robbers are clearly very pleased to have recovered their comrade. They also seem almost as happy with their actions beyond this goal. Schweitzer says: "Besides, our fellows had the chance of plundering scot-free" (82, translation modified). This side remark suggests that the robbers accepted Karl's reason for the attack as its essential feature and that the theft merely occurred as an accident. This robbery was not, however, the only extraneous effect of the attack. After three other robbers describe their plunder, the subject turns to the damage to the town, and, after that, to the populace. Over eighty-three people are said to have been killed in the attack.

It is only after hearing this effect of the side effect of the attack that Karl Moor breaks in, expressing deep despair regarding the use of violence. Early in the scene Ratzmann had expressed his amazement that Karl was not concerned with the plunder of their crimes, and at this point the question of the referent of murder arises again. Karl places the rescued robber in an economic relation: "Roller, your life is dearly bought" (83). The price of his freedom was high; the violence exceeded the amount that one would consider fair. Schufterle (another robber) eagerly provides a detailed description of the victims. His specific accounts replace the anonymous figure of "eighty-three" deaths. He reports that only the weakest were killed, "dregs of the town" (83) who had no power to flee the flames. His list includes "babes in arms still dirtying their linen," "wrinkled grandmothers," "women in childbed," and "poor poets" (83). In a final vignette, he recalls how he threw a baby into the flames.

Now Karl breaks in, throwing Schufterle himself into metaphorical fire: "Did you, Schufterle? And may those flames burn in your breast till the day eternity grows grey!—Away, monster! Never let me see you in my band again" (83–84). The robber hesitates and Karl must repeat his command: "What are you murmuring? Are you hesitating?—Who can hesitate when I command?—Away with him, I say" (84, translation modified). His hesitation could be read either as willful disobedience or simple confusion. After all, Karl never specifically prohibited such behavior. The very undecidability of Schufterle's pause highlights the attack's threat to Karls Moor's authority by demonstrating that the robber's excessive violence does not merely oppose it, but arises from within it. The true risk to the pleasure principle lies in this challenge.

Avital Ronell, who pushes German critical thought into the realm of the contemporary technological scene, points to the difficulty of knowing when one has moved beyond the pleasure principle in a close reading of the step/charge of the Rodney King tape. In 1991, a witness videotaped police brutally beating King following a high-speed chase. As the officers went to trial for the apparent excess of their actions, the tape was broadcast again and again on U.S. television. Ronell looks at the moment of supposed provocation as an ambiguous move forward—was it an innocent step or a guilty charge?—that the court interpreted as aggression. Addressing the repeated segment of video in which this move was excerpted and replayed, she writes of a scene in which "the television watches as the video is on compulsive replay, tripping over this unreadable scene that it has witnessed."[24] Schufterle's hesitation, like King's step and/or charge, indicates a skip or slip which even dedicated repeat viewings cannot define, and which trips up the pleasure principle.

Karl's frustration highlights his difficulty dismissing these uncertainties. The robbers leave the stage and Karl extends his questions alone:

> Hear them not, avenger in heaven! How can I prevent it? How can you prevent it, when your pestilence, your famine, your floods devour the just man with the wicked? Who can command the flame, and bid it spare the hallowed crops when it shall destroy the hornet's nest? (84)

Karl's apparent monologue addresses God, whose very name he transmutes with the title "avenger in heaven." He tries to exculpate himself by controlling what God hears of the robber band's actions as if his intentions could be separated from their effects. Yet how could he presume to command God when his own robbers are uncontrollable? Or does Karl really want God to hear? In the following line he calls God as a witness to the terrible fate of his good intention. His plea takes the form of an excuse rather than an apology; he tries to explain away his debt rather that accepting it unconditionally. Karl metonymically transforms the fire which was the weapon of destruction into other natural threats, thereby shifting the blame from his own shoulders. These natural powers are not the property of men, but of God: "your pestilence, your famine, your floods." Then the fire comes back, but in another context, away from the actual city that was burned, to a metaphorical countryside of hornets and fields.

The three rhetorical questions that Karl asks in the above citation actually suggest a simple answer: man cannot command the flames, God can. In one of his many failed or pseudo-anagnorises (the moment of insight one waits for in a tragedy) Karl seems to recognize this fact: "Oh shame upon the murder of children! Of women! Of the sick! How this deed bows my head! It has poisoned my finest works!" (64). Karl has not been able to restrict the object of his violence and names three separate types of murder for a range of civilian victims. Its effects have spread beyond his control, moving to catch up with his exclamations of universal destruction in act 1, scene 2. Still, he focuses on his "work," as if it had a purpose beyond violence and could be judged independently of it. Confronted in this way with the murders of his gang, Karl declares that he gives up: "Here I renounce the impertinent plan, go to hide myself in some crevice of the earth, where daylight shrinks before my shame" (84).[25] The stage directions that follow show both the desire to enact his intention and the failure to implement his desire: "*As if to flee*" (84). At that very moment though, a robber arrives and announces that they are surrounded by soldiers.

Karl suddenly abandons his intention of leaving. A practical reason suggests itself easily: with his group surrounded, he actually cannot run away. From this point of view, he might be seen to merely hold his ground but he actually goes further, using the attack as a way to reestablish his authority. His first words in reaction to the news are: "I have let them encircle us completely, now these fellows will have to fight in desperation. (*Aloud*) Children! Now's the time!" (85, translation modified). Responsibility for his friends pulls him back. He refers to the robbers for the first time as "children," thereby placing himself in the position of the father. He repeats this address in the remainder of this act as well as in acts 3 and 5. When his relation to his band intensifies he explicitly accepts responsibility for the acts he had just disavowed.

This reversal occurs when, as if conjured by Karl's call to God, a priest enters the camp, accuses him of his crimes, and asks him to surrender. The priest links his charges to the hand:

> Does not the murdered Count's blood stick to your accursed fingers? Have you not with your thieving hands violated the Lord's sanctuary, and villainously seized the consecrated vessels of the sacrament?

> What? Did you not hurl brands of fire into our God-fearing city, and blow up its magazine over the heads of pious Christians? [*Clasping his hands together*] (87).

I have noted above how Karl's right hand serves as the object of the robbers' oath in the first act. The text had already reopened this wound, bloodying this hand in act 2, scene 2 when Hermann recounted an invented story of Karl's death meant to deceive Old Moor and Amalia. He claimed he knew Karl from the army and had seen how his right hand was "shattered" by a bullet, the "flow of blood" (65) that resulted from it and how he had died from this wound. My previous chapter examined the function of the prosthesis of Götz von Berlichingen's hand in figurative terms, and in *The Robbers* the hand, though missing in a different way, also marks a site of power struggle. In this scene the priest repeats the image of the bloody hand from the dream. According to his description the hand signifies a specific death, that of the Count. He then names the "thieving hands" that broke into the church. Finally, the hands are implied as the instruments which "hurl" fire into the city. The priest's clasped hands form a gesture of emphasis, but also one of hands in their peaceful place, folded in prayer to God.

Karl had just repented but now he withdraws this repentance when God's representative formally asks for it. In fact, he now explicitly accepts accountability for what he has done and what has been done in his name: "thus says Moor, captain of murderers [*der Mordbrenner Hauptmann*]" (88). In another resonance of his name, Moor takes the title "*Mord*brenner." He lists his crimes in the mode of a confession: he killed the Count and burned the Dominican church and surrounding city. Rather than announcing the end of his campaign though, as one would expect following a confession, he says "but that is not all" (89), which indicates violence that cannot be circumscribed. Karl then turns from the metaphorical to the literal by extending his actual hand:

> I have done even more. [*Stretching out his right hand*] Do you see these four precious rings that I wear, one on each finger? . . . This ruby I took from the finger of a minister whom I laid low at his prince's feet when he was hunting. He was a man of the common people, who had made his way by flattery to his master's highest favor—his neighbour's fall was the footstool of his exultation—orphan's tears bore him aloft. This diamond I took from a minister of finance, who sold offices and honours to the highest bidder, and turned the sorrowing patriot away from his door. This agate I wear in honor of one of your

> cloth, whom I strangled with my own hands after he lamented in the pulpit, before his congregation, that the Inquisition had declined so.—I could tell even more stories [*noch mehr Geschichten*] of my rings, if it were not that I already regretted the few words I have wasted upon you—. (89, translation modified)

By confronting the Priest's figure of speech with the rings on his fingers, Karl's blood congeals into trophies. He stole these rings, but each one stands primarily as a synecdoche for a person rather than as a signifier of wealth. Each person, in turn, stands for something else. Karl explains to the Priest precisely whom he killed and includes a description of their offense. Here we find the best evidence of Karl as a defender of justice: he kills corrupt officials.[26] Yet instead of focusing on this signification, I wish to emphasize the fact that Karl shows four rings and promises four stories, but only delivers three. The "even more" with which Karl begins his speech has not been fully exhausted. The unexplained fourth ring points to the "even more stories." Displayed but not explained, it leaves open the threat of future violence and the question of the scale of this violence.

Karl sends his threat to the powers of both the church and state, since the Priest arrives with a specific legal offer that indicates his connection to both. He admits guilt only in the afterlife. Otherwise he sees no end point:

> What I have done, doubtless I shall read one day in the ledgers of heaven, but with their miserable hirelings I will waste my words no more. Tell them my craft [*Handwerk*] is retribution—vengeance is my trade [*Gewerbe*]. [*Turning his back on him*] (90)

The hand appears in this citation again in the "craft" or "handwork." Karl's physical hand has served as a placeholder for signifiers that point to his deadly work. Though the actual deeds are those that the Priest originally accused him of, they are now placed in a different context. The detailed descriptions of the previous lines are now replaced with two formulas: "my craft [*Handwerk*] is retribution—vengeance is my trade [*Gewerbe*]." With its implications of an economy based on repayment, Karl's statement appears to allow his violence to be circumscribed. This not only makes the threat to the powerful concrete but also establishes it as an instrument under Karl's control. In the next act, however, we will see that the rhetorical model of uncontainable violence indicated by the violent hand pushes through this model of the limited weapon. Karl will once again face psychic dissolution and only another oath will save him.

Exposing the Oath

As the second scene of act 3 opens, the robbers have escaped from the army sent to capture them. They have emerged from the depths of the forest to look out from a hill over the Donau. Karl asks his comrades for water as he collapses on the ground. Then he turns longingly to the fullness of nature, to the grapes on the vine that he compares to their empty wine flasks. He wishes in vain to linger in this beautiful natural world. At this point he seems close to returning to his decision before the battle to leave the robbers and crawl into a crack in the ground. Here, however, this wish takes on a more sentimental figure, and Karl proclaims: "That I might enter again into my mother's womb!" (99). His desire for the lost mother leads him to tumble into a fit of what would later be termed romantic despair: "Oh, Elysium of my childhood!—will you never return? . . . Gone! Gone beyond recall!" (100). This is the first of Karl's two references to his mother, the second occurring in the monologue where he contemplates suicide. Within a Freudian reading, the absence of the mother in the drama is striking. Indeed, according to the model of the *fort/da*, her absence would be that which structures the entire work.

Here, at the dash of lost nature (which aligns with mother and family), Schweizer comes up to Karl, covered in mud, to deliver water. Again, as in the first act, the robber band brings him back to his senses. After hearing how he fell down a riverbank and while drinking the water he brought back, Karl himself returns from his sentimental thoughts: "Moor [*giving him back his hat, and wiping his face for him*]: Let me—we do not often see the scars the cavalrymen left on your forehead, back there in Bohemia—your water was good, Schweitzer—these scars suit you well" (100). Moor washes Schweizer's face to reveal the scars that have been covered up by mud. These scars, "drawn" in Schweizer's face, are physical marks of his devotion to Karl as real as the water he delivers. Indeed they go even further, signifying not only his past devotion, but his future fidelity to their criminal association. Much open space remains for more battle wounds. Schweizer replies: "Pah! There's room for thirty more!" (100). The lightness of this answer puts Karl at first into a less severe frame of mind, which then shifts again to one of mourning:

> Yes, children—it was a warm afternoon's work—and only one man lost—my Roller died a fine death. There would be a monument on his grave, if he had not died for my sake. This will have to serve [*wiping his eyes*]. How many was it of our enemies that we killed? (100)

Moor again places himself in the role of the father (a role first articulated in the prior act, as I pointed out above), but one who strangely seems not to be upset by the death of one of his sons. Roller's death was beautiful and deserves a beautiful monument. In its place, Karl offers tears. Hearing of the great losses of the army that attacked them, Moor offers an equation: "Three hundred against one!—Each one of you has a claim on this head. [*Baring his head*] Here I raise my dagger—as truly as my soul draws breath I swear—swear I will never forsake you" (100). Karl's own head takes the place of Schweizer's forehead. By taking off his helmet he exposes it to future marks of battle. The death of Roller thus leads to the oath that should guarantee the future of the group and make up for the lost past and nature that Karl laments.

One should remember, however, that they had already pledged their fidelity at the end of act 1, scene 2. Now it seems as if Roller has fulfilled the oath ("till death" [49]) not just for himself, but for everyone. At the same time though, he has weakened its binding power. Karl's proclamation of the new oath here marks a challenge to his authority by indicating that the original founding oath has suffered a fatal blow by Roller's death. As if picking up on this weakness, Schweizer responds to Karl as if the first oath had in fact been annulled: "Do not swear! You do not know if your good luck may yet return, and you will regret it" (100, translation modified). Happiness still exists only outside of the group and he challenges Karl to resist living in this "if." Karl rejects the prospect of peace and announces a new oath that posits the remains of Roller's body as its ultimate referent: "By my Roller's bones! I swear I will never forsake you!" (100). Fleeing from the lost nature of his childhood, Karl tries to form an independent society based on the oath, but this oath fails to ground itself and Karl connects it to a buried body as its guarantor. The motive of the buried body replaces the strong phallic symbol of the "manly" right hand.[27]

The repeated challenge to the oath suggests that it is an oral document that continually needs to be reapproved. Unlike the social contract, which on Hobbes's account takes shape once and for all in the move from nature to culture, the robbers need to restate their commitment again and again. In *Wallenstein's Camp* Schiller returns to the question of the relation between the leader and followers. Learning that the Emperor intended to divide their army, the soldiers come up with the plan of drawing up a "solemn document / declaring we will stay together."[28] The solid voice that they announce with such enthusiasm proves to only be able to be created through deception and ultimately reaches the Emperor's ear at the wrong time. Thus, even in his later years, Schiller remains fascinated with the problem of political representation in its broadest sense and continues to pose questions about the circuit of power from the people to their chosen leaders.

At this point, the aspiring robber Kosinsky appears with a story that interrupts the corresponding oath of the robbers that one expects in reply. The circuit of the oath suffers from this intrusion, since this time the robbers do not explicitly agree. They later act as if they had signed again but never actually do so. To this extent Karl's declaration (and thereby his power) remains precarious. The drama concretely figures the open nature of the oath in the fourth act when Kosinsky's story of his lost beloved, also named Amalia, sends Karl back to his home. Here the drama explicitly reveals the scar of abandonment that lies beneath what Karl called his manly right hand. The servant Daniel recognizes Karl and recounts the story of the childhood accident. Daniel was watching Karl while his parents were away and he severely cut his right hand when he was out of the room ("and it was your right hand too!" [177]). Richard Koc perceptively explains that this accident "implies a double abandonment of the child, first of all by the parents, and secondly by the surrogate to whom they have delegated their responsibilities."[29] The oath founds the robber band, a group of strict belonging, *over* the mark of abandonment. The traumatic wound, Karl's vision of the "phallic ghost" of the anamorphosis thus aligns with the scar, the stain on his own body.

Daniel's story ends with the words: "it all healed up well, but for that wicked scar" (117). The scar has a double function, indicating both healing and incomplete recovery. The skin remains blemished, stained, marked. Karl's right hand, upon which they swear, is not a simple, neutral object.

The Ghost of Roller and Amalia's Corpse

With an understanding of the rhythmic logic of the oath that should incorporate violence, we can now attempt to address the problem named at the start of this chapter: Karl Moor's murder of his beloved Amalia in the final pages of the drama. Following Karl's surprising rescue of his father from Franz's prison, and his resulting death from shock, the robbers announce that they have captured Amalia. She insists on her love for Karl and with three declarations of devotion breaks through his despair and rejection. Karl exclaims that he has found forgiveness: "She forgives me, she loves me!" (156). In reconciliation with his beloved he also returns to nature ("heavenly aether" [156]) and God ("merciful one in heaven"

[156, translation modified]). His inversion moves from despair to totality. This salvation, however, does not extend to the group of robbers as Karl expects: "[*standing up, to the ROBBERS*] So cry too! Cry, cry, you are so happy—O Amalia! Amalia! Amalia! [*He hangs upon her lips, they remain silently embraced*]" (156, translation modified). Of one body, they should all cry together. When this does not happen spontaneously, Karl issues a command. He then meets Amalia's three declarations of devotion with three exclamations of her name. The stage directions mark a silent moment of parousia, as if Karl finally found the full presence of motherly nature ultimately promised by the structure of the *fort/da*.

An unnamed robber responds to Karl's command with a command of his own that breaks the dream of loving and wordless peace: "Stop, traitor! . . . [*He parts them with his sword*]" (156). He not only verbally attacks his leader but physically separates him from Amalia. Then a second robber reminds Karl of his "oaths" (157). Above I considered this plurality as a weakness to the structuring power of the oath but the robbers appeal to it here as a sign of even greater strength, relating it explicitly to the "hand" (157) of the original declaration. A third robber then rhetorically raises the specter of Roller: "The spirit of Roller that died for you [*Der Geist des geopferten Rollers*], Roller who you summoned from the dead to be your witness, will blush from your cowardice, and rise armed from his grave to punish you [*dich zu züchtigen*]" (157, translation modified). The ghost will enforce the economy of Karl's rule even against Karl himself.[30] Roller would provide discipline—*züchtigen* has a pedagogical ring to it—and also in the sense of a demand for *Vergeltung*, repayment. Roller's blush reveals a rush back to life, the flowing of blood. Now the robbers, unnamed throughout their accusations, become a confused, indistinguishable mass, undead bodies that instantiate the power of their sacrificed comrade. They tear their clothes to show their scars, the tears in their bodies that guarantee their hold on their leader. "Do you recognize these scars? you belong to us! We bought you for our bondsman with our heart's blood" (157). Their "heart's blood" provides the liquid currency that has made Karl's very body their own.

The connection between economy and the ghost brings us, via the *oikos* of "economy" (meaning "home") to Derrida's reference to a "domestic specter" in his readings of the *fort/da* game. In the section of *The Post Card* titled "To Speculate—On 'Freud,'" Derrida reads this game as not merely one example among many, but rather as the organizing principle of Freud's investigation of the death drive and as the model of a highly problematic speculative process.[31] In doing so he also sees it as a model of Freud's own rhetorical strategy. Derrida's move from one level of explanation to another highlights the broader implications of Freud's theory, the fact that it can be seen to apply not just to the individual psyche but to broader structures of power. He emphasizes Freud's rhetorical game that "speculates on the return, is completed in coming back."[32] Freudian speculation guarantees the rule of the pleasure principle. Furthermore: "The mastery of the PP [Derrida's abbreviation of 'pleasure principle'] would be none other than mastery in general: there is not a *Herrschaft* [mastery] of the PP, there is *Herrschaft* which is distanced from itself only in order to reappropriate itself: a tauto-teleology which nevertheless makes or lets the other return in its domestic specter."[33] At the end (*telos*), one ends up with the same (*tauto*) according to a logic in which the "specter" that might bring alterity from another realm turns out to be only a ghost produced by, but not threatening to, the dwelling precinct of the system. Derrida shows that Freud never makes the clean step "beyond" the pleasure principle that the title of his text promises.

This phrase, "domestic specter," contains a subtle tension, since while ghosts do tend to haunt houses, they are also one of the key examples of *das Unheimliche*, that strange return of the once familiar. The following lines of *The Robbers* demonstrate the dangerous and uncontrollable nature of a logic that would depend on this ghost.[34] It has returned as promised and appears to have defended the system: Karl turns to lead his thieves away. Amalia resists this decision with her body, demanding that her abandonment be matched by a physical blow. She will not be repressed, and when Karl refuses to kill her she appeals to the robbers: "Then you must take pity on me, you hangman's apprentices! . . . your master is a vain faint-hearted braggart" (158).[35] She challenges the students to rebel against their master and in response a break in their unity does occur. The stage directions first say that the robbers all turn away, but then in the next moment one turns back and aims at Amalia. This turning back may be motivated by pity. At the same time, it must also be an act of rebellion.

Only now does Karl act: "Stop! Would you dare [*Wag' es*]—Moor's love shall die by Moor's hand alone" (158). Karl orders the robber to stop with a command marked with the force of an exclamation mark ("Stop!"). The next phrase disrupts the power of command, though, when it breaks off with a dash that threatens the readability of the scene ("Would you dare—"). Perhaps it topples the authoritative exclamation mark, or perhaps it graphically prefigures the unnamed weapon with which Karl commits murder. As the *Grimm Wörterbuch* tells us, *wagen* refers to a "wager," in other words a "putting in play [*aufs Spiel setzen*]," and also has a speculative resonance. The robber's insubordination has put Karl's authority in play. While the violence that erupts thrusts in the direction of recuperation, it at the same time undermines the conditions of such speculative return. On the one hand, by killing Amalia, Karl accepts the challenge that the robber makes to his authority. On the other hand, he removes the external threat to his group and thus reinforces this authority. Once again, a *fort/da* system: Karl kills Amalia to retain the authority over his robbers that would have allowed him to prevent her murder in the first place, giving up his rule in order to retain it. This is not the forward stride of the speculative dialectic associated with Hegel, but rather what Derrida has called a *demarche*, a step which indebts itself, a "*pas de thèse* which advances without advancing."[36] In the scandal of Amalia's murder the speculative game of authority stumbles.

The robber Grimm attempts to account for the excess in economic terms: "You have paid your debts with interest" (158). He tries, in a sense, to bury Amalia. Karl might be expected to accept this gesture of closure since it offers a way of breaking through a deadlock he faced between Amalia and the robbers, but he rejects any possibility of exchange between them. Upon this refusal to recognize a common currency of exchange, the economy collapses and Karl finally disavows his robber band.

I have followed the drama's consistent staging of threats to Karl Moor's authority, but the murder scene remains an eruption of violence that resists explanation. Amalia, the only woman in the play and the only person killed on stage by Karl Moor—Amalia, whose name means "work" (from *amal* in Gothic and old German), causes the economy to stop working. Perhaps the violent scandal of Amalia's death would be the fact that it is unforeseen, incalculable. It opens a possibility of dislocation in the *fort/da* system at any moment.

Reparation for the Invincible Law

Karl Moor at first figures his murder of Amalia as a sacrifice to the robber band and one robber, Grimm (at this point proper names return), registers his satisfaction, telling Karl to move on. The stage directions provide only the most general information about how Amalia dies, but the drama shows the effect of her death on Karl through his graphic vision of the robbers' demise:

> Oh, I tell you, if every one of you were to walk the scaffold, and to have your flesh torn from your bones, piece by piece with red-hot pincers, that your torments should last eleven summer days long, it would

> not make good these tears. [*With bitter laughter*] The scars, the forests of Bohemia! Yes, yes! Of course that had to be repaid. (159)

Karl digs beneath the scar and removes flesh from the skeleton piece by piece. The rhetorical dismemberment finds nothing upon which the oath to the group could now be founded. The economy of exchange collapses. Karl should have given up Amalia for the maintainence of the group, but instead by giving her up he has dissolved the group as well. From the depths of this collapse and despair Karl renounces his life as a robber for good:

> Oh, fool that I was, to suppose that I could make the world a fairer place through terror, and uphold the cause of justice through lawlessness. . . . oh, childish vanity—here I stand at the limit of a life of horror, and see now with weeping and gnashing of teeth, that *two men such as I would destroy the whole moral order of creation.* (159)

In a phrase that recalls his initial talk with Spiegelberg, Karl refers to the immature nature of his actions. They were pranks. While in the first act he was on the border of Saxony, he now stands at the edge of life. The exclamation ends with a strange reference to "two men." Critical attention to the question of the identity of these "men" reveals a debate over competing aspects of Karl's character. Some scholars propose that the other man is Franz, while others insist that the remark is a merely rhetorical intensification.[37] Spiegelberg would be another candidate, with a doubling function which can be seen in his name (*Spiegel* meaning "mirror"). Karl, however, has always been constitutively split, sending off the part that would then be drawn back to unify his psyche. He continues:

> Mercy—mercy for the youth who sought to anticipate Thy judgment—Thine alone is vengeance. Thou hast no need of man's hand. And now, truly, it is no longer in my power to make up for the past—what is ruined is ruined—what I have overthrown will never rise again. But still something remains that can reconcile me to the laws against which I have offended, and restore the order which I have violated. They must have a sacrifice [*Opfer*]—a sacrifice that will make manifest their invulnerable majesty to all mankind—and I myself shall be the sacrifice. For them I must surely die. (160)

Karl asks forgiveness as a child from God, the Father. He gives up his goal (revenge) and the human hand that was to implement it. The empirical damage that he has caused cannot be reversed but he can still act in the interest of the idea of the law. Benno von Wiese's classic interpretation of *The Robbers* deserves to be reconsidered here. Long regarded as the chief proponent of a reading that emphasizes the reconciliatory role of the divine, von Wiese more specifically argues for the interdependence of heavenly and earthly (societal) law: "Voluntary death in the framework of earthly laws stands as an image for the maintenance of a system of order whose earthly existence can only ever be an allegory for the construction of the ethical world."[38] Karl's submission to the authorities at the end of the drama actually indicates that the law mediates the transcendental.

Von Wiese's argument makes sense of the slippage in Karl's language here between two addressees of his exclamation. At first he speaks to the divine and then to the "law" that seems to be both human and divine. My reading of the drama, however, attunes us to the disjunctive role of the body in this "system of order." Indeed, the German term *Opfer* could be translated either as "sacrifice" or "victim," a distinction that sharply splits the necessary point of view from a contingent one. The sacrifice appears essential in the eyes of power, while the victim sees his punishment as an accident. Karl tries to meld these two viewpoints by taking necessity upon himself. To do so he calls primarily for a body that can be wounded—his own body—in order to demonstrate the invincibility of the law. The law needs a body, that much we know, but the rhetorical struggles around this material referent show that it might not respond to transcendental mobilization. Indeed, when Karl speaks for the law, he announces something that the law would never itself admit. The scaffold becomes a stage and the emphasis moves to the audience of Karl's envisioned death at the hand of the state. He believes this show will have a certain effect, but the following lines of the drama challenge this intention by opening different perspectives on the announced execution.

The opening lines of the monologue do indeed speak of regret for what was done in the past. Karl now not only announces his intent to leave the robbers (as he had a number of times before) but declares that turning himself in will have a higher purpose. With our reading of Freud as a background, the first lesson that suggests itself is that the law will find true unity through the return of the excluded body of the great robber Karl. However, in assuming that the law will return to itself, Karl disregards the lesson of Amalia's murder—she insisted on dying and thus on embodying a *fort* without an accompanying *da*. Like Götz's wife Elizabeth, who opens the future, albeit one that resists stable interpretation, Amalia shifts the interpretive protocols of the *fort/da* game that code violence.

Melanie Klein's work on reparation offers a way to describe an alternative to the closure of the *fort/da* game of aggression that Amalia disrupts. Instead of finally appealing to integration, Klein shows how a (psychic) system can shift in a new direction after violence. In terms of Klein's 1946 article "Notes on Some Schizoid Mechanisms," Karl Moor finds himself at the border between the paranoid-schizoid position and the depressive position. The former describes the earliest stages of the infant's development, in which good and bad objects are seen to be split in a manner that indicates the child's own disunity. In Klein's terminology the child sees the "good breast" that provides nourishment and the "bad breast" that threatens his existence by denying this sustenance.

My reading of Freud in this chapter suggests that the child's "projection" of aggression on the bad object and "introjection" of the good object functions as an early version of the *fort/da* game in that the motions of expulsion and return are both present but not yet connected to each other. Only as the child moves towards the depressive position does a full circuit become productive. At this point the child's fantasy of destroying the mother in reaction to her withdrawal of the breast gives way to regret and the wish to restore her.[39] This constitutes one of Klein's most radical insights: she both posits an originary aggression that she aligns with Freud's work on the death drive and sees this very destructive impulse as a step in the creation of a healthy and unified ego. Specifically, Freud's death drive paves the way for Klein's "drive to make reparation":

> The drive to make reparation, which comes to the fore at this stage, can be regarded as a consequence of greater insight into psychic reality and of growing synthesis, for it shows a more realistic response to the feelings of grief, guilt and fear of loss resulting from the aggression against the loved object.[40]

Aggression produces other emotions that indicate connection, even if this connection at first appears only negatively. The impulse to make a positive counter-action through reparation leads to "synthesis" of the subject and object, which in Klein's work always indicates also the integration of the individual ego. In contrast, other writers in the wake of Freud take trauma to be potentially unresolvable and lead us to be wary of the belief that the past can be left in the past. By naming himself as the victim or sacrifice, Karl himself takes on the role of the ghost, of the domestic specter that would guarantee the authority of the law. He appears to think that this victim allows the "majesty" to analeptically establish itself, that his death will allow its reign to unfold ever more forcefully over men. Indeed, the standard example of *analepsis* in rhetoric (a sentence with the same phrase at the beginning and end) concerns the absence of sovereign power: "The king is dead, long live the king!" Karl attributes the logic of the *fort/da* game to the law itself; the order both needs to be healed and has an "invulnerable majesty." It must give itself up, allow itself to be hurt, in order to produce evidence of its transcendence. The scene of Amalia's murder, however, prevents one from believing that this return would guarantee the solidity and future of the law. Instead it insists on the spectral nature of the authority of the law and the threat of dissolution that haunts it in its very speculation.[41]

Eckart Goebel's work on the connection between Freud and Hobbes allows us to clarify the link between the psychic and the social that I have sought to explicate in *The Robbers*. Goebel convincingly establishes a parallel between "state of nature and state" in the first two parts of the *Leviathan* and "pleasure principle and reality principle" in Freud's 1911 text *Formulations on the Two Principles of Mental Functioning*.[42] Most crucially for Goebel, the underlying force of the drives may never be fully converted into a harmless structure. Instead, just as the state of nature may erupt at any moment, the drives remain a constant threat to the ordering power of the reality principle.

Freudian sublimation operates on the sexual drives. By definition, then, it cannot function in the case of the death drive. Nonetheless, in this chapter I have been following a certain structuring effect of the death drive, and a comparison of this effect to the work of sublimation can help to clarify its operation. The central connection between repetition and the death drive, from Freud's work on returning war dreams and the *fort/da* game, to structuralist readings of Lacan and Žižek, indicate that the death drive induces another type of order. I followed this tendency earlier when I described the *fort/da* game in terms of representational efficacy: the boy places himself at the origin of his mother's absence and, at least within the realm of his psyche, achieves her return.

Karl Moor attempts to operate on this order of symbolization when he manages to solidify his own psyche at the same moment that he founds his robber group over his "manly" right hand. The Freudian logic of the death drive shows itself to be a subtly powerful means of co-opting violence. It allows aggressive impulses to take the foreground but never to wipe out meaning as such. Instead the death drive always shows up in tandem with repetition that tempers violence and renders it perceptible as one facet of a greater order. Karl's violence always has the potential to disrupt representational structures. However, only his murder of Amalia actually forces this disruption, a disruption that I have described as terrorism. This act brings onstage the violence internal to the founding of the robber group that he had kept hidden but which had never truly been transformed.

Witnessing his speech of repentance, the robbers first think that Karl intends to kill himself. When they hear he plans to turn himself in, one says: "Chain him! He is raving mad [*rasend*]" (160). With this description as "raving mad [*rasend*]," a term earlier applied specifically to Amalia, Karl takes his lover's place as that which resists the system. In fact, Amalia has in a sense still slipped under my critical sights even as I have tried to focus on her. She actively *provokes* Karl to his final murder and in doing so disrupts the logic that would incorporate violence both in individual and social terms. What critics persist in calling her extreme sacrifice does not restore any economy but causes a greater rupture than had previously seemed possible.

In his final monologue, Karl appears oblivious to Amalia's lesson. The Kleinian reading of the death drive can help us learn from it though, especially when we highlight the theatrical nature of Karl's presentation. He says he will "manifest" the power of the law for "mankind." Yet once he brings the law out of itself and into his body on the stage of the scaffold, he cannot guarantee its interpretation. In response to his speech, the robbers exclaim that he only seeks "idle admiration [*eitle Bewunderung*]" (160). From their point of view, the only reason their leader would turn himself in would be for his own fame and glory. Klein's version of the death drive as an original aggression that can lead to reparation helps us see Karl's surrender in terms of a displacement of structuralist interpretations of the death drive that emphasize rhythmic repetition. For Klein there is only a single transition to the depressive position (which of course does not prevent relapses to the paranoid-schizoid position in the future.) From this point of view, Moor's appeal to the law's "invulnerable majesty" in the wake of Amalia's murder appears as a re-description of his violence as that which cannot be immediately reinscribed according to previous protocols, and which demands an unforeseen shift in the relation between state and subject.

Replying to the robbers, Karl says: "I might be admired for it [*Man könnte mich darum bewundern*]" (160). Though his tone is hard to interpret here, it seems that he admits the possibility that the robbers are right, but in acting as he announced, he also thinks *he* may be right. A range of possibilities suggest themselves between these two extremes of the personal and political. To suggest only one, perhaps the people who see Karl die will take him as an example for future rebellion against the law. The drama ends with a turn to the spectators and leaves their response open. Indeed, with an ironic twist, it concludes before showing Karl's punishment. *The Robbers* shows Amalia's senseless death and not Karl's supposedly meaningful one. In so doing it leaves us with the homonymic resonance of "wound [*Wund*]" and "wonder [*Wunder*]," and the decision of how to interpret Karl's deeds.

Chapter 4

Who Reads Terrorism?

The Mandate of *Michael Kohlhaas*

Michael Kohlhaas recounts scenes of murder and arson. These scenes, vivid yet complex in their unfolding, both urgently demand to be read and at the same time continually resist the framework necessary for reading. Kleist tells a story of a raid on material constructs as well as on political semiology, but the qualities of the objects or emblems under assault cannot be quantified in fixed terms: it is neither simply a tale of revenge that would restore a pre-given economy, nor merely one of a failed call for revolution. In this chapter I argue that Kleist's novella exposes an intrinsic dislocation between violence and discursive attempts to frame violence, and stages the consequences of this dislocation in terms of a displacement of political, historical, and narrative schemas of representation. My reading follows the stages of destruction, tracing violence as it metonymically cuts through the narrative boundaries that have traditionally been understood to rein it in. A subterranean logic that has escaped critical notice links Kohlhaas's original acceptance of a call to action with his manifestos and the concluding fortune-teller episode. Toward its conclusion, the work begins to track the makings of a counter-history, one that reviews the narrative strategies on which Kohlhaas the character as well as historians have hitherto relied. Somewhat surprisingly, the possibility of rewriting his own history erupts under the sign of the feminine—a gendered character, a woman, changes the possibilities of historical and narrative recounting.

In examining Kleist's novella in terms of terrorism, I focus on a subset of critics who move beyond the debate over how to categorize Kohlhaas's violence in terms of its means or ends and instead point to moments of his attacks that exceed even the explanation he offers. Carefully following this excessive violence through the framing devices of Kohlhaas's manifestos allows me to describe the way in which it changes our understanding of terrorism: it is an attack not only on specific people and things but on political representation itself. Kleist's novella takes a specific narrative stand on this representational attack by describing the historical shift that opens when the people question their identification with the sovereign without replacing him with either the rebel challenger or a legitimate successor.

Unlike the majority of critics, including Bloch, Bohnert, Boockmann, and Skrotzki, I seek to avoid the question of whether Kohlhaas is or is not a certain type of terrorist. Instead, I agree with Ratmoko that the novella changes our understanding of terrorism itself. Sendler, Kittler, and Wittkowski make an important advance in this discussion when they speak of Kohlhaas's terrorism, not in the vague sense of an individual's violent campaign against a government, but in terms of a specific moment in the novella (roughly around the burning of Wittenberg and Leipzig) in which his violence goes beyond any definition of a rational target.[1] Yet while these three critics admit the rupture of any system of means and ends in Kohlhaas's murder of innocent people, each claims that the narrative places a definite limit on this threat. I follow the insight of these scholars into excessive violence even further, and argue that the terrorist force does not simply erupt at a specific instance and then recede, but instead acquires an independent momentum that displaces power until the very end of the text. These shock waves suggest that Kohlhaas's terrorism does not merely attack specific manifestations of state power, but representational potency itself.

My reading draws on two aspects of Hannah Arendt's late work *On Violence*, which combines precise theoretical definitions of political terms with subtle and searching interpretations of contemporary protest movements. I propose that she offers an unacknowledged resource for describing power differently, as that which can be simply abandoned and lie in need of assumption. Specific attention to the repercussions of the fortune-teller's prediction can help us think through the prospect of a transfer of power that is not logically determined in advance, a shift not constrained and compelled but nonetheless *propelled* by unique historical circumstances. The novella recounts neither the violent reinforcement of a preexisting law nor the founding of a new one, but a long breakdown of power that could not be calculated ahead of time. In the course of this breakdown, and in the midst of what appears to be a fierce battle of man against man, a third party marked as feminine—*die Zigeunerin* (the "gypsy" fortune-teller)—guides a threat that sends history in another direction.[2]

I begin by tracing key steps of Kohlhaas's struggle to measure the injury that he incurs upon the maltreatment of his prized horses. What at first seems to be potentially reducible to a private slight becomes a matter of public concern through a series of confrontations with violence in changing contexts. Seen in this way, the first decree that Kohlhaas composes appears not as a sudden burst of irrationality, but as an effort to cast himself as a representative figure that organizes violence. He claims to stand in for all of the people that Von Tronka has hurt and will hurt and justifies his threat against the nobleman from this position. Yet this grounding moment occurs over paradoxes of representation that point to a disjunction between violence and power. The brutal attacks that follow escape even the boundaries that Kohlhaas sets for them, thereby highlighting, rather than resolving, this disjunction. Finally, Kohlhaas issues a mandate that calls for a new society in a manner that lays bare the performative structure of power as thoroughly dependent on context. The people clearly do not respond to this call for a new regime. With its public staging though, the following story of the mysterious capsule text provided by the fortune-teller keeps the threat of rebellion open, re-broadcasting the mandate's earlier threat to power with a new inflection.

Taking the Call to Violence

A brief review of *Michael Kohlhaas*'s arc will set the stage for a reading of the graphic violence that propels it. Facing not only the seizure and abuse of his prized horses by the nobleman Wenzel von Tronka, but also the corruption of the legal system that should punish this crime, the horse dealer Michael Kohlhaas engages in an ever-expanding campaign of fiery attacks that ultimately engulfs entire Saxon cities. After a meeting with Martin Luther, Kohlhaas enters into an amnesty agreement that allows him to pursue his claim in the courts again. At this point, however, a conflict between Kohlhaas and the Elector of Saxony takes over the story. Due to the corruption of his advisors, the Elector presses the Emperor to prosecute Kohlhaas just before he realizes that Kohlhaas possesses a mysterious amulet containing a prophecy related to the fall of the Saxon ruling family. In the final scene, the court decides Kohlhaas's suit regarding the horses in his favor, but at the same time condemns him to death for his violent attacks. Just before he dies he swallows the prophecy, causing the Elector of Saxony to pass out in what resembles a psychosomatic attack.

The text opens in the middle of a history of death and interruption. The old nobleman has died, and the next link in the signifying chain of genealogy—the son—has set up a roadblock to enforce rules supposedly overlooked by his father. Even before this, however, the narrator sets himself up on another point of passage that belies an impasse. After opening with a description of Kohlhaas's many virtues, the text offers an early explanation of what is to come: "But his sense of justice turned him into a robber and a murderer [*Das Rechtgefühl aber machte ihn zum Räuber und Mörder*]" (87, translation modified).[3] Provisionally, this "sense of justice [*Rechtgefühl*]," which could be colloquially translated as the "sense of what's right," might be considered a synthesis of the two terms, as the anchoring of the objective rules of what is right in subjective feeling. This presumed synthesis falters, however, when the term appears again in the course of the more detailed narrative. A close reading of the way in which Kohlhaas comes to make his case against Wenzel von Tronka will show that he does not merely generalize from his personal injury to a greater sense of public injustice but stakes a claim to a universal position whose representational potency the novella undermines from the very start. In this light we will be able to resist the temptation to see the manifestos and attacks that follow in terms of a simple expansion of destruction to reach a preconceived goal. Instead, we will trace how Kohlhaas's efforts to frame violence change in response to attacks that repeatedly exceed their stated target.

In order to focus quickly on the problem of containing violence, I want to pick up the path to Kohlhaas's attacks at the point where he has just seen that his horses have been worked nearly to death on Wenzel von Tronka's field. Von Tronka denies any wrongdoing and his castellan threatens Kolhlhaas, sending the horse dealer's pulse rising. He experiences a forceful impulse to physically attack. Just as suddenly, however, this urge encounters an impasse that leads to its dissolution: "But his sense of justice, which was as delicate as a gold balance, still wavered; he could not be sure [*noch nicht gewiß*], before the bar of his own breast, whether the man was really guilty of a crime" (92, translation modified). Kohlhaas stops himself from bursting into violence. Yet the scale, which suggests rational calculation in the sense of equivalency that would allow restitution, is located not, as one might expect, in his head. Instead, Kohlhaas's predicament is located in his "breast," a rhetorical site that suggests a more immediate decision, one perhaps unfettered by logic. Through the use of the phrase "he could not be sure [*noch nicht gewiß*]" we are brought into the vicinity of the German term *Gewissen*, which like its English counterpart "conscience" both etymologically indicates knowledge and at the same time implies a moral sense that resists the standard topography of rational thinking.

Kohlhaas faces the dilemma of reading violence, a violence that, while having been inflicted on his horses and his servant Herse, he experiences as an injury against himself. Shortly thereafter, riding away from Tronka Castle, he reweighs the possibilities in a scene beginning, once again, in the realm of the private or subjective. Here Kohlhaas swings between two "feelings," one that suggests resignation and one that suggests action. His internal scales of right and wrong are clearly still in a state of flux, tipping only when he hears from other people of the many other abuses perpetrated by von Tronka. He then begins to believe "it was his duty [*in der Pflicht verfallen sei*] to the world to do everything in his power to get satisfaction for himself for the wrong done to him, and a guarantee against future ones for his fellow citizens" (95). When these witnesses appear on the scene, they give voice to a call that surpasses his internal feelings and becomes a demand. He does not make a calculated step, but loses his footing in a fall into duty. Yet "duty [*Pflicht*]" has not simply overcome the private concerns associated with "inclination [*Neigung*]" in the Kantian vocabulary. Kohlhaas does not simply submit to the moral law. Instead, he accepts a call that is both internal and external, articulating a claim to fight not only for himself (for his horses) but for others as well, drawing on the injury he suffered in the past to become a representative figure who takes responsibility for the future.[4]

Attention to the structure of this call can help map Kohlhaas's leap from his struggle to contain his injury to the broadcast of his own proclamations. The call is not a simple transition system: while it grants violence a certain legibility, a closer look at its logic warns against hopes that it might provide a firm foundation for a recuperative operation. In *The Telephone Book*, Avital Ronell reads the call via Heidegger's call of conscience (*Gewissensruf*) as that which both constitutes and de-constitutes its own subject. She writes: "Insofar as the call comes from beyond me and over me, it commands a power post of sorts, it lords over me from beyond my station and puts me in its place—*my* place, for the call also comes from me."[5] What seems to be the most internal, the call from within, turns out also to have an origin beyond the subject. It marks the assumption of a paradoxical autonomy since in taking the call one posits one's very power to do so. This movement explains how, while Kohlhaas first pursues his concern for right within the bounds of the law, his description of his task in terms of a call already prefigures an insistence on the independence of these two concepts. Kohlhaas's conscience makes him stand up for the law, but in putting himself directly in a position to enforce the law he already commits himself in principle to breaking it by ignoring its set procedures.

Kohlhaas's wife Lisbeth appears at first merely to add to the list of plaintiffs in his case, reaffirming the necessity of acting for others and adding that he would also be doing the will of God. However, her death marks a break at which Kohlhaas abandons the legal system and declares his own authority. After one of the Elector of Brandenburg's guards accidentally kills her as she attempts to deliver an appeal from her husband, Kohlhaas composes his first written demand:

> He sat down and drew up a decree [*verfaßte einen Rechtsschluß*] that, by virtue of the authority inborn in him, commanded the nobleman von Tronka, within three days of its receipt, to bring back to Kohlhaasenbrück the pair of black horses he had stolen from him and worked to death in the fields, and to fatten them in person in Kohlhaas's stables. (111)

By writing this document, Kohlhaas solves his interpretive problem of how to locate the physical violence committed against his horses: he establishes the crime which has been perpetrated and names the victim of this crime. As the *Schluß* [end] of *Rechtsschluß* suggests, he does so by closing off other options to posit an organic source of authority, speaking of an "inborn power." This singular authority has, in turn, one target of attack, Wenzel von Tronka. Kohlhaas's document splits off from the legal order to install its own clear delimitations of right: it recounts a crime, a victim, and orders a specific person to perform a certain action in a set amount of time.[6]

By describing Kohlhaas's phrase "inborn power" in terms of "authority" I seek to indicate the pre-institutional character of his claim and thus open a space between the proclamation of power and formalized power. Kohlhaas claims authority as an author, he attempts to write his way to power. The novella tells the story of the struggle to grasp injury in writing. The many victims named up to this point do not ground this proclamation but rather highlight its disjunctive positing, indicating that when he composes his documents ("verfaßte") he will fail to grasp (*fassen*) power. Kohlhaas chooses a referent of violence from within a field of targets that cannot be totally reconciled. This is not to say that the choice is arbitrary, but rather that it proceeds from a system of links and jumps rather than rational reflection. First of all, Kohlhaas forwards his call of conscience and proclaims his own power, not mentioning the people, God, or Lisbeth, all of whom he elides. He also effaces the wounds of his servant Herse and other targets that could have easily been named in these circumstances: the castellan demanded the passport at first and then reminded von Tronka of it again as Kohlhaas began to leave. At the other end of the social spectrum, the Elector of Brandenburg might have been chosen as the target in that Lisbeth was killed trying to reach him and he ultimately holds responsibility for the behavior of his guards. While Kohlhaas does not merely leave the choice of targets to chance, his document obscures his intention. Kohlhaas needs this obscurity to justify himself but because of it he can never simply impose his will.

Decrees of Terror or How Performance Fails

With his first decree, Kohlhaas channels authority and thereby assumes a position that can pronounce judgment. In the scenes that follow he turns to terrible attacks as a means of enforcing this judgment but his intention is repeatedly thwarted. In terms of the story's violent trajectory, these attacks can be seen as another series of attempts to contain an injury, this time not by seeking its cause, but rather by channeling it in a specific direction. This goal ultimately appears to be the origin of society itself, and thus might in Walter Benjamin's terms be considered an attempt to engage in law-making violence (in distinction to the law-preserving violence that maintains a system already in existence). If this is such an attempt, however, it repeatedly proves unsuccessful.[7] Yet its failure still has an impact, and following it closely suggests that Kleist's novella challenges Benjamin's conception of law-making violence, at least to the extent that it belongs to the dialectical tradition of Hegel and Marx. Hannah Arendt's definition of violence in *On Violence* provides a necessarily provocative guide to my reading. In her view "violence can destroy power; it is utterly incapable of creating it."[8] Power, as she defines it, comes from elsewhere. Arendt's semicolon marks an abyss and Kleist steers us right toward it. Yet power does not simply collapse in *Michael Kohlhaas*. Instead, in the various written texts (decrees, mandates, etc.) thematized within the larger narrative, there is always a gesture towards an alternate power that never manages to consolidate itself. Close attention to the circumstances of this non-consolidation will point to a displacement of power that operates between its destruction and creation.

Strangely, Kohlhaas's first "decree" makes no mention of the specific consequence that would result from a failure to comply. It gives no warning that violence will follow, offers no enforcement plan. Yet when the stipulated three days have passed, Kohlhaas and his men attack Tronka Castle and burn it to the ground in one of the most violent passages in German literature. The tollkeeper and gateman fall below their attackers' horses as Kohlhaas's group storms the castle. Herse assaults the castellan and steward. The decree, we learn, has both reached its destination and failed to deliver its intended message: Wenzel von Tronka is reading it aloud to great laughter. Entering the hall to find his target already gone, Kohlhaas immediately grabs Wenzel's relative Hans von Tronka, throwing him with such rage, "that his brains splattered over the stone floor" (112). The attack ends with the bodies of the castellan and the steward flying out the windows, along with those of their wives and children. Kohlhaas's turn to violence in an effort to enforce the authority he claimed turns out to undermine that very authority. The "inborn power" that he announced before his attack has failed in its first attempt at realization. He has not succeeded in capturing Wenzel von Tronka, and in the process people unnamed in his "decree" have become its objects and victims. This splattering of blood and murder of innocent family members initiates an escalation of rhetorical violence that will itself, in turn, be surpassed by physical violence. Kohlhaas now believes that Wenzel von Tronka has fled to his aunt's convent. In response we are told that he

> drew up a so-called "Kohlhaas Manifesto [*Kohlhaasisches Mandat*]," in which he called upon the country to give no aid or comfort to the nobleman Wenzel von Tronka, against whom he was waging a righteous war, but instead required every inhabitant, including relatives and friends, to hand him over forthwith on pain of death and the certain incineration of everything they call their own. (114)

How are we to read the title of this document? Of undetermined origin, it comes to us in quotation marks that indicate the narrator's skeptical distance. "So called," it could have, and perhaps should have, been called something else. The document is not another "decree [*Rechtsschluß*]," and the standard translation of "manifesto" suggests that there has been a movement from the earlier closure of the "Schluß" to an opening or disclosure of manifestation. Yet the content of this document fails to provide the justification or grounding movement one expects in a "manifesto." Instead, as a "mandate [*Mandat*]" it appears to merely command and like "decree [*Rechtsschluß*]," it implies a legal framework for its order that is absent.

This passage begins with a metonymy in which "the country" presumably replaces the people of the country. This trope not only has a specific rhetorical function but also indicates the missive's broader metonymic logic—the way it locks on to a series of different targets that do not have a necessary relation to its true goal. While the document aims at the capture of Wenzel von Tronka, Kohlhaas must route it through the convent.

Yet it does not address the specific relative (the aunt), but rather "every inhabitant." Although the manifesto says that *even* relatives and friends must obey, it actually figures all people as "relatives" of Wenzel von Tronka. The manifesto thus employs a series of substitutions to greatly expand the scope of the object that Kohlhaas will attack. However, this articulation does not merely arise from a twist in language but follows Kohlhaas's metonymic attack on Hans von Tronka in the place of Wenzel von Tronka and his men's murder of innocent people. The weapon in question, fire, which had spread in an uncontrollable manner through the castle, now enters the language of the manifesto and becomes the master trope for an absolute threat.

Put another way, the manifesto's fiery language ignites retroactively as if to account for the physical violence already committed. This accounting, however, does not contain the preceding events but rather amplifies their strength by emphasizing the lack of warning or explanation that had preceded them. While Kohlhaas fails to carry out his threat at the convent, he takes his incendiary campaign to Wittenberg, sending one of his men to set fire to the city while its inhabitants sleep.

As a rule, Kleist scholarship has placed the written texts of this section of *Michael Kohlhaas* in the disciplinary context of political theory and the law.[9] While such approaches have resulted in rich insights into the background of the story, they thrive at the expense of its victims, seeing Kohlhaas's most horrible moments as no more than an extreme way of posing questions about the legitimacy of rebellion. Critics who speak of Kohlhaas as a terrorist in this sense can be said to rightly emphasize the contemporary relevance of Kleist's novella.[10] My interest, however, lies in an important subset of these scholars who go further, seeing in Kohlhaas not just a provocation to reexamine the questions of rebellion and power in terms of an already given history of ideas and laws, but as a challenge to the very contours of this tradition. Nonetheless, while they acknowledge a radical conceptual threat in Kohlhaas's attacks, they are also particularly careful to place borders that limit the damage he does in the novella and the damage that might be done to his reputation. Consideration of the work of three of the most insightful of these scholars will allow me to more clearly articulate the unanswered challenge of the attacks. In addition it will set the stage for the confrontation between their uncontainable force and Kohlhaas's apparent call for a grounding moment of a state from Lützen.

Wolf Kittler faces the excessive nature of Kohlhaas's violence directly. While he argues against Carl Schmitt that Kohlhaas is indeed a partisan (fighting for a "party" that will eventually occupy territory), he also recognizes a terrorist moment in the story that resists this categorization. Under the heading "Insurrection as Citizen's Duty" Kittler defends the proposition that Kohlhaas fights not for his own property rights but for the legal order that guarantees all rights of property. The horse dealer is vindicated when the Elector of Brandenburg restores these rights at the end of the story. Kittler points out, however, that certain of Kohlhaas's actions resist this categorization:

> I call actions like the incineration of the greater part of Wittenberg terrorist, since it is a matter neither of the irregular battle of partisans against the regular troops of an occupation, nor of revenge against a personal enemy, but rather of a targeted and extortionate attack on the life and property of an uninvolved third party.[11]

Kittler thus places Kohlhaas's terrorism within a detailed taxonomy of violence. It indicates attacks that are on the one hand not merely personal and on the other hand not purely political (in the sense of having an army as its target). Terrorism targets the third and is itself the third. In my reading of the fortune-teller episode, I will argue that this third party (the civilians) remains central to the trajectory of Kohlhaas's threat to power. Horst Sendler approaches the question of terrorism in Kohlhaas from another angle, examining at length a number of commonalities between Kohlhaas and the modern terrorist. Two aspects of his analysis are particularly relevant for my argument. First, Sendler emphasizes that Kohlhaas uses unrestricted methods of fighting. Beginning with his murder of Hans von Tronka, "anyone" can be a target of Kohlhaas's attacks.[12] Second, this unlimited violence is tied to a total claim: "this corresponds with an absolute claim [*Absolutheitsanspruch*], a claim that as absolute is also pushed through with absolute means" (Sendler, *Über Michael Kohlhaas* 27). In the previous section we have seen how Kohlhaas first articulates his claim, and further attention to the interplay of the texts and violence in the novella will demonstrate the precise sense in which he gestures to an absolute (fully self-contained) system to satisfy this claim.

Sendler, for his part, identifies this threat of the absolute, but sees it as one that the narrative ultimately reins in. He identifies a number of differences between Kohlhaas and the modern terrorist, the most significant of which is Kohlhaas's renunciation of violence after his meeting with Luther. According to Sendler, a modern terrorist would never give up his general campaign for justice in favor of his own grievance as his goal is not private but universal. One of the fascinating aspects of Kleist's story, however, is that Kohlhaas redefines his goal a number of times such that the boundary between him and the general populace, at least momentarily, collapses.

In the end, Sendler sees Kohlhaas as "half" a terrorist (Sendler, *Über Michael Kohlhaas* 34) and this proves to be a commonality with Wolfgang Wittkowski's interpretation in his article "Is Kleist's Michael Kohlhaas a Terrorist?" Wittkowski provides a less subtle attempt to rein in charges of terrorism against Kohlhaas, but appeals to a similar logic, answering his title question in the negative and describing Kohlhaas rather as "an exemplary resistance fighter."[13] Seeing him as a secular warrior on behalf of Enlightenment ideals, Wittkowski goes to great lengths to counter positions claiming that "the injuries Kohlhaas inflicts are out of proportion with the losses he has suffered" (Wittkowski, "Is Kleist's Michael Kohlhaas a Terrorist?" 478). His fundamental strategy is to separate these terrible episodes from Kohlhaas's attitude before and after this violence. Indeed, Wittkowski mounts a kind of insanity defense for the horse dealer. At the height of his violent campaign Kohlhaas goes "half mad," but this madness is short-lived, ending with his meeting with Luther. The periods before and after this madness supposedly show that he is eminently reasonable and ready to compromise.

The efforts of Sendler and Wittkowski to locate Kohlhaas's violence and to calculate his guilt in terms of a fraction do point to a strategy employed by specific characters (such as Luther and the Elector of Saxony) that have an interest in setting a strict limit to the impact of his attacks. Yet the violence that erupts in this section of the novella does not simply recede. Instead, I wish to point to an unstoppable interplay of texts and violence, to the manner in which Kohlhaas's manifestos create an expectation of signification that the attacks then undermine. Once unleashed, this violence continues to disrupt its frame of reference even after Kohlhaas himself surrenders. "Terrorism" would then in these discussions function not as a concept, but at most a pseudo-concept, an attempt to name a force that cannot be calculated. In this crisis of naming, however, we gain an important insight into the gap between word and deed that the terrorist unleashes.

In her recent analysis of *The Battle of Hermann* (*Hermannsschlacht)* and *Penthesilea*, Elizabeth Krimmer points out that the wars in both dramas also "lose sight of their initial objectives."[14] For example, the introduction of a brutal battle between Achilles and Penthesilea displays a violence that resists being instrumentalized in the service of the official aims of the Trojan or Amazon wars. This provides an illuminating analogy to the trajectory of Michael Kohlhaas, who at this moment of the novella unleashes a violence that does not fit into the plans of any government powers. On the other hand, *The Battle of Hermann* portrays a violence that, as errant as it may be, ultimately achieves Hermann's original aim of defeating the Romans. They fail to control the effect of their violence, but their destruction of a village under Hermann's rule does not introduce a change in the course of the conflict. Instead it only contributes one more reason for the German people to rise up against them.

The remaining attacks follow this incalculable force to a paradoxical, if provisional, conclusion that promises foundation. After Kohlhaas's attack on Wittenberg another document immediately follows that attempts to claim both the power of the disjunctive movement under way, and also ensures that it is anchored in a subject:

> Kohlhaas stuck a notice up on the door of the church saying that "he, Kohlhaas, had set the city afire, and, if the nobleman were not surrendered to him, he would raze the place so thoroughly that," as he put it, "he would not have to hunt behind any walls to find him." (116)

Kohlhaas signs for the fire, claiming the destruction that has occurred and promising its continuance. Once again, the word attempts to catch up with the act; the actual lighting of the fire in many places at once has given rise to the rhetorical expression of a hope for a destruction so complete that all barriers to sight would be removed. Kohlhaas has fallen into a delusional hope for omniscience that is expressed in a figure of speech ("as he put it") that moves from the physical destruction of walls to the figurative destruction of obstacles to his search.

After setting fire to Wittenberg two more times, Kohlhaas moves on to burn Leipzig, where he issues a terrible double call:

> In a manifesto [*Mandat*] which he scattered abroad on this occasion, he called himself "a lieutenant [*Statthalter*] of the Archangel Michael, come to punish with fire and sword . . . all those who should take the side of the nobleman in this quarrel." And from the castle at Lützen . . . he summoned the people [*das Volk*] to join him to build [*zur Errichtung*] a better order of things. With a kind of madness the manifesto [*Mandat*] was signed: "Done at the Seat of Our Provisional World Government, The Chief Castle at Lützen." (121)

At the heart of this passage lie both an act of self-naming and the broadcast of an appeal. The authority that Kohlhaas claims derives from the fact that he is not merely himself, but one who has responded to a divine call. Having metonymically produced the absolute target of "das

Land [the country]," he now creates the divine warrior who could battle the entire world for its rule. As the etymology of *Statthalter* suggests, Kohlhaas "takes the place" of the Archangel. This turn to the angelic occurs, however, only *after* the judgment day scenes of destruction in the previous pages. The "fragile state of the world [*gebrechliche Einrichtung der Welt*]" (94, translation modified), toward which Kohlhaas earlier in the story shows such sensitivity, has now collapsed, destroyed by his fiery attacks. Having demonstrated its precarious *Einrichtung*, Kohlhaas now actively calls "for the construction [*zur Errichtung*]" of a new world. In this phrase we can also hear a resonance of "right [*Recht*]," indicating the imposition of a system of right that he has authored. Kohlhaas calls on the people to tie themselves to him and thereby to the Archangel. The incalculable power of his own attacks forced him to abandon the intermediate goal (the restoration of the horses) that might have maintained the current order in its precariousness, and he instead projects a future vision of "a better order of things."

The origin of this enunciation, however, can claim none of the certainty of Kohlhaas's rhetoric. He speaks from the place of "Our Provisional World Government" in which neither the people that are to join him nor the ruling institution he speaks of yet exists. And while he issues the call, it cannot be said to be grounded in his subjectivity either, since his source of authority is always overdetermined. The structural paradox of the call of conscience is thus repeated on another level: Kohlhaas issues a call from within him (as grounded in the divine) and beyond him (from an as of yet nonexistent world government). J. Hillis Miller reads this manifesto as a performative speech act that seeks to establish a new set of laws for a group of people when, in fact, neither the law nor the people exist before their linguistic enunciation. He continues, however, to describe it more accurately as an "infelicitous performative" in that it does not lead to the actual institution of a new regime.[15] Indeed, shortly hereafter Luther persuades Kohlhaas that his legal appeal could still receive a fair hearing, at which point he abandons his army. Kohlhaas turns himself in and the performative does not succeed. Yet for this performative to conclusively *fail* the representatives of the state would have to frame it as a limited threat belonging to the past.[16] And while an uncanny sense of calm settles upon the story after this point, these figures are each unable to contain the violence as focused by Kohlhaas's final manifesto. His terrorism does merely employ violence in service of a specific political goal at a specific moment in time, but disrupts power in a manner that it cannot reconstitute itself. This will become clear through brief attention to Luther's attempt to contain the violence and his insistence that the people can no longer be counted on to answer to their ruler. With this background, I will conclude by turning to the fortune-teller story, which both sets the stage for Kohlhaas's campaign and re-broadcasts the internal danger that threatens the Elector of Saxony's rule. Through the fortune-teller's intervention the structural dislocation of power will be seen not merely as a moment of paralysis but as the gateway to a temporality that opens an alternative history.

The Fortune-Teller's Audience: Representation in Contexts

Kleist not only tells the story of power near its zero point, but holds and extends this condition, forcing us to keep straining for hints of power in its near absence. Rather than an injury to a system of power that manages to recover, or the fall of one system of power in the face of another, we see the founding impulse of power in conflict with the very actions that attempt to instantiate and extend that impulse. In their meeting, Luther tells Kohlhaas that he should give up his violent campaign because the Saxon officials had perverted the course of the law without the knowledge of the Elector of Saxony. Luther then makes his attempt at ending the bloodshed by proposing an amnesty. He speaks not of repairing an injustice of the state, however, but of the threat that faces it:

> Public opinion, Luther remarked, was on his side to a very dangerous extent, so much so that even in Wittenberg, which had been set on fire three times by him, it was still possible to hear a voice [*eine Stimme*] in his favor; and since Kohlhaas would undoubtedly let the people know about it if his proposal were refused, as well as make his own malicious commentary on the matter, the populace might easily be misled so far that the state would find itself powerless to act against him. (129)

Kohlhaas does not attempt to contain violence within a theological or political framework, but instead struggles with a threat that may pull down that framework itself. This threat can be seen in the rhetorical indeterminacy of the voice that can still be heard for Kohlhaas. Literally read, "a voice" as *one* voice would hardly be a matter of concern. However, this voice can be heard out of the ashes of Wittenberg, acquiring a ghostly quality, as if even the dead support him. The trope's effectiveness stems from the fact that it combines both a synecdoche and an understatement. A part of the person (his "voice") stands for the person as a whole, and this reference to a totality shades the reference to the "one" that is clearly more than one. In fact it implies a totality, the possibility that all of the people might support Kohlhaas, which is almost certainly not the case. Relying on a synecdoche in which a part stands in for a whole, but a whole of uncertain size, the threat expands to be one that promises to undermine the state. Furthermore, while the voice implies the mouth, Luther's letter also refers to the people's receptivity, and thus to their eyes and ears. Kohlhaas has a huge audience for his manifestos and the next one could be a devastating best seller.

Indeed, Luther's letter not only warns of future manifestos, it itself functions as a manifesto that both provisionally contains and, at the same time, perpetuates the threat it deals with. It names the danger, but only as that which threatens any circumscription.[17] In *Michael Kohlhaas* the excess ascribable to the terrorist, the absolute violence that knows no restriction of scale or target, is one that may begin on the inside but ultimately undoes all borders between the internal and external. A horse dealer from Brandenburg, Kohlhaas first gathered his men and crossed the border to attack von Tronka. Through his manifestos, however, he has summoned a ghostly force from within the Saxon state that poses its most serious threat in that it, as figured in Luther's letter, may steal the body politic from the sovereign. A process has been set in motion and the danger grows over time: the future of power is open.

Kleist's earlier story "The Earthquake in Chili" offers a contrast to the negotiations of *Michael Kohlhaas* in two extreme reactions to violence. First, it offers a vision of a completely new society following a terrible earthquake. The disaster frees the adulterers Jeronimo Rugera and Donna Josepha from their prison cells, and they escape to the countryside of Santiago to find not only a clean slate for them personally, but a social utopia. The formerly poor and rich are brought to the same level and are seen to be "commiserating with one another, helping one another, gladly sharing whatever they might have saved to keep themselves alive, as if the general disaster had united all survivors into a single family."[18] The divisions wrought by economics fall away and natural order returns (more Rousseau's nature than Hobbes's) in which all people act as if they were blood relations. Then, following a sermon by a high priest that restores the morality of society with a brutal vengeance, the people turn on the couple and murder them in a mob. In this second version of a response to the violence of the earthquake, society does not move forward, but backward to something even worse than the state of nature. In *Michael Kohlhaas*, we see a middle path, a way to respond to violence that is neither utopian nor reactionary.

Unlike the priest in "The Earthquake in Chili," Luther acts as a mediating figure in his letter by marking the temporal challenge of dealing with violence. The mysterious episode of the fortune-teller that comprises the last fifth of the story intensifies this challenge to the future of power. As the Elector of Brandenburg's men transport Kohlhaas to Brandenburg to stand trial, a chance encounter leads the Elector of Saxony to meet the famous outlaw in person. Kohlhaas tells him of his encounter with a fortune-teller who gave him a piece of paper that she promised would save his life. Later, the Elector of Saxony recounts the story from his own perspective in more detail. On his account, the Elector of Brandenburg, having joined him for a hunting trip at the border of their two states, takes it upon himself to ruin the reputation of a highly admired fortune-teller. When he demands a prediction that can be tested that very day, the fortune-teller says that a certain prized roebuck will come to meet them in the square before they leave. The Elector of Brandenburg then orders the slaughter of this animal, apparently overriding the fortune-teller's prophetic authority.

Though described as a joke, this encounter between the sovereign and the fortune-teller in fact has very serious political implications. The narrator describes this episode from the very beginning in terms of performance, as a staging "in front of all of the people [*im Angesicht alles Volks*]" (170) who show the utmost interest in the scene. The role of the public intensifies when, after the fortune-teller promises the Elector of Brandenburg a prosperous future, the Elector of Saxony is prompted to ask for his own fortune. Confronted with a double negative that seems to mark the first disruption of his sense of control, the Elector of Saxony asks for the details of the threat to come: "'she has nothing very pleasant to say to me, it seems' . . . she whispered distinctly in my ear, 'No!'" (171). It is the fact that the Elector thinks he knows how to interpret the fortune-teller's answer that sets him up for a fall. The whisper here only tempts one to amplify it and clarify it.[19]

The Elector of Saxony asks for the origin of the danger and she follows his lead, writing on a piece of paper a number of facts related to the end of his rule. She announces this, as the Elector emphasizes, "before the eyes of all of the people [*vor den Augen allen Volks*]" (172, translation modified), appropriating the topographical and political center, but only to displace it. She gives the piece of paper, before he can read it, to a man at the back of this crowd who turns out to be Kohlhaas. Just then a dog walks into the square, dragging the dead roebuck along and fulfilling the prophecy that was meant to test the fortune-teller. Once again, violence in the story has completely unexpected consequences. Not only does the order to kill the roebuck allow the prophecy to come true, but his appearance in the square strikes the Elector of Saxony like a bolt of lightning in winter. This metaphorical blow, described via violence out of season and out of context, impels him to order an intensive search for the man with the paper containing the prophecy that the fortune-teller announced.

If Kohlhaas destroys faith in the Elector with his attacks (as we saw was the case in Luther's letter), the amulet can only become so important after these attacks because it marks a shift in power, an appropriation if not an empowerment. The people do not rise up, they do not "empower" Kohlhaas in Arendt's sense of choosing him as their representative (this definition occurs in the same section of *On Violence* that I cited above when discussing her definition of violence). Instead the non-reconcilable opposition between violence and power that Arendt points out has another consequence; it leads to power being shifted in another direction by a single person in the right context. Later in *On Violence* Arendt provides another reading of violence that aligns much less easily with a representative theory of power. Here she speaks instead of times when "power is already in the street" and "some group of men prepared for such an eventuality is needed to pick it up" (*On Violence* 49). With its intricately embedded introduction of the fortune-teller story, *Michael Kohlhaas* recounts this kind of shift in power, one that is not in principle opposed to a representative structure but suggests that this representation will always occur in a specific context.

The fortune-teller episode marks an *anachrony*, which Genette defines as "discordance between the two orderings of story and narrative" (Genette, *Narrative Discourse* 34). According to his schema, these disruptions are further classified as either *analepsis* or *prolepsis*, depending on whether the narrative sequence is disrupted to recount an event in the future or the past. As analepsis, the fortune-teller episode would seem merely to interrupt the narrative sequence in order to provide information that would ensure the establishment of a greater totality. After all, it provides a missing aspect of the story that results in a fuller description of the event it relates. Yet this view obscures the fact that this anachrony raises an episode of the past that has become of the utmost importance in the wake of Kohlhaas's attacks because it contains a proleptic threat. The incredible anxiety that this piece of paper provokes in the Elector would not only, or even primarily, be the anxiety produced by the supernatural knowledge of the end of his reign. It instead marks a real political danger. Reconstructing the narrative we see that the fortune-teller deprives the Elector of the future in the eyes of a people that are then called to rebellion by Kohlhaas in connection with violence that backs up this call.[20]

As the announcement of a performative speech act that cannot yet be determined to be either successful or unsuccessful, the text hidden in the amulet replaces Kohlhaas's final mandate. In both cases rhetorical violence precedes a physical violence that neither follows nor can be comfortably ruled out. That the content of the capsule remains a mystery points to a violence in the future that is unknown. It announces a violence that only the revelation of its content could delimit. By guarding its secret, Kohlhaas deprives the Elector of the unquestioning presence of his subjects. Indeed the fact that the Elector physically collapses at the mention of the paper can be read as a literalization of the loss of the political body that Luther warned of in his letter. The fortune-teller's prophecy repeats Kohlhaas's earlier threat against the state and prevents his uprising and manifestos from being appropriated as a temporary and limited disruption of authority. The Elector's power depends on the strength of a tradition that should in principle not come to an end. Its announced demise would be enough to undermine this power by implying the existence of another regime that is to follow him. However, by only announcing that there is an end but not saying when, we have another confrontation with a power that is not yet destroyed but nonetheless hollowed out.[21]

If the Elector of Saxony receives the impact of future violence on his body in the present, the Elector of Brandenburg seems to raise himself above the all-threatening currents by ordering a mighty spectacle that preserves his authority. His court rules in Kohlhaas's favor against Wenzel von Tronka, whose men deliver the horses in a state of perfect health. Kohlhaas himself receives the death sentence in the suit prosecuted by the Emperor for breaking the peace, and the people gather around in great masses to witness the downfall of the famous outlaw. In the "execution [*Hinrichtung*]" the state finally gets "right [*Recht*]" back on its side alone. Famously, Kohlhaas reads the secret text and then devours it just before the executioner beheads him.

The novella thus ends with both an affirmation and denial of authority, a solution which could be seen either as a delicate balance or a paradox. Yet while the Elector of Brandenburg appears to uphold justice for all involved, his motives are not as pure as they seem. First of all, throughout the story he engages in a rivalry with the Elector of Saxony and the latter's humiliation surely pleases him (after all, the fortune-teller announced a long and prosperous reign for the house of Brandenburg). More importantly, however, we know that he did not prosecute the Emperor's case only for the sake of justice. Even after the Saxon authorities intercepted the letter that would have reunited Kohlhaas with the bandit Nagelschmidt, the latter, calling himself "Kohlhaas's lieutenant [*Statthalter des Kohlhaas*]" (146), has continued his attacks over the border to Brandenburg (169). Just as Kohlhaas called himself a "Statthalter," literally a "placeholder" of the archangel Michael, Nagelschmidt himself claims a place in the violent chain of substitutions. In another twist of supplementary logic, the Elector of Brandenburg says that the Emperor's case must go forward to make a "chilling example [*abschreckende*[*s*] *Beispiel*]" (97) of Kohlhaas. The Elector of Brandenburg's satisfaction at the end of the story would ultimately, on this reading, be based on the belief that he had stopped the violence of Kohlhaas's call by cutting off its referent and bringing terror, in the *Schrecken* of *abschrecken*, back to the side of state power. Nagelschmidt, however, is conspicuously absent from the otherwise meticulous list of actors and offenses that fall into balance at the end.

If close attention to the content of the story raises doubts that the Elector of Brandenburg succeeds in mastering the violence unleashed by Kohlhaas's attacks, attention to its form only redoubles these doubts. Here it is not just a matter of successfully accounting for particular violent events, but of a stylistic and narrative collision that questions the very possibility of narrating violence. The 1810 version of the story has the heading "from an old chronicle [*Aus einer alten Chronik*]" (85), a genre marker, which, as an appeal to history from within a fictional text, both imposes a method of reading attuned to mimetic correspondence and alerts the reader to problems of representation. On the one hand, Kleist did draw the story from the *Chronic of the Margraviate* (*Märkische Chronik*) composed by Peter Hafftitz in the middle of the sixteenth century. As Cixous notes in her work on the relation between law and guilt in Kleist, *Michael Kohlhaas* begins its narrative account "seemingly in the most innocent mode," eliding the paradoxes of reflection that are to come.[22] This mark of innocence reinforces the sense of objectivity established by the appeal to the historical source. There actually was a horse dealer (named Hans Kohlhase) whose horses were stolen by a Saxon nobleman, and who subsequently led attacks on the country in an attempt to win them back. On the other hand, the story does not only repeatedly depart from the historical account, but also suddenly shifts from its original realistic style to the fantastic style of the fortune-teller episode.

Even the earliest critics of the story raise the question of how to relate these two aspects of the text. Indeed, in the introduction to the first edition of Kleist's collected stories, Ludwig Tieck described the last section as "a fantastic dream world."[23] Tieck's judgment influenced a long tradition of condemning the story aesthetically on grounds of disunity, an anathema to nineteenth-century narrative precepts. In the twentieth century, however, Kleist criticism has made an integral reading of the novella one of its main tasks.[24]

Attention to terrorism in the story sheds new light on the stylistic break of the fortune-teller episode in that it reveals the challenge of rebellion for historical narratives. Here the violence that is the subject of the text is mirrored in disjunctive narrative and morcellated storytelling. Tieck's important structural observation noting the text's change of genre from one of the chronicle to one of the romantic fairy tale actually serves the interest of a narrator whose interests are aligned with those of the Elector of Brandenburg.[25] The careful restoration of legal economy at the end of the story, which ends both in Kohlhaas's satisfaction in the case of his horses and his death for the crimes he has committed, would be matched by the restoration of a narrative economy that masters the stylistic break associated with his violence.[26] After all, Kohlhaas received the paper from the fortune-teller on his way to his first attack. It would portray the threat in terms of a supernatural element that would then be reincorporated within the historical frame.[27]

Indeed, the text does not only indicate an origin in history, but sends the reader back to history in its final lines. The text first announces its conclusion in a lapidary tone worthy of a fairy tale: "Here ends the story of Kohlhaas" (141–42, translation modified). While the story is said to end, the text continues to briefly recount Kohlhaas's burial, the knighting of his sons, and the Elector of Saxony's return to Dresden "where what happened subsequently must be gleaned from history [*wo man das Weitere in der Geschichte nachlesen muß*]" (183, translation modified). A victory, in short, not only for history but for the possibility of history, a victory of temporal placement, a victory of chronos over anachrony. Kohlhaas's attacks are contained by the history books. Yet a closer reading reveals that this attempt to frame violence under the genre marker of the chronicle is, like those that parallel it, doomed to failure. It attempts to suppress the fact that in German "Geschichte" can mean both "history" and "story"—a fateful homonymy. While history tries to hide its disruption as fantasy, history itself suffers a break from within that undermines its victory.

To see how this happens, we must return to the anachrony discussed above, to the break at the level of narration that occurs at the moment of Kohlhaas's turn to violence, but which only comes to the reader's attention after this violence has been unleashed and has thereafter repeatedly resisted attempts to contain it. At issue here is a contradiction in what Genette calls the "reach" of the anachrony, the amount of time between the earlier episode and the narrative present (Genette, *Narrative Discourse*

48). The narrator first says that Kohlhaas sent his "decree" to Wenzel von Tronka the day after his wife died and he left for Tronka castle the "third day" (111) after its delivery. However, when Kohlhaas himself tells how he came into possession of the capsule, he says: "Seven months ago, I think it was, exactly on the day after my wife's funeral" (162, translation modified). He notes some uncertainty as to just how much time has passed, but none about the day in question. Roland Reuß writes that this contradiction "disrupts the appearance of coherence" that underlies the story's realist tone.[28] In the context of my reading, however, I wish to emphasize that this "disruption" occurs within the historical presentation itself. The anachrony in question here is not merely a structural "discordance" of the type Genette names, but a challenge to time as the collapse of the border between the fictional and the historical. Tied to the origin of Kohlhaas's attacks, and amplifying these attacks even more radically than the mandates that accompanied them, the fantastic fortune-teller story marks a stylistic revolution at the point of the highest danger of political revolution. It is a further consequence of terrorism, another sign of violence that cannot be appropriated. The Elector of Brandenburg's glorious future thus remains enmeshed in fantasy, having been announced by the fortune-teller and recounted in a manner that, in the face of violence, destabilizes our faith in the consistency of historical narrative.

Conclusion

✦

Acting on Violence—*Impartially*

From one point of view, the election and reelection of Barack Obama as the president of the United States could be seen as the type of minoritarian swerve that I have drawn out in my readings of classic German literature. The choice of an African American ruptured many long-held prejudices about the U.S. electorate and the conventional wisdom of political scientists. Those who elected him, especially in the minority and progressive wings, certainly hoped for a change in policy that was equally surprising. Indeed, in Obama's own use of "hope" we can see him in the lead-up to the 2008 election as a sort of fortune-teller in the Kleistian sense, announcing a change of the national narrative "before the eyes of all of the people."

The fact that the improvement that many people set their sights on has not come to pass does not rule out the possibility of future unexpected and not-yet perceivable fundamental shifts. However, from the standpoint of foreign policy and rhetoric, Obama has proven remarkably consistent with his predecessor. In my first chapter, I read selections of President George W. Bush's speech on the day of 9/11 as an indication of the necessity of confronting terrorism as a test, even while arguing that we had not yet passed it. By returning to the words of another commander-in-chief, I want to consider the way that the sovereign controls the perception of the public, how he orients the audience of citizens.

In Bush's speech on September 11, I focused in on the line "We will show the world that we will pass this test." Bush's words echo those of Weislingen, who advised the Emperor to destroy Götz von Berlichingen as a leader "in the eyes of the world." They also resonate with the language that President Obama employed when on May 2, 2011 he reported the killing of Al Qaeda leader Osama bin Laden. In a televised address, he announced that "on nights like this one, we can say to those families who have lost loved ones to Al Qaeda's terror: Justice has been done."[1] "Justice" in the context of immediate blood relations has the limited sense of revenge, of an eye for an eye. However, the phrase "families who have lost loved ones" clearly serves as a metonym, setting up the "family" as a stand-in for the nation as a whole. At this level, the family of the nation should feel a sense of direct justice as well.

Obama's May 2 speech reduces the scope of justice from a general principle to an organic reaction when it relies on the family in this manner. The phrase also indicates that an action has been taken for once and for all. Obama and the military have "done" justice in the sense of making it and, at the same time, the pronouncement implies that doing justice is over, that it is "done" in the sense of "finished." Days later, the president's announcement of the decision not to release photographs of Osama bin Laden suggested an anxiety over the completion of justice. In an interview he said: "It is very important for us to make sure that very graphic photos of somebody who was shot in the head are not floating around as an incitement to additional violence—as a propaganda tool."[2] Obama decided that there would be a sea burial in order to prevent the creation of a land-based memorial, but the circulating effect of the sea enters his rhetoric, raising the possibility that the photograph would bring bin Laden back like stray jetsam.

While I am not suggesting that releasing the photos would have been a better decision, I do want to interrogate the logic guiding President Obama's insistence on hiding the body from view as a way of controlling who can see violence. Readers of the intricate staging of executions in *The Robbers* and *Michael Kohlhaas* would not expect this move. The latter text especially provides a paradigmatic example of how to re-center sovereign power by putting the criminal on the executioner's block in front of everyone while the sovereign looks on as well. Staying a bit longer with the sovereign's reluctance to show his power in violence allows us to look back more clearly at how, and with what implications, the errant readers of violence (Götz's wife Elizabeth, Karl Moor's Amalia, and the fortune-teller in *Michael Kohlhaas*) operate.

Walter Benjamin offers one reason why an execution would be better off not shown: such displays reveal something rotten in the law itself. His article "Critique of Violence" reformulates the role of violence in legal theory by questioning the readability of violence. This text, though most famous for its rich theoretical terminology, operates not by consistently applying a set mode of analysis but by developing new modes of perception in the face of the example. It repeatedly calls witnesses to testify to the connection between violence and the law. Among these figures, those of the general strike and police have received great attention from critics, while the figure of the criminal has gone relatively unnoticed. This neglect is surprising since he has a privileged place in the series of examples, and allows Benjamin to point to, if not immediately show, violence beyond the representational schema of positive law.

Written in the immediate aftermath of World War I and the fall of the German monarchy in 1918, "Critique of Violence" deals with the collapse of sovereignty. Its spectacular and combustive combination of political analysis and religious interpretation provokes and breaks off suddenly, coming to us as a short article rather than as a part of the larger political project originally planned from 1919. Benjamin first considers the example of the criminal in his discussion of the role of punishment in preserving the state's monopoly on violence. The punishment meted out by the state aims not primarily at ensuring that specific laws are not broken again in the future but rather in defending its exclusive right to violence. To this extent, Benjamin makes a point essential to social contract theory, if one traditionally hidden from view by its explicit attempts to couch its model in wholly rational terms. In fact, the social contract depends on a total use of violence once it is established, as we saw in chapter 1 and later in chapter 2 in Agamben. Benjamin calls on the criminal to present the reticent and fugitive aspect of the law's violence. When he does so, he routes his attention not through the criminal alone, but through the spectator. He raises the issue of

> how often the figure [*Gestalt*] of the "great" criminal, however repellent his ends [*Zwecke*] may have been, has aroused the secret admiration of the public. This can result not from his deed but only from the violence to which it bears witness.[3]

The quotation highlights the context of the criminal's greatness. He appears as a foreign body that the people encase but do not fully enclose. He both belongs to society and remains external to it. Beyond this specific instance, however, Benjamin's investigation into responses to violence employs a broader logic of citationality. His method develops as he separates the "figure" of the criminal from his "ends." In other words, the people do not admire the fact that a specific law was broken. The breaking of the law merely points to, or as Benjamin says, "witnesses" violence. A second level opens beyond the binary of witness and witnessed in that the people *see* the breaking of the law, which in turn reveals violence.

In response to this circuit of testimony, the audience reacts with a power expressed by affect. Continuing his attention to that which one can barely perceive, Benjamin speaks first of the "secret admiration" of the people. His rhetoric initially indicates that he has succeeded in making violence appear by following the mediating power of witnessing: "In this case, therefore, the violence that present-day law is seeking in all areas of activity to deny the individual appears really threatening, and arouses even in defeat the sympathy of the masses [*Menge*] against the law" ("Critique of Violence" 239). Importantly, this example speaks through the eyes of the people not under the immediate and everyday point of view in which the criminal would be a potential threat, but rather to the criminal's relation to the law. In another adjective of emotion, the people are now described as sympathetic as they join the criminal as opponents of the law. The descriptive change from the earlier term "admiration" indicates an intensification and loss of distance. At this point, Benjamin chooses "Menge," a mass or vaguely defined group rather than the more stable, if still supposedly pre-political "people [*Volk*]."

At this point the precise nature of the people's admiration remains undefined, but it takes on clearer contours when, after brief discussions of the strike and military violence, Benjamin calls the criminal to the stand again to describe the "law-making [*rechtsetzender*] character" of all violence that takes place outside the ruling system of law: "In the great criminal this violence confronts the law with the threat of declaring a new law, a threat that even today, despite its impotence, in important instances horrifies the public [*das Volk . . . erschaudert*] as it did in primeval times" (241). While the essay's first consideration of the audience employed the positive terms of "admiration" and "sympathy," the audience now reacts negatively. In *erschaudern* one hears a primal shaking, an effect on the body as well as the spirit. We are reminded of the Elector of Saxony's corporeal reaction to Kohlhaas's ingestion of the capsule, as the material aspect of the body asserts primacy over the structures of historically anchored legitimacy.

The reference to the "primeval times" indicates a primordial aspect of this violence, a kind of Ur-violence of the *Urzeit* (perhaps the time of Hobbes's state of nature) that always exists despite the specific historical regimes and legal systems that come and go. The moment of originary shaking offers at least two possibilities for reading that it then combines. It may be that the challenge to the old law causes the people to shudder, or it could be the possibility of being present at the annunciation of a new law. In terms of Benjamin's argument, the important point is that this shaking combines the two dangers, that in an attack on a specific law, the law's legitimacy as such suffers at the most fundamental level.

In a shift of perspective, Benjamin's treatment of the criminal concludes with the insight that the state fears the violence of the criminal as well, but only has to recognize it in the cases of strike or war. Shortly thereafter, however, Benjamin returns to the criminal and focuses explicitly on how in the death penalty the state does recognize, if obliquely, the impossible challenge that the criminal poses to its regime. What first appears to be merely an effort to maintain the law in fact reveals its founding function. Or, to use Benjamin's terminology, "law-preserving" violence reveals "law-making" violence. Here we have another kind of testimony, the death penalty as a testament to the origin of the law. Staying tuned into affect, Benjamin refers to critics of the death penalty, and then to those who oppose these critics because they feel that their objection aims not at one law among others, but at "law itself" (242).

In a characteristic second-level analysis, Benjamin picks up on these critics of the critics and takes their objection in another direction. He suspects "where the highest violence, that over life and death, occurs in the legal system, the origins of law jut [*hineinragen*] manifestly and fearsomely [*furchtbar*] into existence" (242). The description "fearsomely [*furchtbar*]" indicates a cut that links the shaking body of the audience in the earlier example to an emotionally described reaction of the law itself. Capital punishment represents the origin of the legal order in *the legal order itself* through a puncture or topographical imposition, as the term *hineinragen* suggests. According to Benjamin, in the death penalty the law strengthens itself and in this sense terror connects with strength. At the same time though, it unveils "something rotten in the law" (242). The violence of the death penalty both strengthens the law and reveals that the law is rotten.

Following Benjamin, the sovereign does not come back to himself in the execution; instead, the question of violence stays open, and even moves to a higher level in an awareness of the violence of the state itself. The dramas *Götz von Berlichingen* and *The Robbers* elicited passionate responses from their audiences when they were first performed. According to reports, this energy was connected primarily to the lead male heroes, and by reaction, the figures of power that they opposed. My analyses of these dramas have gone another route, looking at the minority that reads in secret, the feminine figure who secrets away another passage of power within plain view. While shifting genres in the final chapter, I maintained an attunement to dramatic questions of performance and the spectator in my reading of *Michael Kohlhaas*. When set against the earlier dramas and considered a post-Sturm und Drang work, the novella form of *Kohlhaas* opened the path to a much more explicit treatment of the audience.[4]

Returning to the difficult connection between violence and action that I briefly raised in my first chapter suggests a way of responding to the question between the spectators and violence in a broader way. While an adequate discussion would demand a lengthy engagement with Arendt's work of the 1960s and 1970s, I want to return to this problem here to more clearly suggest its importance. Violence, like action, has an interruptive function. It does not power history in the Hegelian sense. In short, the relationship between power and violence is asymmetrical, and here I wish to return to a phrase that informed my reading of *Kohlhaas*: "Violence can destroy power; it is utterly incapable of creating it."[5] We have seen in my reading of Goethe, Schiller, and Kleist that a third figure arises unexpectedly to frame violence in unique ways, and this is only possible because neither the ruler nor the outlaw is able to command meaning. The later chapters of *On Violence* help describe the fall of power when Arendt associates power with opinion as the number of people who support an institution. Acting in accordance with the directions of the law extends the agreement which occasioned its founding. Such extension is temporal; it sustains the decision that grounded the institution. Since this is the case, it follows that power can be lost at any moment:

> When we say of somebody that he is "in power" we actually refer to his being empowered by a certain number of people to act in their name. The moment the group, from which the power originated to begin with (*potestas in populo*, without a people or group there is no power), disappears, "his power" also vanishes. (*On Violence* 44)

While violence is distinct from power, Arendt says that they rarely occur in their pure states, and she offers a number of examples that demonstrate their relations. The guiding logic of these relations is prosthetic. Violence stands in not only for strength, but for power as well. In the case of the latter, however, the substitution does not succeed. While it may maintain an institution, it at the same time brings to light this institution's loss of power as support. Arendt treats revolutions as privileged examples in that they are successful against superior means of violence when the power "behind" this violence falls. When a government has already lost its power, as in France in 1968, students are able to be a threat without violence. In contrast, Vietnam shows that superior violence fails against the power of an organized movement.

In each of my literary readings, the structure of political representation suffers a blow as the result of attacks. There are moments when the "the group . . . disappears" as Arendt put it above. The sovereign loses the body politic and power lies "in the street" (*On Violence* 49). Arendt's *Lectures on Kant's Political Philosophy* helps us to further follow the break between violence and the reaction to violence. Here she picks up on

Kant's fraught engagement with the French Revolution. As an observer, he admires the actual revolution while at the same time condemning the act that made it possible. Arendt cites Kant from *The Conflict of the Faculties* that "this event [the French Revolution] consists neither in momentous deeds nor misdeeds committed by men . . . It is simply the mode of thinking of the spectators which reveals itself publicly in this great game of transformations."[6] He continues with an explicit acknowledgment that the revolution may succeed or fail, but that is not the point. Instead, Kant emphasizes the "exaltation of the uninvolved public" (Arendt, *Lectures* 45). Commenting on this passage, Arendt writes: "Without this sympathetic participation, the 'meaning' of the occurrence would be altogether different, or simply non-existent" (46). Picked up in quotation marks, meaning gets carried away by those uninvolved with the original event.

Earlier in the same lectures, Arendt comments on Kant's remarks on the importance of considering other points of view when creating judgments. She writes that for Kant "*impartiality* is obtained by taking the viewpoints of others into account; impartiality is not the result of some higher standpoint that would then actually settle the dispute by being altogether above the meleé" (Arendt, *Lectures* 42). In my readings, violence caused a break in ruling frames of reference, forcing the observer into this kind of situation where no higher vantage point is possible. Instead, the minority figures appropriate and interpret from within a conflict. In this light, violence is not a part of something greater, as Schmitt suggests in his reading of the partisan, but rather compels impartiality. Even if each third party sets itself up as the start of a greater cause, the observer of these interpretations can consider them as unique appropriations that expand the range of possible responses to violence.[7]

Arendt tells us that while Kant was an acute observer of revolution and the structural mappings of the spectator, he did not speak of action in her sense of men coming together to create something new. My readings of classic German rogues suggest, however, that extreme violence can be an impetus to impartial reflection in Arendt's sense.[8] As such it would have a role in the difficult endeavor of working out the condition of possibility of action by compelling consideration of truly new options of response.

Looking back at my readings of Goethe, Schiller, and Kleist allows me to make new connections between close reading and political theory through the role of the spectator by further developing the "making" of the terrorist that I explicitly conceptualized in my introduction and first chapter. In the first sense of my title, I placed a great deal of emphasis on how the sovereign "makes," or creates, the terrorist as a justification for increasing his power. I suggested the term "rogue" as a way to back off epistemologically from this heavy-handed and automatic response.

Over the course of my literary readings, the second sense of "making" grew in importance: the making of violence that cannot immediately be appropriated. One way of synthesizing or condensing this problematic (and even obscene) production is to recall how *Götz von Berlichingen* and *The Robbers* track a disjunction between the hand and the head. These figures showed action's tendency to go awry and leave behind the plans of the mind. Alternatively, one can recall the role that writing plays in the texts of Goethe and Kleist. Götz writes his history and Kohlhaas writes manifestos, neither of which can ensure an intended meaning.

It may not surprise students of the classical tradition that the "making" of the terrorist goes wrong in these texts by escaping its originator's intention. After all, Greek tragedy on the model of Sophocles teaches us that humans cannot control the results of their actions in general and must resign themselves to the knowledge that fate, not will, guides the world. The texts I have examined also show acts that in their violence radically break with intention. By keeping the emphasis on the social world even in the face of extreme metaphysical temptations (most powerfully in the final scene of *The Robbers*), however, these modern texts show that we, as a society, are still responsible for our actions. We have to respond to violence on its own terms without relegating it to either fate or, in a contemporary way of similarly evading the implications of the unexpected, to an origin in a specific actor that would take all the blame.

In a striking manner, each text concludes with the question of the heirs as a way of figuratively suggesting the need to respond to violence. In German, *Nachkommenschaft* nicely suggests that time does not stop, that something has to come after (*nach*). Most conventionally and directly, the Elector of Saxony collapses when he cannot be sure of the security of his family line. Karl Moor's last words refer to a man with "eleven children living" (160) that he intends to help by allowing him to claim the reward money. In *Götz von Berlichingen*, the heirs that Elisabeth names are not his literal family but presumably those people who wish to follow his spirit of independence. In fact, Elisabeth's recommendation that her husband write his memoirs could extend Weislingen's fear that Götz is the enlivening "spirit" of the rebellion even beyond his death. The question that remains is how to convert *Nachkommenschaft* into a vigorous guarantor of futurity.

By endowing the heirs with a figural stamina, *Götz von Berlichingen* imports a lineage that undoes the family bloodline and sustains a notion of disruptive kinship that bears political consequences. We tend to see the heir as representing more of the same, genetically and politically speaking. In principle, the child of a king will rule "in their name," as history says, even if they change the sovereign parental policy. When one assumes the name, however, one also highlights a shift from a purported natural relation to a figural appropriation of succession that opens a new terrain of potential freedom, while also inheriting the transmitted burdens of the past and a mark of death—part of the package deal of assumed inheritance. Still, even genetic combination creates not only variation but at times the more decisive departure of mutation, which, in a biological cast, performatively illustrates the interruption of ruling traditions. The feminine readers, the stealth activists, in the past chapters do not just passively issue an heir: they subtly offer a birth of history, but a *figural* one that no longer relies on organic or even conventional precepts of legitimacy. Now the "making" of my title takes on yet a third significance in addition to the "making" of the terrorist by the sovereign and the "making" of excessive violence by the terrorist. Violence leaves both its victims and witnesses speechless, as it fundamentally disables political and semantic representation. Only through the detour of a third figure marginalized by social dictum but empowered to perceive and able to succumb to epistemological fissures can there be a new interpretation of violence that begins to "make" something of it. If the "rogue" earlier offered a way to step back from the term "terrorist," here we can, on yet another register, speak of the emergence of a *rogue reader*. Trained but unbound by the strictures of conventional regimes of signification, shocked to the bone by trauma but still responsibly oriented—if, indeed, on shaky ground—such a reader takes account of persistent damage to political representation. Acknowledging the irreversibile dimensions of damage done, she invites us to look defiantly ahead to a facet of genuine futurity which, radically open, may well come around the bend unrecognizably.

NOTES

Preface

1. Tom Cohen, *Ideology and Inscription: "Cultural Studies" after Benjamin, De Man, and Bakhtin* (Cambridge, Eng.: Cambridge University Press, 1998), 205.

Introduction

1. 22 United States Code, Section 2656(f), 2008.
2. See the July 3, 1773 letter from Mattius Claudius reprinted in Volker Neuhaus, *Johann Wolfgang Goethe: Götz von Berlichingen: Erläuterungen und Dokumente* (Stuttgart: Reclam, 1991), 129–30.
3. Andreas Huyssen, *Drama des Sturm und Drang: Kommentar zu einer Epoche* (Munich: Winkler, 1980), 26–30.
4. Attention to the limit of the Enlightenment reading of Sturm und Drang compels me to reevaluate, with caution and disclaimer, German scholars implicated in the Nazi regime. The current generation of scholars in Germany and the United States rarely cite the work of such writers as Hermann August Korff, at one time an eminent presence in the field of Germanistik due to his work *Geist der Goethezeit.* Beyond recovering specific insights of their research, I wish to raise the issue of the relation between literary scholars and those equally compromised philosophers usually who have been granted academic security clearance, even if they are still subject to repeated searches (such as Carl Schmitt and Heidegger).

Chapter 1

1. In *Stupidity*, Avital Ronell suggests that seeing Bush as sovereign may seem derisory, but the sovereign was always a prop and a barred subject, so he fits the job description joltingly well, in fact, and comes up from central casting of psychoanalytical and historical insight. Ronell cites Lacan's "idiot king" for instance, and many other treatments of sovereign emblematics covering over a mark of deficiency. Avital Ronell, *Stupidity* (Urbana: University of Illinois Press, 2002).
2. George W. Bush, *Public Papers of the Presidents of the United States: George W. Bush*, 2001–, vol. 1, bk. 2 (Washington, D.C.: Government Printing Office, 2004), 1098.
3. Bush, *Public Papers of the Presidents of the United States: George W. Bush*, 1099.
4. Avital Ronell, *The Test Drive* (Urbana: University of Illinois Press, 2005), 168.
5. In dealing with questions of political theater and theatrics, I engage what Philippe Lacoue-Labarthe calls "national aestheticism." Philippe Lacoue-Labarthe, *Heidegger, Art, and Politics: The Fiction of the Political* (Oxford: Blackwell, 1990). See also Samuel Weber's "'War,' 'Terrorism,' and 'Spectacle': On Towers and Caves," in *Theatricality as Medium* (New York: Fordham University Press 2009), 326–36.

6. Gerd Van den Heuvel provides the most thorough and concise overview of the origin of the word "terrorist." Gerd Van den Heuvel, "Terreur, Terroriste, Terrorisme," in *Handbuch politisch-sozialer Grundbegriffe in Frankreich 1680–1820*, ed. Rolf Reichardt and Eberhard Schmitt (Munich: Oldenbourg, 1985), 89–132.

7. "Terrorist," in *The OED Online* (Oxford University Press, 2009), http://dictionary.oed.com/cgi/entry/50249599.

8. Rudolf Walter, "Terror, Terrorismus," in *Geschichtliche Grundbegriffe: Historisches Lexikon zur politisch-sozialen Sprache in Deutschland*, ed. Otto Brunner, Werner Conze, and Reinhart Koselleck, 8 vols. (Stuttgart: Klett-Cotta, 1972–97) 6:323–444.

9. Walter Laqueur, *No End to War: Terrorism in the Twenty First Century* (New York: Continuum, 2003). For a collection of the manifestos written by the most prominent of those termed terrorists, see Walter Laqueur, ed., *Voices of Terror: Manifestos, Writings & Manuals of Al Qaeda, Hamas, & Other Terrorists from around the World & Throughout the Ages* (New York: Reed, 2004).

10. Brynjar Lia, *Globalization and the Future of Terrorism: Patterns and Predictions* (London: Routledge, 2005), 10.

11. For a review of the contemporary debate over the term "terrorism," see Lia (9–15). For his own research, Lia favors the criteria set out by the U.S. State Department in 1983: "premeditated, politically motivated violence perpetrated against non combatant targets by subnational groups or clandestine agents, usually intended to influence an audience" (quoted in Lia, 11). This definition, 22 USC Sec. 2656(f) 2008, cited above.

12. Hobbes uses the phrase "The naturall condition of mankind" in *Leviathan*, but the now more common phrase "state of nature" in his earlier work *De Cive, or the Citizen* (1642).

13. Carl Schmitt, *The "Leviathan" in the State Theory of Thomas Hobbes: Meaning and Failure of a Political Symbol* (Chicago: University of Chicago Press, 2008), 31. Translation modified.

14. Thomas Hobbes, *Leviathan*, in *The English Works of Thomas Hobbes of Malmesbury*, vol. 3, ed. Sir Williams Molesworth (London: John Bohn, 1839).

15. Jacques Derrida, *The Beast and the Sovereign*, vol. 1, ed. Geoffrey Bennington and Peggy Kamuf (Chicago: University of Chicago Press, 2009).

16. In a critical reading of Arendt that extends to Kojève and beyond, Avital Ronell tracks "the forgetting of authority" with particular emphasis on the effort of philosophers to separate authority from violence. From this perspective, Hobbes offers the paradigmatic modern account of the move from violence to authority. Avital Ronell, *Loser Sons: Politics and Authority* (Urbana: University of Illinois Press, 2012), 26.

17. Parts of my reading here originally appeared in Jeffrey Champlin, "Introduction," *Terror and the Roots of Poetics*, ed. Jeffrey Champlin (New York: Atropos, 2013), 10–12.

18. In his reading of Hobbes in *The Beast and the Sovereign*, Derrida offers the telling, and troubling, phrase: "terror or terrorism as knowing-how to make fear reign." Jacques Derrida, *The Beast and the Sovereign*, vol. 1 (Chicago: University of Chicago Press, 2009), 39. From the perspective of my effort to uncouple knowledge and terror in this chapter, I wish to highlight how Derrida's reading

slips behind the sovereign's effort to instrumentalize fear and terror. Ultimately the sovereign's efforts fail because he is unable to monopolize terror. Instead, "terror is both what motivates respect for laws and the transgression of laws" (41).

19. Paul Fleming's work on the exemplary allows us to draw out the key tension between institution and origination in Hobbes's logic. While Fleming is chiefly concerned with poetics, I see important political implications in his emphasis on the generative aspect of the example. According to Fleming, classical poetics in the work of Aristotle and Horace emphasized the correct application of rules and thus reinforced tradition. "Modern exemplarity no longer consists in adhering to canonical texts and established procedure but in establishing a new rule for aesthetic judgement via originality." Paul Fleming, *Exemplarity and Mediocrity: The Art of the Average from Bourgeois Tragedy to Realism* (Stanford, Calif.: Stanford University Press, 2008), 11. In Hobbes's explication of the subject who provides the model of how to fear, we see a type of originary exemplarity. At the same time, the irreversibility of the social contract connects this example with the imposition of tradition.

20. G. W. F Hegel, *Political Writings*, ed. Lawrence Dickey and H. B. Nisbet (Cambridge, Eng.: Cambridge University Press, 1999), 218. G. W. F. Hegel, *Vorlesungen über die Philosophie der Weltgeschichte*, vols. 2–4 (Hamburg: Felix Meiner, 1968), 930.

21. Hegel, *Political Writings*, 218. Translation modified.

22. Ibid.

23. Ibid.

24. The representational challenge that I describe here in political terms takes on its full dimensions in Rebecca Comay's reading of Hegel on the Law of Suspects: "Suspicion is both the epistemology and poetics of a world devoid of enduring objects." Rebecca Comay, *Mourning Sickness: Hegel and the French Revolution* (Stanford, Calif.: Stanford University Press, 2010), 71.

25. Maurice Blanchot, *The Infinite Conversation* (Minneapolis: University of Minnesota Press, 1993), 238.

26. Ibid., 238–39.

27. De Man's reading of Rousseau is particularly important for the question of the suspect since it names the estranged individual within a model of political representation that carries over the clash of models I described in Hobbes. "The double relationship of the individual toward the State is thus based on the coexistence of two distinct rhetorical models, the first self-reflective or specular, the other estranged. But what the individual is estranged from is precisely the executive activity of his own state as *souverain*." Paul de Man, *Allegories of Reading* (New Haven, Conn.: Yale University Press, 1979), 261.

28. In a study that ranges from ancient Roman fable to East German film and contemporary photography, John Hamilton develops the delicate interdependences of security and its opposite: "Feeling secure means feeling secure-from and therefore involves the recognition of our insecurity, our vulnerability." John Hamilton, *Security: Politics, Humanity, and the Philology of Care* (Princeton, N.J.: Princeton University Press, 2013), 296.

29. Jacques Derrida, *Rogues: Two Essays on Reason* (Stanford, Calif.: Stanford University Press, 2004).

30. Ibid., 93–94.

31. Jacques Derrida, *Philosophy in a Time of Terror: Dialogues with Jürgen Habermas and Jacques Derrida*, ed. Giovanna Borradori (Chicago: University of Chicago Press, 2003), 93.

32. Ibid., 94.

33. Ibid.

34. Derrida, *Rogues*, 64.

35. In moving to the RAF in this section, I jump over an explicit discussion of Marx, which would have led the investigation too far into the complex late nineteenth-century debates over violence. Jacques Lezra offers a powerful reading of Hegel and Marx on the concept of the state that goes further than historical review. Drawing on the work of Althusser, he suggests that "terror" is one of the concepts that "are no longer (as in Kant) *representationes communes* but emerge as non-representational expressions, in line with a specific literary materialism." Jacques Lezra, *Wild Materialism* (New York: Fordham University Press, 2010), 31. See especially chapter 4, "*Materia* in the Critique of Autonomy," 110–49.

36. Jürgen Habermas, *Habermas and the Public Sphere*, ed. Craig Calhoun (Cambridge, Mass.: MIT Press, 1993), 467. For Habermas's explicit discussion of terrorism following 9/11, see his section in *Philosophy in a Time of Terror: Dialogues with Jürgen Habermas and Jacques Derrida*. There he says that violence generally does not erupt in Western countries because people of those countries share the same cultural background that establishes the precondition of reasoned debate.

37. Habermas, *Habermas and the Public Sphere*, 467.

38. ID Verlag, ed., "Über den bewaffneten Kampf in Westeuropa," in *Rote Armee Fraktion: Texte und Materialien zur Geschichte der RAF* (Berlin: ID Verlag, 1997), 49–111. Translations are my own.

39. Jeremy Varon provides an accessible and enlightening account of the RAF in English that emphasizes twentieth-century cultural reaction (including Böll and Marcuse). Jeremy Varon, *Bringing the War Home: The Weather Underground, The Red Army Faction, and Revolutionary Violence in the Sixties and Seventies* (Berkeley: University of California Press, 2004).

40. Carl Schmitt, *Theory of the Partisan: Intermediate Commentary on the Concept of the Political*, trans. G. L. Ulmen (New York: Telos, 2007), 14–22.

41. Hannah Arendt, *On Violence* (New York: Harcourt, Brace and World, 1970). Hereafter cited in the text by page number.

42. Arendt's comparison of theories of growth seeks to find the place for violence in relation to power and the place of the students with respect to Marx and Mao. Looking at her analysis in terms of a double paternity, Arendt can be seen to make an important feminist intervention here. Despite the profound differences that she insists on, Arendt sees Marx and Mao as sharing the common assumption of "man creating himself" (*On Violence*, 12). This can be understood as an anthropomorphism of Hegel's *Sichselbstproduzieren*, spirit's act of "producing itself." With her language of birth, and insistence that man does not create himself, Arendt mobilizes the feminine to displace one of the most tenacious traditions of philosophy since the nineteenth century. While Arendt never explicitly mobilized her thought in the name of feminine difference, her work contains important resources for this endeavor, as the collection *Feminist Interpretations*

of Hannah Arendt, edited by Bonnie Honig, has shown. *Feminist Interpretations of Hannah Arendt* (University Park: Pennsylvania State University Press, 1995).

43. That the RAF, Schmitt, and Arendt all respond to Mao at central points in their texts points to his central position as a writer on guerilla tactics. Beyond this specific relevance, he also indicates a limit of one strain of Hegelian-Marxist thought.

44. Derrida, *Rogues*, 68.

Chapter 2

1. J. W. von Goethe, *Goetz von Berlichingen with the Iron Hand*, in *Early Verse Drama and Prose Plays*, ed. Cyrus Hamlin and Frank Ryder, trans. Cyrus Hamlin (New York: Suhrkamp, 1988), 1–82. Hereafter cited in the text by page number. For the German I refer to *Sämtliche Werke nach Epochen seines Schaffens*, Munich Edition, ed. Karl Richter (Munich: Hanser, 1985–98).

2. In using the term "apotrope" to refer to a specific instance of rhetorical defense, I follow Derrida's *Glas*, which I discuss below. "Apotropaic" usually applies to magic and is the broader and more common phrase from which "apotrope" derives.

3. Friedrich II von Preußen, *De la littérature allemande*, in *Goethes Werke: Hamburger Ausgabe in 14 Bänden,* 4:493–94. Translations are my own. While the content of Frederick's criticism is largely derivative, repeating earlier French reviews, my reading here insists on the importance of the rhetorical aspect of this particular articulation.

4. Hans-Eugen Schramm reports this continuing popularity in 1960. *L.m.i.A. Des Ritters Götz von Berlichingen denkwürdige Fensterrede* (Tübingen am Neckar: Verlag Fritz Schlichtenmeyer, 1960). As is often the case, the obscenity here resists direct translation. Literally, it would be translated as "He can lick my ass" and the shortened version is "He can . . ." The translations I choose here retain the more common obscenity in English in the longer version and keep a bit more of the quote in the second (cutting out only the key part which is consistent with the obscure function of the apotrope).

5. Herder, letter to Goethe, published in J. W. von Goethe, *Sämtliche Werke nach Epochen seines Schaffens*, Munich Edition, ed. Karl Richter (Munich: Hanser, 1985–98), vol. 16, p. 604. Translations are mine.

6. Ibid., 605.

7. Ibid. My translation. Since the adverbs can also be interpreted as adjectives in the German original, these sentences can take on two meanings: both Goethe and his passion are unconscious, both Adelheid and Goethe's writing are lovable. "Besonders gegen das Ende, riβ mich eine wundersame Leidenschaft unbewβt hin. Ich hatte mich, indem ich *Adelheid* liebenswürdig zu schildern trachtete, selbst in sie verliebt."

8. Ibid.

9. Jakob Michael Reinhold Lenz, "Über Götz von Berlichingen," in *Goethe im Urteil seiner Kritiker*, ed. Karl Robert Mandelkow (Munich: C. H. Beck, 1975), 26. My translation. This review was published for the first time only in the nineteenth century.

10. G. W. F. Hegel, *Aesthetics: Lectures on Fine Art*, trans. T. M. Knox, 2 vols. (Oxford: Clarendon, 1975), 1:196.

11. G. W. F. Hegel, *Aesthetics: Lectures on Fine Art*, 2:1231. Hegel compares Götz with Wallenstein in the earlier passage as well.

12. Hegel, *Ästhetik*, 2:581. At the same time, Hegel is far from claiming that the drama is a historical drama in the sense that it faithfully reproduces the details of the period. In fact, he points out what he sees to be some of the historical inaccuracies of the drama. First of all, Brother Martin, who Hegel interprets as suggesting Martin Luther, does not speak piously as the real Luther would have. Secondly, the scene in which Götz's son mechanically repeats the information he has learned about his father's castle is said to reflect eighteenth-century concerns. For Hegel a historical drama stages the movement of history, not particular historical details. Hegel, *Aesthetics: Lectures on Fine Art*, 1:296–97.

13. Rainer Nägele, "Götz von Berlichingen," in *Goethes Dramen: Neue Interpretationen*, ed. Walter Hinderer (Stuttgart: Reclam, 1980), 65–77. Ilse Appelbaum Graham inaugurates a line of inquiry that focuses on the figure of the hand itself in the drama. "Götz von Berlichingen's Right Hand," *German Life and Letters* 16 (April–July 1963): 212–28.

14. Nägele, "Götz," 71. Translation is mine.

15. Heinrich Meyer-Benfey, *Goethes Götz von Berlichingen* (Weimar: Hermann Böhlaus Nachfolger, 1929). Emil Staiger connects Götz to Goethe's concept of "Nature" ("Natur") which he defines as "eternal and original creative power." Staiger, *Goethe*, vol. 1 (Zürich: Atlantis Verlag, 1964), 85. Translation mine.

16. It thus suggests the embrace at the end of *Torquato Tasso*, which, as Avital Ronell writes, could either be a gesture of attack or one of reconciliation. Ronell, *The Test Drive*, 305. See also Avital Ronell, "Taking it Philosophically: Torquato Tasso's Women as Theorists," in *Finitude's Score: Essays for the End of the Millennium* (Lincoln: University of Nebraska Press, 1994), 129–58.

17. Susan E. Gustafson, "Male Desire in Götz von Berlichingen," in *Outing Goethe and His Age*, ed. Alice Kuzniar (Stanford, Calif.: Stanford University Press, 1996), 115–16.

18. Jonathan Culler, *The Pursuit of Signs: Semiotics, Literature, Deconstruction* (Ithaca, N.Y.: Cornell University Press, 1981), 152.

19. Ibid., 153.

20. The rebellious "people," complaining or fighting, are the cause *and* the effect of the trouble. However, there is a distinction here: the merchants oppose Götz and are on the side of the princes while the peasants are on his side. See Engels for the development of the dynamic between Götz and the peasants. Friedrich Engels, *Der Deutsche Bauernkrieg* (Berlin: Dietz, 1955). In the broader sense of the narratology of political theory, Engels's investigation offers a fascinating effort to appropriate the direct appeals for change that emerged in the peasant uprising. Engels supports the goals of the peasants but places them in the context of a *process* of social change over time. By extension, he offers his readers a vision for the future that participates in this already ongoing process.

21. Götz von Berlichingen, *Lebens-Beschreibung* (Hildesheim: Georg Olms Verlag, 1977), 125. My translation. A note on the terminology is necessary at this point. "Acht" and "Bann" can be used as synonyms. See Adalbert Erler and Ekkehard Kaufmann, eds., *Handwörterbuch zur deutschen Rechtsgeschichte*, 5 vols. (Berlin: Erich Schmidt Verlag, 1971–1998), 1:26. In *Götz von Berlichingen* specifically, "Bann" is used to refer to a territory; the Emperor wishes that Götz

and his people be ordered not to leave their "Bann." "Acht" is used to refer to the Emperor's declaration itself.

22. Horst Lange, "Wolves," 15. Lange's article "Weislingen: Goethe's Politics of the Ego" reads the character Weislingen not only as the key to *Götz* as *Charakterdrama*, but as the figure that connects such readings to a greater historical context. *Goethe Yearbook* 11 (2002): 177–96.

23. Cited in Horst Lange, "Wolves, Sheep and the Shepherd: Legality, Legitimacy, and Hobbesian Political Theory in Goethe's Götz von Berlichingen," *Goethe Yearbook* 10 (2001): 22.

24. Lange, "Wolves," 22.

25. Lange shows that this explains why the drama's early readers quickly took Götz's side. He had to be presented sympathetically to overcome the viewers' prejudice for the modern legal system in which he lived. Violence is on both sides: Götz attacks his enemies in his feuds and the Emperor attacks Götz. Illegitimacy is also on both sides: Götz does not have the right to feud, but the Emperor is also unjust in forcing Götz to submit to a contract he didn't sign. Goethe himself cannot, therefore, be seen to have promoted one party over the other.

26. Giorgio Agamben, *Homo Sacer: Sovereign Power and Bare Life*, trans. Daniel Heller-Roazen (Stanford, Calif.: Stanford University Press, 1998), 28.

27. Ibid., 29.

28. Ibid., 111.

29. Jhering quoted in Agamben, *Homo Sacer*, 104. Agamben cites Nancy as the source of his notion of the ban: Jean-Luc Nancy, "Abandoned Being," in *The Birth to Presence*, trans. Brian Holmes (Stanford, Calif.: Stanford University Press, 1993).

30. Quoted in Agamben, *Homo Sacer*, 105–6.

31. Agamben, *Homo Sacer*, 109.

32. Ibid.

33. Ibid., 107.

34. Ibid.

35. Ibid., 109.

36. Throughout, Götz predicts what the other side will do. Later in this act Lerse suggests negotiating a retreat, to which Götz responds that they will instead demand house arrest. That this in fact is what the Emperor intended could indicate a connection between the sovereign and the outlaw. In Heilbronn, Götz is freed by Sicklingen and sets his own punishment, again house arrest. What does this desire to return to the house signify? It is as if his failure to engage in an external economy sends him back to the literal *oikos*, the place where he is unchallenged in his actions.

37. See Naphtali Lewis and Meyer Reinhold, *Roman Civilization: Selected Readings* (New York: Columbia University Press, 1990), 15–19.

38. Horst Lange is an exception to those who ignore the Citation, reading it as a sign of Götz's failure to give up the feudal contract. Lange, "Wolves," 7.

39. Maximilian Müller-Jabusch, *Götzens grober Gruss* (Munich: Pohl, 1956).

40. "Apotropaic, a," in *The OED Online* (Oxford University Press, 2009), http://dictionary.oed.com/cgi/entry/50010540. Common apotropaic objects include amulets or icons meant to ward off evil or bad luck.

41. Jahn quoted in Müller-Jabusch, *Götzens grober Gruss*, 268. Translation mine.

42. "It insults the gaze and throws it back" ("Es beleidigt den Anblick und stößt ihn zurück"), Jahn quoted in Müller-Jabusch, *Götzens grober Gruss*, 268.

43. In *Civilization and Its Discontents* Freud claims that man's evolution into an animal that walks upright resulted in the exposure of the genitals, which had been protected. This new vulnerability led to shame (Freud, *Civilization*, 46). The move to the realm of morality, where honesty is possible, happens only by way of the transition to standing up. This change is also associated with the loss of the power of the sense of smell and its replacement by the sense of sight. Ronell points to the connection between Freud's postural morality and Nietzsche's critical deployment of the terms "anständig" and "aufrichtig." Ronell, *Finitude's Score*, 162.

44. Johann Wolfgang von Goethe, "Prometheus," in *The Collected Works*, vol. 1: *Selected Poems*, ed. Christopher Middleton, trans. Cyrus Hamlin (New York: Suhrkamp, 1983), 29.

45. The paradoxical wish of Sturm und Drang invective to take down God by calling on him that we see here acquires theoretical articulation in the twentieth century, as Arnd Wedemeyer shows in his reading of Schmitt and Buber. Wedemeyer argues that "the fate of political theology beyond its allegedly retrograde inclinations is tied to the curse's force, which always already includes its peculiar attenuations and constitutive weaknesses." Arnd Wedemeyer, "Herrschaftszeiten! Theopolitical Profanities in the Face of Secularization," *New German Critique* 105 (Fall 2008): 129.

46. Jacques Derrida, *Glas* (Lincoln: University of Nebraska Press, 1986), 42. Derrida's reading follows Hegel's early text *The Spirit of Christianity and Its Fate*.

47. Derrida, *Glas*, 46.

48. Letter to Heinrich Christian Boie, July 8, 1773, in Neuhaus, *Johann Wolfgang Goethe: Götz von Berlichingen*, 131.

49. That part of the *Quote* was partially effaced in editions after the original printing of 1773 indicates a textual amputation that repeats the physical amputation of its main character. It changes the character of the scene, replacing a specific threat (at least rhetorically) with an *aposiopesis* (from the Greek "becoming silent"), a sudden break that leaves the threat open: "Er aber, sag's ihm, er kann mich . . ." *Aposiopesis* implies that the reader would add the end of the sentence himself as he reads. Left open, demanding a prosthetic act from the reader, the threat is even *more* obscene, so terrible that it can't be signified on the page.

50. Susan Bernstein, *Housing Problems: Writing and Architecture in Goethe, Walpole, Freud, and Heidegger* (Stanford, Calif.: Stanford University Press, 2008), 26.

51. Ibid., 34.

52. The absurdity of Götz's hopes here is marked by the fact that he orders a copy of the contract to be sent "to all your troops" (70) when these masses are farmers who obviously cannnot read. See Bruce Kieffer, *The Storm and Stress of Language* (University Park: Pennsylvania State University Press, 1986). Kieffer analyzes Götz's emphasis on fidelity to the oath and notes that in his interaction with the rebelling peasants "the limitations of the knightly oath finally prove fatal for Götz" (33). Andrea Bartl also addresses the difficulty of keeping one's word in this drama. "He [Götz] rejects all ineffective, content-free speech but is on the other hand unable to find an influential language whose reception can be

calculated." Andrea Bartl, *Im Anfang war der Zweifel: Zur Sprachskepsis in der deutschen Literatur um 1800* (Tübingen: Francke, 2005), 107. My translation. Bartl's discussion focuses on the first version of the drama, but emphasizes that the second version also supports this reading. She connects Götz's devaluation of writing towards the end of the drama (in both versions) with Derrida's critique of this writing in Rousseau. When Götz declares that he shows the court how to "keep their word" he denies the type of semantic dissemination that Derrida sees as being demonstrated in writing, not only in the strict sense, but also in the broader sense of *écriture*.

53. In a sense, Elisabeth's subtle intervention here continues the feminine disruption of the drama that Goethe thought he had contained by removing the scenes devoted to the passionate and violent Adelheid.

54. H. A. Korff, *Geist der Goethezeit* (Leipzig: J. J. Weber, 1923), 226–30, here 226. My translation. Any discussion of the political aspects of Korff's classic work of *Ideengeschichte* is necessarily problematized by his later complicity in the Nazi regime. I limit myself here to marking this difficulty.

55. Ibid., 230.

56. Johann Wolfgang von Goethe, *Egmont*, in *Early Verse Dramas and Prose Plays*, ed. Cyrus Hamlin and Frank Ryder, trans. Cyrus Hamlin (New York: Suhrkamp, 1988), 151. Translation modified.

57. Kenneth Weisinger, "*Götz von Berlichingen*: History Writing Itself," *German Studies Review* 9 (1986): 211–32.

58. Horst Lange should also be mentioned in this review of interpretations that are concerned with history. Lange wonders how Götz could be considered to be a "positive hero" when he seems to love violence for its own sake. Lange, "Wolves," 2. I discuss Lange's article, which examines the drama by demonstrating the emergence of the sovereign as outlined in Hobbes's social contract theory, in greater detail later in this chapter.

Chapter 3

1. Staiger, *Goethe*, 1:87. Translation mine. As I emphasized in my previous chapter, Götz does lead a violent campaign, despite his intention.

2. Michael Patterson, "Aspects of Terrorism in the Work of Piscator and Brecht," in *Terrorism and Modern Drama*, ed. John Orr and Dragon Klaic (Edinburgh: Edinburgh University Press, 1990), 84.

3. Friedrich Engels, "Die wahren Sozialisten," in *Karl Marx—Friedrich Engels—Werke*, vol. 4 (Berlin: Dietz, 1972), 248–90. Translation mine. In an essay which opens with the same citation as *The Robbers*, Bakunin refers to Karl Moor as a model for the Russian terrorists of his day: "Deeds to which Karakosov, Beresowski and others took the initiative, have to constantly increase and multiply and become acts of collective masses, like the comrades of Schiller's Karl Moor." Michael Bakunin, "Die Prinzipien der Revolution," in *Sozial-Politischer Briefwechsel mit Alexander Iw. Herzen und Ogarjow* (Stuttgart: Cotta, 1895), 358–64. My translation.

4. Korff, *Geist der Goethezeit*, 231. My translation.

5. Benno von Wiese argues for a personal origin in his study *Schiller* (Stuttgart: J. B. Metzlersche Verlagsbuchhandlung, 1959). Patrick Häffner, like Korff, argues for a mixture of the two influences in *Widerstandsrecht bei Schiller* (Frankfurt

am Main: Peter Lang, 2005). Häffner divides Schiller's characters into "resistance fighters" and "terrorists." While Tell and Johanna von Orleans lead legitimate battles of liberation, Demetrius, Fiesco, and Wallenstein work for their own advantage. Franz Moor, unsurprisingly, falls in with the latter. Karl, however, is also judged harshly because his motivations are not pure. At times he justifies his acts ideologically, while at others psychological factors are paramount.

6. The *Oxford English Dictionary* indicates that "rogue" is perhaps derived from "roger," a slang term from the sixteenth-century meaning: "A begging vagrant pretending to be a poor Oxford or Cambridge scholar."

7. Friedrich Schiller, *The Robbers*, in *The Robbers and Wallenstein*, trans. F. J. Lamport (New York: Penguin, 1979). Hereafter cited in the text by page number. *Schillers Werke: Nationalausgabe* (Weimar: Böhlaus Nachfolger, 1953), 3:20.

8. In the pseudonymous "Selbstbesprechung im Wirtembergischen Repertorium" Schiller speaks of the author of *The Robbers* as a doctor who prefers "*starke Dosen* in Emeticis." For a detailed reading of the literary and theoretical history of the term, see Winfried Menninghaus, *Ekel* (Frankfurt: Suhrkamp, 1999).

9. Jacques Lacan, *Four Fundamental Concepts of Psychoanalysis* (New York: W. W. Norton, 1981), 88. For a further elaboration of the anamorphosis, see Jacques Lacan, *The Ethics of Psychoanalysis* (New York: W. W. Norton, 1997), 139–54.

10. For a review of the most important readings of this line of criticism, which was especially prominent among Marxist critics, see David Pugh, *Schiller's Early Dramas: A Critical History* (Rochester, N.Y.: Camden House, 2000), 144–58.

11. This very same line was appropriated by the Nazi reading of the play as proof that Karl specifically *denies* democratic ideals. Rome and Sparta are glossed as "Republics, in which nobles, not the majority decided, in which true national character, not peaceful cosmopolitanism, created form." Hans Fabricius, *Schiller unser Kampfgenosse* (Berlin: Verlag Deutsche Kultur, 1940), 10.

12. Bruce Kieffer notes that Karl reads the letter, leaves the stage, then returns to declare his rage. He says that during this time Karl connects the specific injury he has suffered at the hands of his father and the hypocritical nature of society that he had previously spoken so eloquently against. Expanding on this interpretation, one could say that Karl's father no longer provides the protection, the shade that he expected ("Im Schatten meiner väterlichen Haine"). Karl's absence from the stage signifies his speechlessness; he returns when he can say something. The automatic, instinctive reaction to the letter occurs only after a delay. Kieffer, *The Storm and Stress of Language*, 117.

13. For a thorough classification of the drama's stylistic devices, see H. B. Garland, *Schiller: The Dramatic Writer* (Oxford: Clarendon, 1969), 4–39.

14. Slavoj Žižek, "Grimaces of the Real, or When the Phallus Appears," *October*, vol. 58 (Fall 1991): 66.

15. Hans-Jürgen Schings explicates the power of this break in terms of a cut in the great chain of being. Hans-Jürgen Schings, "Schillers Räuber: Ein Experiment des Universalhasses," in *Friedrich Schiller: Kunst, Humanität und Politik in der späten Aufklärunged*, ed. Wolfgang Wittkowski (Tübingen: Niemeyer, 1982), 23.

16. Peter Michelsen points out that the presence of the sword is anachronistic. He accounts for this by pointing out its importance in the operatic tradition and argues that incorporating this tradition is key to understanding the play.

Insisting on the sword, Schiller emphasizes "signifying power" over realism. Peter Michelsen, *Bruch mit der Vaterwelt: Studien zu Schillers "Räubern,"* supplement to *Euphorion* 16 (Heidelberg: Winter, 1979). See especially pages 57–58.

17. Karl Moor does not free himself when he proclaims that he has "no father." Instead, in a movement that Avital Ronell links to the "loser son," he converts the negative energy of the father who rejects him into "megalomanic certitudes" that evince an almost supernatural boost of superego. Ronell continues: "Loser sons need and feed on a simplified notion of enmity. They trail around an enemy hit list." Avital Ronell, *Loser Sons: Politics and Authority* (Urbana: University of Illinois Press, 2012), 5. From this perspective, Karl Moor reroutes, but by no means escapes, the power of the father in the moment of these declarations. Ronell contrasts the unconscious and nihilating force of the superego in the loser sons George W. Bush, Osama bin Laden, and Mohammed Atta, with the neurotically refined tactics of evasion mobilized by the alternate loser son Franz Kafka. Right until the end of the drama, the question remains open as to whether or not Karl Moor's wavering between violence and regret might offer an alternate modality of the parental takedown.

18. Bruce Kieffer sees the robber band as offering Karl the "linguistic faithfulness he was unable to find in either society or family." The oath is perhaps the strongest example of this faithfulness, of a deed directly tied to words. Kieffer, *The Storm and Stress of Language*, 118.

19. Slavoj Žižek, *The Metastases of Enjoyment: On Women and Causality* (London: Verso, 1994), 95.

20. Sigmund Freud, *Jenseits des Lustprinzips*, in *Gesammelte Werke*, vol. 13 (Frankfurt: Fischer, 1940), 9. My translation. "möglichst niedrig oder wenigstens konstant."

21. Ibid., 16. My translation. "Das war also das komplette Spiel, Verschwinden und Wiederkommen."

22. Ibid., 17. My translation. "große kulturelle Leistung des Kindes."

23. In his reading of expectation in Jean Paul, Paul Fleming develops a reading of the *fort/da* game that focuses not on the return of the desired object but rather on its "holding back" and "suspension." Paul Fleming, *The Pleasures of Abandonment: Jean Paul and the Life of Humor* (Würzburg: Königshausen und Neumann, 2006), 72. In this light we could say that Karl Moor's power derives from such an absence but fails to ever totally escape the potentially deflationary return of the cast-off object.

24. Avital Ronell, "TraumaTV: Twelve Steps Beyond the Pleasure Principle," in *Finitude's Score: Essays for the End of the Millennium* (Lincoln: University of Nebraska Press, 1994), 322.

25. This wish relates to the desire to return to the mother's womb that Friedrich Kittler analyzes in *Dichter—Mutter—Kind* (Munich: Wilhelm Fink Verlag, 1991) and that Karl explicitly names in the next act.

26. Cannac reports that the victims Karl mentions represent actual people that would have been easily recognized by the reader at the time. René Cannac, *Théâtre et révolte: Essai sur la jeunesse de Schiller* (Paris: Payot, 1996).

27. I return to the question of the ways in which the performative that attempts to found a social group can fail and how to read the implications of such failures in my reading of Michael Kohlhaas's call to the people to rise up in my next chapter.

28. Friedrich Schiller, *Wallenstein,* in *The Robbers and Wallenstein,* trans. F. J. Lamport (New York: Penguin, 1979), 211.

29. Richard Koc, "Fathers and Sons: Ambivalence Doubled in Schiller's Räuber," *The Germanic Review* 61, no. 3 (Summer 1986): 98. Koc's article is one of the few to consider *The Robbers* in light of Freud. His reading considers Franz and Karl to be representations of two sides of a single son and draws its theoretical framework from *Totem and Taboo.* See also John D. Simmons, "In Errato Veritas: Schiller and Freud on Slips," *The German Quarterly* 56, no. 1 (1983): 14–27. For an account of Schiller's influence on Freud, see Liliane Weissberg, "Freuds Schiller," in *Friedrich Schiller und der Wed in der Moderne* (Würzburg: Konigshausen and Neumann, 2006), 421–34.

30. In her reading of Freud's *Traumdeutung* Elke Siegel identifies an "ambivalence of love and rivalry" in the friend as *revenant.* In the case of Karl Moor, this ambivalence shows that the friend must guarantee the unity of the group but at the same time threatens to destroy it. Elke Siegel, *Entfernte Freunde: Nietzsche, Freud, Kafka und die Freundschaft der Moderne* (Würzburg: Königshausen und Neumann, 2009), 159.

31. Jacques Derrida, *The Post Card* (Chicago: University of Chicago Press, 1987), 302.

32. Ibid., 313.

33. Ibid., 317. "PP" is also is the common French way of calling grandfather, like "poppy," or "pa." Freud is the grandfather in this scene and has given up his proper name when his daughter married and unloaded "Freud."

34. Roller's destabilizing climb out of the grave should be thought of as an instance of what Susan Bernstein calls "the ambulatory uncanny." Bernstein follows figures of the uncanny on the move as challenges to reading protocols that seek to stabilize meaning around presence and absence. Susan Bernstein, "It Walks: The Ambulatory Uncanny," *Modern Language Notes* 118, no. 5 (December 2003): 1111–39.

35. The term "pity [*Erbarmen*]," as an appeal to inner motion, fuels the *Drang* of this Sturm und Drang drama, its variations appearing twenty-nine times in the text.

36. Derrida, *The Post Card,* 293.

37. Hans-Jürgen Schings takes the latter position. Schings, "Schillers Räuber: Ein Experiment des Universalhasses," in *Friedrich Schiller: Kunst, Humanität und Politik in der späten Aufklärung,* ed. Wolfgang Wittkowski (Tübingen: Niemeyer, 1982), 23.

38. Von Wiese, *Schiller,* 167. Translation mine.

39. In terms of another key Kleinian concept, Karl Moor's relation to the law will thus be one of a move from what Laurence Rickels has described as a negative to "a more positive" transference. In her treatment of the ten-year-old Richard during World War II, Laurence Rickels describes how Klein must first stage an antagonistic encounter before she can help him move beyond his anxiety. Laurence Rickels, *Nazi Psychoanalysis,* vol. 2: *Crypto-Fetishism* (Minneapolis: University of Minnesota Press, 2002), 109.

40. Melanie Klein, "Notes on Some Schizoid Mechanisms," in *The Selected Works of Melanie Klein* (New York: Free, 1986), 189.

41. Oskar Seidlin points out the importance of the letter in Franz's attack on the world of nature, God, and the father. Oskar Seidlin, "Schiller's 'trügerische

Zeichen,'" in *Schiller: Zur Theorie und Praxis der Dramen*, ed. Klaus Berghahn and Reinhold Grimm (Darmstadt: Wissenschaftliche Buchgesellschaft, 1972), 178–205. He utilizes the letter's indirectness to divert the sign from its meaning. Karl rebels against the sign as well, but in the other direction, in favor of immediacy: "He rebels against the unchangeable will of the highest, that *this* world, *this* justice is no more than a mediating sign in which pure being cannot be directly present in an unbroken state" (185–86). My translation.

42. Eckart Goebel, *Jenseits des Unbehagens "Sublimierung" von Goethe bis Lacan* (Bielefeld: Transcript, 2009), 130.

Chapter 4

1. Ratmoko provides a concise overview of authors who have addressed the problem of terrorism in *Michael Kohlhaas*. He also argues that the novella changes our understanding of terrorism, seeing Kohlhaas engaged in "unintentional 'strategies' of imploding legal space." David Ratmoko, "Das Vorbild im Nachbild des Terrors: Eine Untersuchung des gespenstischen Nachlebens von *Michael Kohlhaas*," *Kleist Jahrbuch* (2003): 224, my translation. My reading focuses instead on the chain of violent effects and the continued challenge they pose. I discuss the work of Sendler, Kittler, and Wittkowski in more detail below.

2. In tracing the links, however tenuous and tentative, between the violent breakdown of political representation and the mechanics of history in *Michael Kohlhaas*, my reading responds to two key aspects of Derrida's work on terrorism. The first, which I introduced in chapter 1, is his insistence that the 9/11 attacks injure not only specific people and things but representational schemas themselves. The second is his argument for the reevaluation of the temporality of trauma in the wake of these attacks. They opened a wound that does not only continually return from the past to disrupt the present, but threatens in the future and by the future: "It is the future that determines the unappropriability of the event, not the present or the past. Or at least, if it is in the present or the past, it is only insofar as it bears on its body the terrible sign of what might or perhaps will take place, which will be worse than anything which has ever taken place" (Derrida, *Philosophy in a Time of Terror*, 97).

3. Translations from *Michael Kohlhaas* are from Martin Greenberg, with occasional modifications when required by my readings of the original. *Michael Kohlhaas*, in Heinrich von Kleist, *The Marquise von O. and Other Stories*, trans. and ed. Martin Greenberg (New York: Criterion, 1960), 87–183.

4. For Kant (in *Metaphysics of Morals*) and Kohlhaas, duty is both individual and universal. In the most recent book-length treatment of the topic, James Phillips reviews the relevant scholarship and makes a case for the interconnection of the epistemological, aesthetic, and ethical aspects of the much discussed Kleist–Kant relationship. James Phillips, *The Equivocation of Reason: Kleist Reading Kant* (Stanford, Calif.: Stanford University Press, 2007).

5. Avital Ronell, *The Telephone Book: Technology—Schizophrenia—Electric Speech* (Lincoln: University of Nebraska Press, 1989), 33.

6. The *Adelung Wörterbuch* defines "Rechtsschluß" as "eine im Hochdeutschen ungewöhnliche Benennung eines Gutachtens oder Bedenkens eines oder mehrerer Rechtslehrer, eines rechtlichen Gutachtens." Kohlhaas thus installs himself in the position of the judge. Boockmann argues that Kohlhaas's "Rechtsschluß" and

the "Mandat[e]" that follow it should be seen in the tradition of letters that accompanied feuds ("Fehdebriefe"). As Boockmann notes, however, the *Ewige Landfrieden* of 1495 outlawed feuds. Set in the middle of the following century, *Michael Kohlhaas* confronts us on yet another level with an anachronistic violence, with violence not sanctioned by its time.

7. Žižek claims that Kohlhaas participates in both types of violence: "In a paradigmatic dialectical reversal, Kohlhaas's very unconditional sticking to the rules, his *law-preserving violence*, turns into *law-making violence*." Slavoj Žižek, *Did Somebody Say Totalitarianism?* (London: Verso, 2001), 33. Strictly speaking, however, Kohlhaas's violence is never simply law-preserving. Even when his demands align with the previously existing law he always posits an alternate authority that contradicts the law. While I wish to focus on Arendt's proposal, a cross-reading of Benjamin and Arendt on this point may be productive for our understanding of both authors. Arendt's notion of a non-dialectical violence may allow a more precise understanding of the kind of stop to the law suggested by Benjamin's divine violence. On the other hand, Benjamin perhaps provides a unique pivot for Arendt's reliance on power as "empowering."

8. Arendt, *On Violence*, 56.

9. In other words, these attempts to provide a way to read Kohlhaas's attacks are all too successful, at the price of ignoring the excessive, the murdered civilians and nightmare scenes of inferno that infuse their investigations with urgency. Lützeler provides the best review of legal and political examinations of *Kohlhaas*. Paul Michael Lützeler, "Heinrich von Kleist, Michael Kohlhaas," in *Romane und Erzählungen der deutschen Romantik: Neue Interpretationen*, ed. P. M. Lützeler (Stuttgart: Reclam, 1982), 213–39. Important research on this topic that has come after Lützeler's article includes that of Kittler, Wittkowski, and Schmidt.

10. In addition to Bloch, Bohnert, and Skrotzki (who I cite earlier in this chapter), Apel also falls into this category with his proposal of an analogy between the "Baader-Meinhof-Komplex" and a "Kleist-Kohlhaas-Komplex." Friedmar Apel, ed., *Kleists Kohlhaas: Ein deutscher Traum vom Recht auf Mordbrennerei* (Berlin: Wagenbach, 1987), 149.

11. Wolf Kittler, *Die Geburt des Partisanen aus dem Geist der Poesie: Heinrich von Kleist und die Strategie der Befreiungskriege* (Freiburg: Rombach, 1987), 304.

12. Horst Sendler, *Über Michael Kohlhaas—damals und heute* (Berlin: Walter de Gruyter, 1985), 24.

13. Wittkowski proposes that Kleist is on the side of the Enlightenment ideals put forth in the *Gesetzbuch für die Preußischen Staaten* (*Code of Laws of the Prussian States*) of 1792. He would therefore be protesting against the withdrawal of rights in this code as a reaction to the French Revolution in the 1794 *Allgemeines Preußisches Landrecht*. Wittkowski demonstrates that many of the abuses that Kohlhaas suffers were in fact codified and prohibited in the reform of 1792. These prohibitions were revoked in the later law which restored greater power to the sovereign. Wolfgang Wittkowski, "Is Kleist's Michael Kohlhaas a Terrorist?" *Historical Reflections / Relexions Historiques* 26, no. 3 (2000): 485.

14. Elizabeth Krimmer, "The Gender of Terror: War as (Im)Moral Institution in Kleist's Hermannsschlacht and Penthesilea," *The German Quarterly* 81, no. 1 (Winter 2008): 77.

15. J. Hillis Miller, "Laying Down the Law in Literature: The Example of Kleist," *Cardozo Law* 11 (1990): 1504.

16. In an analysis of contemporary terrorist attacks anchored in the field of religious studies, Mark Juergensmeyer describes "performance violence" as violence that does not have a clear strategic objective but instead functions as a ritual that forces spectators into the "alternative view of the world" held by the terrorist. Mark Juergensmeyer, *Terror in the Mind of God: The Global Rise of Religious Violence* (Berkeley: University of California Press, 2003), 125. By synthesizing insights of J. L. Austin and Pierre Bourdieu, he draws attention to the specific social background that determines whether or not a certain performance of violence will induce a shift to the alternative legitimacy that the terrorist attack implies. In terms of my reading of *Michael Kohlhaas*, the key point will be that this social background itself remains in flux even after Kohlhaas's attacks, deferring resolution to the end of the novella and beyond.

17. Luther's reading of the "one voice" in Kohlhaas's letter works along the same lines as the threat of "total war" that Thomas Keenan analyzes in contemporary political discourse while inverting the scale of the trope. Keenan reveals a devastating rhetorical contradiction: "as long as escalation is possible, as long as still more destruction remains to come, then so does the possibility of less, and hence there is an offer being made, a proposition, a move in a negotiation. Each attack, up to a certain limit (it seems), always means—in addition to whatever specific message it enunciates—that things 'could always get worse.' " Thomas Keenan, "A Language That Needs No Translation, or: Can Things Get Any Worse?" in *Terror and the Roots of Poetics*, ed. Jeffrey Champlin (Dresden: Atropos, 2013), 95.

18. Heinrich von Kleist, "The Earthquake in Chile," in *The Marquise von O. and Other Stories*, trans. and ed. Martin Greenberg (New York: Criterion, 1960), 259.

19. The fortune-teller's double negation opens an obscure space for interpretation that recalls Kleist's account of Mirabeau's rejection of Louis XVI's Master of Ceremonies in the meeting of the French General Assembly on June 20, 1789. In his essay "On the Gradual Production of Thoughts Whilst Speaking," Kleist offers a scene where the Master of Ceremonies asks Mirabeau if the Assembly had heard the royal command to disband. When he first replies in the affirmative, Kleist offers the commentary that "I am certain that beginning thus humanely he had not yet thought of the bayonets with which he would finish" and then continues to report the scene: " 'Yes, my dear sir,' he repeated, 'we have heard it.' " Mirabeau does not just stall while he thinks of how to phrase his objection; he actively pushes himself to a new thought. When Kleist refers to "the bayonets with which he would finish," he suggests the future violence of the French Revolution. In fact though, Mirabeau ends up only refusing to move and announcing resistance to the King's violence. The "bayonets" named at the end are instruments of state power. It is as if the saying of "yes" opens a program of repetition that Mirabeau then decides to extend and embody: in acting as the ear of the assembly, he hears the command but cuts it off from the expected compliance. Heinrich von Kleist, "On the Gradual Production of Thoughts Whilst Speaking," in *Selected Writings*, ed. and trans. David Constantine (Indianapolis, Ind.: Hackett, 2004), 406.

20. Zachary Sng notes that Kleist doubles back in other narratives as well and offers a particularly insightful reading of "The Duel" that links the story to *Kohlhaas* through its emphasis on "an interposed thirdness that undermines the entire structure of decision, conflict, and resolution." Zachary Sng, "The Poetics of the Middle in Kleist's 'Michael Kohlhaas,'" *The Germanic Review* 85, no. 3 (2010): 184–85.

21. I thus wish to emphasize the political context and repercussions of the epistemological challenge that Carol Jacobs identifies in the capsule text. Her reading indicates an openness to this question when she writes that Kohlhaas's satisfaction with regards to the Elector of Saxony "is less the satisfaction of exchanging things of equal value (*Wechseln*) and of the fulfillment of the significance of the law (as authored text) than one of joy in the text as privation of knowledge, satisfaction through negation of meaning, the celebration of a text precisely insofar as it denies the presence of its own authority." Carol Jacobs, *Uncontainable Romanticism: Shelley, Brontë, Kleist* (Baltimore: Johns Hopkins University Press, 1989), 148–49.

22. Helène Cixous sees Kohlhaas's fate as one tied to the paradoxical nature of innocence: that it wants to be recognized. Helène Cixous, "Grace and Innocence: Heinrich von Kleist," in *Readings: The Poetics of Blanchot, Joyce, Kafka, Kleist, Lispector, and Tsvetayeva*, trans. Verena Andermatt Conley (Minneapolis: University of Minnesota Press, 1991), 42.

23. Cited in Kleist, *Sämtliche Werke und Briefe*, vol. 3: *Erzählungen, Anekdoten, Gedichte, Schriften*, ed. Klaus Müller-Salget (Frankfurt: Deutscher Klassiker Verlag, 1990), 715. Translation mine.

24. Scholars who have addressed this question include Schultze-Jahde, Jacobs, Koelb, Reuß, and Gailus.

25. Andreas Gailus provides a very insightful reading of the manner in which the Elector of Brandenburg acts as the stage director of justice in his final "aesthetic production of sovereignty" and argues that with *Michael Kohlhaas*, Kleist himself intervenes in the politics of the day with a text designed to incite national passions. Andreas Gailus, *Passions of the Sign: Revolution and Language in Kant, Goethe, and Kleist* (Baltimore: Johns Hopkins University Press, 2006), 144. Seán Allan sees Kolhaas going along with this show of power and also getting his message across clearly in the end: "In surrendering his life he demonstrates before the assembled crowd that he behaved in an altruistic fashion, that what he did was not for the sake of his horses, nor for the sake of personal enrichment, but for the sake of justice for all." Seán Allan, *The Stories of Heinrich von Kleist: Fictions of Security* (Rochester, N.Y.: Camden House, 2001), 72. On his reading, accepting the Elector of Brandenburg's punishment calmly shows a fundamental devotion to order despite his earlier violent acts. Roger Berkowitz offers a way to conceptualize the difficult relationship between revenge and justice that such an acceptance demonstrates. He considers the killing of Osama bin Laden in light of an interpretation of Hannah Arendt's suggestion that it might have been better to kill Eichmann immediately in Argentina. Then the killer could have turned himself in and have argued in court that this was just. On Berkowitz's reading of Arendt, "Revenge . . . can be just when done in certain ways—namely, when the avenger submits the justice or injustice of his act to the legal verdict of a jury." Roger Berkowitz, "Assassinating Justly: Reflections on Justice and Revenge in the

Osama bin Laden Killing," in *Terror and the Roots of Poetics*, ed. Jeffrey Champlin (Dresden: Atropos, 2013), 188.

26. Werner Hamacher carefully explicates a similar restoration at the end of the "The Earthquake in Chili," with important but subtle differences (which are primarily evident in the character of Don Fernando). Werner Hamacher, "Das Beben der Darstellung," in *Positionen der Literaturwissenschaft*, ed. David Wellbery (Munich: Beck, 1985), 149–73.

27. The fortune-teller episode would thus be a further case of the type of hermeneutic struggle that Paul de Man identifies in his text "Kleist's *Über das Marionettentheater*." De Man writes of the importance of the authorial feint as "perhaps the only proof of his mastery over meaning, that he is free to decree it, at his own will, as genuine or fake." Paul de Man, *The Rhetoric of Romanticism* (New York: Columbia University Press, 1984), 282. Seen from this perspective, the narrator of *Michael Kohlhaas* attempts such a feint with his fantastic interlude so as to ensure that the genuine thrust of history reaches its target.

28. Roland Reuß, "'Michael Kohlhaas' und 'Michael Kohlhaas,'" *Berlin Kleist Blätter* 3 (1990): 42.

Conclusion

1. Mark Mazzetti, "Osama Is Dead, Obama Says," *New York Times*, May 2, 2011, http://www.nytimes.com/2011/05/02/world/asia/osama-bin-laden-is-killed.html.

2. Mark Mazzetti, "Account Tells of One-Sided Battle in Bin Laden Raid," *New York Times*, May 4, 2011, http://www.nytimes.com/2011/05/05/us/politics/05binladen.html.

3. Walter Benjamin, "Critique of Violence," trans. Edmund Jephcott, in *Walter Benjamin, Selected Writings*, vol. 1: *1913–1926*, ed. Marcus Bullock and Michael W. Jennings (Cambridge, Mass.: Harvard University Press, 1996), 239.

4. Could we imagine Kleist rewriting *Michael Kohlhaas* as a drama, perhaps the equal of such important works as *Penthesilea* or *Prinz Friedrich von Homburg*? Miloš Forman's 1981 film *Ragtime*, working through the intermediary of Doctorov's novel, shows that the core experience of injustice crosses genre boundaries without difficulty. However, the complicated indication of the "chronicle" and the intricate temporal markers noted by the narrator allow the novella to address the extended impact of violence to even form itself.

5. Arendt, *On Violence*, 56.

6. Hannah Arendt, *Lectures on Kant's Political Philosophy*, ed. Ronald Beiner (Chicago: University of Chicago Press, 1992), 45.

7. Ronald Beiner suggest that Arendt's project in the Kant lectures is to "detranscendentalize" Kant's aesthetics "by playing up the continuity between the third Critique's theme of communicability and the theme of sociability as found in some of the pre-critical writings." Ronald Beiner, "Rereading Hannah Arendt's Kant Lectures," *Philosophy and Social Criticism* 23, no. 1 (1997): 28. A new conception of political philosophy would emerge from this combination of the pre-critical writings with the *Critique of Judgment*. This formulation suggests a strong affinity between Arendt and the post-Kantian thinkers of the late eighteenth and early nineteenth centuries. Arendt wanted to write her second academic book (*Habilitationsschrift*) in the German university system about

romanticism but was prevented by growing anti-Semitism. In this light, Arendt can be seen to offer another type of *Aesthetic Education*, to quote the title of Schiller's letters (the model for Fichte, Schelling, and Hegel in so many regards).

8. Speaking of Arendt's work on literature specifically, Susannah Gottlieb writes "just as political judgment creates public space, aesthetic judgment, which suspends direct involvement in all *pragmata*, grants access to political *time*." Susannah Gottlieb, "Introduction," in *Hannah Arendt: Reflections on Literature and Culture* (Stanford, Calif.: Stanford University Press, 2007), xiii. The narrative disjunctions in the texts I have examined especially highlight this sense of suspension as an occasion for reflection on "political time."

WORKS CITED

Adelung, Johann Christoph. "Rechtsschluß." In *Grammatisch-kritisches Wörterbuch der Hochdeutschen Mundart, 1009.* Vienna: Bauer, 1811.

Agamben, Giorgio. *Homo Sacer: Sovereign Power and Bare Life.* Trans. Daniel Heller-Roazen. Stanford, Calif.: Stanford University Press, 1998.

Allan, Seán. *The Stories of Heinrich von Kleist: Fictions of Security.* Rochester, N.Y.: Camden House, 2001.

Apel, Friedmar, ed. *Kleists Kohlhaas: Ein deutscher Traum vom Recht auf Mordbrennerei.* Berlin: Wagenbach, 1987.

Appelbaum Graham, Ilse. "Götz von Berlichingen's Right Hand." *German Life and Letters* 16 (April and July 1963): 212–28.

Arendt, Hannah. *Lectures on Kant's Political Philosophy.* Chicago: University of Chicago Press, 1992.

———. *On Violence.* New York: Harcourt, Brace and World, 1970.

Baer, Ulrich. *Remnants of Song: Trauma and the Experience of Modernity in Charles Baudelaire and Paul Celan.* Stanford, Calif.: Stanford University Press, 2000.

Bakunin, Mikhail. "Die Prinzipien der Revolution." In *Michail Bakunins sozialpolitischer Briefwechsel mit Alexander Iw. Herzen und Ogarjow,* 358–64. Stuttgart: Cotta, 1895.

Bartl, Andrea. *Im Anfang war der Zweifel: Zur Sprachskepsis in der deutschen Literatur um 1800.* Tübingen: Francke, 2005.

Beiner, Ronald. "Rereading Hannah Arendt's Kant Lectures." *Philosophy and Social Criticism* 23, no. 1 (1997): 21–32.

Benjamin, Walter. "Zur Kritik der Gewalt." In *Gesammelte Schriften,* vol. 2.1, ed. Rolf Tiedemann and Hermann Schweppenhäuser. Frankfurt am Main: Suhrkamp, 1972–1989.

Berkowitz, Roger. "Assassinating Justly: Reflections on Justice and Revenge in the Osama bin Laden Killing." In *Terror and the Roots of Poetics,* ed. Jeffrey Champlin, 181–89. Dresden: Atropos, 2013.

Berlichingen, Götz von. *Lebens-Beschreibung, 1731.* Hildesheim: Georg Olms Verlag, 1977.

Bernstein, Susan. *Housing Problems: Writing and Architecture in Goethe, Walpole, Freud, and Heidegger.* Stanford, Calif.: Stanford University Press, 2008.

———. "It Walks: The Ambulatory Uncanny." *Modern Language Notes* 118, no. 5 (December 2003): 1111–39.

Blanchot, Maurice. *The Infinite Conversation.* Minneapolis: University of Minnesota Press, 1993.

Bloch, Ernst. *Naturrecht und menschliche Würde.* In *Gesamtausgabe,* vol. 6. Frankfurt: Suhrkamp, 1961.

Bohnert, Joachim. "Kohlhaas der Entsetzliche." *Kleist Jahrbuch* (1988–89): 404–31.

Boockmann, Hartmut. "Mittelalterliches Recht bei Kleist: Ein Beitrag zum Verständnis des *Michael Kohlhaas*." *Kleist Jahrbuch* (1985): 84–108.

———. "Über Horst Sendler: Über Michael Kohlhaas—damals und heute." *Kleist Jahrbuch* (1985): 177–79.

Bush, George W. *Public Papers of the Presidents of the United States: George W. Bush*, 2001–, vol. 1, bk. 2, pp. 1098–99. Washington, D.C.: Government Printing Office, 2004.

Butler, Judith. "Critique, Coercion, and Sacred Life in Benjamin's 'Critique of Violence.'" In *Political Theologies*, ed. Hent de Vries. New York: Fordham University Press, 2006.

Cannac, René. *Théâtre et révolte: Essai sur la jeunesse de Schiller*. Paris: Payot, 1996.

Cixous, Helène. "Grace and Innocence: Heinrich von Kleist." In *Readings: The Poetics of Blanchot, Joyce, Kafka, Kleist, Lispector, and Tsvetayeva*, trans. Verena Andermatt Conley, 28–73. Minneapolis: University of Minnesota Press, 1991.

Cohen, Tom. *Ideology and Inscriptions: "Cultural Studies" after Benjamin, De Man, and Bakhtin,* 205. Cambridge, Eng.: Cambridge University Press, 1998.

Comay, Rebecca. *Mourning Sickness: Hegel and the French Revolution*. Stanford, Calif.: Stanford University Press, 2010.

Culler, Jonathan. *The Pursuit of Signs: Semiotics, Literature, Deconstruction*. Ithaca, N.Y.: Cornell University Press, 1981.

De Man, Paul. *Allegories of Reading*. New Haven, Conn.: Yale University Press, 1979.

———. *The Rhetoric of Romanticism*. New York: Columbia University Press, 1984.

Derrida, Jacques. *The Beast and the Sovereign*, vol. 1. Chicago: University of Chicago Press, 2009.

———. *Glas*. Lincoln: University of Nebraska Press, 1986.

———. *Philosophy in a Time of Terror: Dialogues with Jürgen Habermas and Jacques Derrida*. Ed. Giovanna Borradori. Chicago: University of Chicago Press, 2003.

———. *The Post Card*. Chicago: University of Chicago Press, 1987.

———. *Rogues: Two Essays on Reason*. Trans. Pascale-Anne Brault and Michael Naas. Stanford, Calif.: Stanford University Press, 2004.

Engels, Friedrich. *Der Deutsche Bauernkrieg*. Berlin: Dietz, 1955.

———. "Die wahren Sozialisten." In *Karl Marx—Friedrich Engels—Werke*, vol. 4, 248–90. Berlin: Dietz, 1972.

Erler, Adalbert, and Ekkehard Kaufmann, eds. *Handwörterbuch zur deutschen Rechtsgeschichte*. 5 vols. Berlin: Erich Schmidt Verlag, 1971–1998.

Fabricius, Hans. *Schiller unser Kampfgenosse*. Berlin: Verlag Deutsche Kultur, 1940.

Fleming, Paul. *Exemplarity and Mediocrity: The Art of the Average from Bourgeois Tragedy to Realism*. Stanford, Calif.: Stanford University Press, 2008.

Freud, Sigmund. *The Ego and the Id*. New York: Norton, 1962.

———. *Gesammelte Werke*. Frankfurt: S. Fischer Verlag, 1946.

Gailus, Andreas. *Passions of the Sign: Revolution and Language in Kant, Goethe, and Kleist*. Baltimore: Johns Hopkins University Press, 2006.

Garland, H. B. *Schiller: The Dramatic Writer.* Oxford: Clarendon, 1969.

Genette, Gérard. *Narrative Discourse: An Essay in Method.* Trans. Jane E. Lewin. Ithaca, N.Y.: Cornell University Press, 1980.

Goebel, Eckart. *Jenseits des Unbehagens "Sublimierung" von Goethe bis Lacan.* Bielefeld: Transcript, 2009.

Goethe, Johann Wolfgang von. *Egmont.* In *Early Verse Dramas and Prose Plays*, ed. Cyrus Hamlin and Frank Ryder, trans. Cyrus Hamlin. New York: Suhrkamp, 1988.

———. *Goetz von Berlichingen with the Iron Hand.* In *Early Verse Drama and Prose Plays*, ed. Cyrus Hamlin and Frank Ryder, trans. Cyrus Hamlin, 1–82. New York: Suhrkamp, 1988.

———. "Prometheus." In *The Collected Works*, vol. 1: *Selected Poems*, ed. Christopher Middleton, trans. Cyrus Hamlin, 27–29. New York: Suhrkamp, 1983.

———. *Sämtliche Werke nach Epochen seines Schaffens.* Münchner Ausgabe, ed. Karl Richter. Munich: Hanser, 1985–98.

———. *Werke in 14 Bänder.* Hamburg: Christian Wegner Verlag, 1951.

Gottlieb, Susannah. "Introduction." In *Hannah Arendt: Reflections on Literature and Culture.* Stanford, Calif.: Stanford University Press, 2007.

Gustafson, Susan E. "Male Desire in Götz von Berlichingen." In *Outing Goethe and His Age*, ed. Alice Kuzniar, 111–24. Stanford: Stanford University Press, 1996.

Guthrie, John. "Schiller's Early Styles: Language and Gesture in *The Robbers.*" *The Modern Language Review* 94, no. 2 (April 1999): 438–59.

Habermas, Jürgen, *Habermas and the Public Sphere*, ed. Craig Calhoun. Cambridge, Mass.: MIT Press, 1993.

Häffner, Patrick. *Widerstandsrecht bei Schiller.* Frankfurt: Peter Lang, 2005.

Hamacher, Werner. *"Das Beben der Darstellung."* In *Positionen der Literaturwissenschaft*, ed. David Wellbery, 149–73. Munich: Beck, 1985.

Hamilton, John. *Security: Politics, Humanity, and the Philology of Care.* Princeton, N.J.: Princeton University Press, 2013.

Hegel, Georg Wilhelm Friedrich. *Aesthetics: Lectures on Fine Art.* Trans. T. M. Knox. 2 vols. Oxford: Clarendon, 1975.

———. *Grundlinien der Philosophie des Rechts.* Berlin: Akademie Verlag, 1997.

———. *Vorlesungen über die Philosophie der Weltgeschichte*, vols. 2–4. Hamburg: Felix Meiner, 1968.

Heuvel, Gerd van den. "Terreur, Terroriste, Terrorisme." In *Handbuch politisch-sozialer Grundbegriffe in Frankreich 1680–1820*, ed. Rolf Reichardt and Eberhard Schmitt, 89–132. Munich: Oldenbourg, 1985.

Hobbes, Thomas. *The English Works of Thomas Hobbes.* Ed. Sir William Molesworth. Vol. 3. London: John Bohn, 1839.

Hoeps, Thomas. *Arbeit am Widerspruch: "Terrorismus" in deutschen Romanen und Erzählungen (1837–1992).* Dresden: Thelem, 2001.

Huyssen, Andreas. *Drama des Sturm und Drang: Kommentar zu einer Epoche.* Munich: Winkler, 1980.

Jacobs, Carol. *Uncontainable Romanticism: Shelley, Brontë, Kleist.* Baltimore: Johns Hopkins University Press, 1989.

Juergensmeyer, Mark. *Terror in the Mind of God: The Global Rise of Religious Violence.* Berkeley: University of California Press, 2003.

Keenan, Thomas. "A Language That Needs No Translation, or: Can Things Get Any Worse?" In *Terror and the Roots of Poetics*, ed. Jeffrey Champlin, 92–109. Dresden: Atropos, 2013.

Kieffer, Bruce. *The Storm and Stress of Language: Linguistic Catastrophe in the Early Works of Goethe, Lenz, Klinger, and Schiller*. University Park: Pennsylvania State University Press, 1986.

Kittler, Friedrich. *Dichter—Mutter—Kind*. Munich: Wilhelm Fink Verlag, 1991.

Kittler, Wolf. *Die Geburt des Partisanen aus dem Geist der Poesie: Heinrich von Kleist und die Strategie der Befreiungskriege*. Freiburg: Rombach, 1987.

———. "Militärisches Kommando und tragisches Geschick: Zur Funktion der Schrift im Werk des preußischen Dichters Heinrich von Kleist." In *Heinrich von Kleist*, ed. Dirk Grathoff, 56–68. Opladen: Westdeutscher Verlag, 1988.

Klein, Melanie. *The Selected Works of Melanie Klein*. New York: Free, 1986.

Kleist, Heinrich von. *Michael Kohlhaas*. In *The Marquise von O. and Other Stories*, trans. and ed. Martin Greenberg, 87–183. New York: Criterion, 1960.

———. *Michael Kohlhaas, Sämtliche Werke und Briefe*, vol. 3: *Erzählungen, Anekdoten, Gedichte, Schriften*. Ed. Klaus Müller-Salget. Frankfurt: Deutscher Klassiker Verlag, 1990.

———. "On the Gradual Production of Thoughts Whilst Speaking." In *Selected Writings*, ed. and trans. David Constantine, 406. Indianapolis, Ind.: Hackett, 2004.

Koc, Richard. "Fathers and Sons: Ambivalence Doubled in Schiller's Räuber." *The Germanic Review* 61, no. 3 (Summer 1986): 91–104.

Koelb, Clayton. "Incorporating the Text: Kleist's Michael Kohlhaas." *PMLA: Publications of the Modern Language Association of America* 105, no. 5 (October 1990): 1098–1107.

Korff, H. A. *Geist der Goethezeit*. Leipzig: J. J. Weber, 1923.

Krimmer, Elizabeth. "The Gender of Terror: War as (Im)Moral Institution in Kleist's Hermannsschlacht and Penthesilea." *The German Quarterly* 81, no. 1 (Winter 2008): 66–86.

Kubiak, Anthony. *Stages of Terror: Terrorism, Ideology, and Coercion as Theatre History*. Bloomington: Indiana University Press, 1991.

Lacan, Jacques. *The Ethics of Psychoanalysis*. New York: W. W. Norton, 1997.

———. *Four Fundamental Concepts of Psychoanalysis*. New York: W. W. Norton, 1981.

Lange, Horst. "Weislingen: Goethe's Politics of the Ego." *Goethe Yearbook* 11 (2002): 177–96.

———. "Wolves, Sheep and the Shepherd: Legality, Legitimacy, and Hobbesian Political Theory in Goethe's Götz von Berlichingen." *Goethe Yearbook* 10 (2001): 1–30.

Laqueur, Walter. *Voices Of Terror: Manifestos, Writings & Manuals of Al Qaeda, Hamas, & Other Terrorists from Around the World & Throughout the Ages*. New York: Reed, 2004.

Lenz, Jakob Michael Reinhold. "Über Götz von Berlichingen." In *Goethe im Urteil seiner Kritiker*, ed. Karl Robert Mandelkow. Munich: C. H. Beck, 1975.

Lezra, Jacques. *Wild Materialism*. New York: Fordham University Press, 2010.

Lewis, Naphtali, and Reinhold Meyer. *Roman Civilization: Selected Readings*. New York: Columbia University Press, 1990.

Lia, Brynjar. *Globalization and the Future of Terrorism: Patterns and Predictions.* London: Routledge, 2005.

Lukács, Georg. *Deutsche Literatur in zwei Jahrhunderten.* Neuwied: Luchterhand, 1964.

Lützeler, Paul Michael. "Heinrich von Kleist, Michael Kohlhaas." In *Romane und Erzählungen der deutschen Romantik: Neue Interpretationen*, ed. P. M. Lützeler, 213–39. Stuttgart: Reclam, 1982.

Marx, Karl, and Friedrich Engels. *Karl Marx—Friedrich Engels—Werke*, vol. 4. Berlin: Dietz, 1972.

Mazzetti, Mark. "Account Tells of One-Sided Battle in Bin Laden Raid." *New York Times*, May 4, 2011, http://www.nytimes.com/2011/05/05/us/politics/05bin laden.html.

———. "Osama Is Dead, Obama Says." *New York Times*, May 2, 2011, http://www.nytimes.com/2011/05/02/world/asia/osama-bin-laden-is-killed.html.

Menninghaus, Winfried. *Ekel.* Frankfurt: Suhrkamp, 1999.

Meyer-Benfey, Heinrich. "Die innere Geschichte des *Michael Kohlhaas.*" *Euphorion* 15 (1908): 101–3.

———. *Goethes Götz von Berlichingen.* Weimar: Hermann Böhlaus Nachfolger, 1929.

Michelsen, Peter. *Bruch mit der Vaterwelt: Studien zu Schillers "Räubern."* Supplement to *Euphorion* 16. Heidelberg: Winter, 1979.

Miller, J. Hillis. "Laying down the Law in Literature: The Example of Kleist." *Cardozo Law* 11 (1990): 1491–1514.

Müller-Jabusch, Maximilian. *Götzens grober Gruss.* Munich: Pohl, 1956.

Müller-Seidel, Walter. *Versehen und Erkennen: Eine Studie über Heinrich von Kleist.* Cologne: Böhlau, 1961.

Nägele, Rainer. "Götz von Berlichingen." In *Goethes Dramen: Neue Interpretationen*, ed. Walter Hinderer, 65–77. Stuttgart: Reclam, 1980.

Neuhaus, Volker. *Johann Wolfgang Goethe: "Götz von Berlichingen," Erläuterungen und Dokumente.* Stuttgart: Reclam, 1991.

The OED Online. December 2009. Oxford University Press. http://dictionary.oed.com/.

Patterson, Michael. "Aspects of Terrorism in the Work of Piscator and Brecht." In *Terrorism and Modern Drama*, ed. John Orr and Dragon Klaic. Edinburgh: Edinburgh University Press, 1990.

Phillips, James. *The Equivocation of Reason: Kleist Reading Kant.* Stanford, Calif.: Stanford University Press, 2007.

Pugh, David. *Schiller's Early Dramas.* Rochester, N.Y.: Camden House, 2000.

Ratmoko, David. "Das Vorbild im Nachbild des Terrors: Eine Untersuchung des gespenstischen Nachlebens von 'Michael Kohlhaas.' " *Kleist Jahrbuch* (2003): 218–31.

Reuß, Roland. " 'Michael Kohlhaas' und 'Michael Kohlhaas.' " *Berlin Kleist Blätter* 3 (1990): 3–43.

Rickels, Laurence. *Nazi Psychoanalysis*, vol. 2: *Crypto-Fetishism.* Minneapolis: University of Minnesota Press, 2002.

Robespierre, Maximilien. *Oeuvres de Robespierre.* Ed. A. Vermorel. Paris: F. Cournol, 1866.

Ronell, Avital. *Dictations: On Haunted Writing*. Bloomington: Indiana University Press, 1986.

———. *Finitude's Score: Essays for the End of the Millennium*. Lincoln: University of Nebraska Press, 1994.

———. Introduction to *Scum Manifesto*, by Valerie Solanas. London: Verso, 2004.

———. *Loser Sons: Politics and Authority*. University of Illinois Press, 2012.

———. *Stupidity.* Urbana: University of Illinois Press, 2002.

———. *The Telephone Book: Technology—Schizophrenia—Electric Speech*. Lincoln: University of Nebraska Press, 1989.

———. *The Test Drive*. Urbana: University of Illinois Press, 2005.

Schiller, Friedrich. *Schillers Werke: Nationalausgabe*. Vol. 3. Weimar: Böhlaus Nachfolger, 1953.

Schings, Hans-Jürgen. "Schillers Räuber: Ein Experiment des Universalhasses." In *Friedrich Schiller: Kunst, Humanität und Politik in der späten Aufklärung*, ed. Wolfgang Wittkowski, 1–25. Tübingen: Niemeyer, 1982.

Schmidt, Jochen. *Heinrich von Kleist: Die Dramen und Erzählungen in ihrer Epoche*. Darmstadt: Wissenschaftliche Buchgesellschaft, 2003.

Schmitt, Carl. *The "Leviathan" in the State Theory of Thomas Hobbes: Meaning and Failure of a Political Symbol*. Chicago: University of Chicago Press, 2008.

———. *Theory of the Partisan: Intermediate Commentary on the Concept of the Political*. Trans: G. L. Ulmen. New York: Telos, 2007.

Schramm, Hans-Eugen. *L.m.i.A. Des Ritters Götz von Berlichingen denkwürdige Fensterrede*. Tübingen am Neckar: Verlag Fritz Schlichtenmeyer, 1960.

Schultze-Jahde, Karl. "Kohlhaas und die Zigeunerin." *Jahrbuch der Kleist Gesellschaft* 17 (1933–37): 108–35.

Seidlin, Oskar. "Schiller's 'trügerische Zeichen.'" In *Schiller: Zur Theorie und Praxis der Dramen*, ed. Klaus Berghahn and Reinhold Grimm, 178–205. Darmstadt: Wissenschaftliche Buchgesellschaft, 1972.

Sembdner, Helmut, ed. *Heinrich von Kleists Lebensspuren: Dokumente und Berichte der Zeitgenossen*. Bremen: Schünemann, 1957.

Sendler, Horst. *Über Michael Kohlhaas—damals und heute*. Berlin: Walter de Gruyter, 1985.

Siegel, Elke. *Entfernte Freunde: Nietzsche, Freud, Kafka und die Freundschaft der Moderne*. Würzburg: Königshausen und Neumann, 2009.

Simmons, John D. "In Errato Veritas: Schiller and Freud on Slips." *The German Quarterly* 56, no. 1 (1983): 14–27.

Skrotzki, Ditmar. "Ist Kleists Erzählung von Kohlhaas wirklich die Geschichte des Rebellen Kohlhaas? Oder: wie stoppt man den Teufel, der auf zwei Rappen durch Sachsen reitet?" *Heilbronner Kleist-Schriften* 3 (1993): 7–19.

Sng, Zachary. "The Poetics of the Middle in Kleist's 'Michael Kohlhaas.'" *Germanic Review* 85, no. 3 (2010): 92–109.

Staiger, Emil. *Goethe*. 3 vols. Zurich: Atlantis Verlag, 1964.

Varon, Jeremy. *Bringing the War Home: The Weather Underground, The Red Army Faction, and Revolutionary Violence in the Sixties and Seventies*. Berkeley: University of California Press, 2004.

Walter, Rudolf. "Terror, Terrorismus." In *Geschichtliche Grundbegriffe: Historisches Lexikon zur politisch-sozialen Sprache in Deutschland*, ed. Otto

Brunner, Werner Conze, and Reinhart Koselleck, 8 vols., 6:323–444. Stuttgart: Klett-Cotta, 1972–1997.
Wedemeyer, Arnd. "Herrschaftszeiten! Theopolitical Profanities in the Face of Secularization." *New German Critique* 105 (Fall 2008): 121–41.
Wellbery, David E. *The Specular Moment.* Stanford, Calif.: Stanford University Press, 1996.
Weisinger, Kenneth. "*Götz von Berlichingen*: History Writing Itself." *German Studies Review* 9 (1986): 211–32.
Weissberg, Liliane. "Freuds Schiller." In *Friedrich Schiller und der Wed in der Moderne*, ed. Walter Hinderer, 421–34. Würzburg: Konigshausen and Neumann, 2006.
Wiese, Benno von. *Schiller*. Stuttgart: J. B. Metzlersche Verlagsbuchhandlung, 1959.
Wittkowski, Wolfgang. "Is Kleist's Michael Kohlhaas a Terrorist?" *Historical Reflections / Relexions Historiques* 26, no. 3 (2000): 471–86.
Žižek, Slavoj. *Did Somebody Say Totalitarianism?* London: Verso, 2001.
———. "Grimaces of the Real, or When the Phallus Appears." *October* 58 (Fall 1991): 44–68.
———. *The Metastases of Enjoyment: Six Essays on Woman and Causality.* London: Verso, 1999.

INDEX